Modernizing Legacy Systems

Software Technologies, Engineering Processes, and Business Practices

Robert C. Seacord
Daniel Plakosh
Grace A. Lewis

✦ Addison-Wesley

Boston • San Francisco • New York • Toronto
London • Munich • Paris • Madrid
Capetown • Sidney • Tokyo • Singapore • Mexico City

**Carnegie Mellon
Software Engineering Institute**

The SEI Series in Software Engineering

The publisher offers discounts on this book when ordered in quantity for special sales. For more information, please contact:

U.S. Corporate and Government Sales
(800) 382-3419
corpsales@pearsontechgroup.com

For sales outside of the U.S., please contact:

International Sales
(317) 581-3793
international@pearsontechgroup.com

Visit Addison-Wesley on the Web: www.awprofessional.com

Library of Congress Cataloging-in-Publication Data

Seacord, Robert C.
   Modernizing legacy systems software technologies, engineering
processes, and business practices / Robert C. Seacord, Daniel Plakosh,
Grace A. Lewis.
       p. cm. —(The SEI series in software engineering)
   Includes bibliographical references and index.
   ISBN 0-321-11884-7 (Paperback : alk. paper)
    1. Software reengineering. 2. Software maintenance—Management. I.
Plakosh, Daniel. II. Lewis, Grace A. III. Title. IV. Series.

QA76.758 .S42 2003
005.1—dc21
2002152730

ISBN 0-321-11884-7
Text printed on recycled paper
1 2 3 4 5 6 7 8 9 10—CRS—0706050403
First printing, February 2003

In the spirit of recognizing our legacies, I am dedicating this book to the memory of my grandparents, Charles, Ruth, Andrew, and Flora; to my parents, Charles and Adrienne; and to my wife, Rhonda, and our children, Chelsea and Jordan.

—rCs

To my wife, Judy, for her love and support; and to my parents, Charles and Dolores, for the gift of an education.

—Dan

This book is dedicated to the people who make my life wonderful: my husband, Mike, for his love and support; my "Mami," Graciela, for leading me to where I am today; and my sister, Ingrid, for always being there.

—Grace

Contents

Preface

Software systems become legacy systems when they begin to resist modification and evolution. However, the knowledge embodied in legacy systems constitutes a significant corporate asset. Assuming that these systems still provide significant business value, they must then be modernized or replaced. This book describes a risk-managed approach to legacy system modernization that applies a knowledge of software technologies and an understanding of engineering processes within a business context.

Audience

Modernizing Legacy Systems: Software Technologies, Engineering Processes, and Business Practices should be useful to anyone involved in modernizing a legacy system.

- For a *software engineer*, the book should help you understand some of the larger business concerns that drive a modernization effort.

- For a *software designer*, this book should help you understand the impact of legacy code, coupled with incremental development and deployment practices, on design activities.

- For a *system architect*, this book explains the processes and techniques that have failed or succeeded in practice. It should also provide insight into how you can repeat these successes and avoid the failures.

- For an *IT manager*, this book explains how technology and business objectives influence the software modernization processes.

In particular, the book should help you answer the following questions:

- When and how do I decide whether a modernization or replacement effort is justified?
- How do I develop an understanding of the legacy system?
- How do I gain an understanding of, and evaluate the applicability of, information system technologies that can be used in the modernization of my system?

- When do I involve the stakeholders, and how can I reconcile their conflicting needs?
- What role does architecture play in legacy system modernization?
- How can I estimate the cost of a legacy system modernization?
- How can I evaluate and select a modernization strategy?
- How can I develop a detailed modernization plan?

Organization and Content

Modernizing Legacy Systems: Software Technologies, Engineering Processes, and Business Practices shows how legacy systems can be incrementally modernized. It uses and extends the methods and techniques described in *Building Systems from Commercial Components* [Wallnau 01] to draw on engineering expertise early in the conceptual phase to ensure realistic and comprehensive planning.

This book features an extensive case study involving a major modernization effort. The legacy system in this case study consists of nearly 2 million lines of COBOL code developed over 30 years. The system is being replaced with a modern system based on the Java 2 Enterprise Edition (J2EE) architecture. Additional challenges include a requirement to incrementally develop and deploy the system. We look at the strategy used to modernize the system; the use of Enterprise JavaBeans, message-oriented middleware, Java, and other J2EE technologies to produce the modern system; the supporting software engineering processes and techniques; and the resulting system.

Chapter 1 provides an introduction to the challenges and practices of software evolution. Chapter 2 introduces the major case study in the book. Chapter 3 introduces the risk-managed modernization (RMM) approach, which is elaborated in Chapters 4 through 17 and illustrated by the case study. At the beginning of Chapters 4 through 17, we provide an activity diagram of RMM as a road map to the chapter. Chapter 18 provides some recommendations to help guide your modernization efforts, although these recommendations cannot be fully appreciated without reading the main body of the book.

Throughout this book, we use the Unified Modeling Language (UML) to represent architecture drawings and design patterns. A brief introduction to UML is provided in Chapter 6.

Updated information, events, and news related to *Modernizing Legacy Systems: Software Technologies, Engineering Processes, and Business Practices* can be found at http://www.sei.cmu.edu/cbs/mls.

Acknowledgments

First, we want to thank Santiago Comella-Dorda, Vivian Martin, Len Bass, Felix Bachmann, Paul Clements, David Garlan, James Ivers, Reed Little, Robert Nord, Judith Stafford, Lutz Wrage, Russ Bunting, Dennis Smith, Liam O'Brien, Scott Tilley, David Zubrow, Brad Clark, and Wolf Goethert for their contribution of chapters in this book. Many people also contributed material either directly or indirectly, including John Robert, Patrick Place, Scott Hissam, Kurt Wallnau, Mark McLaughlin, and Robert Graham. We also owe a debt of gratitude to our manager, John Foreman, for his strong support, without which we would not have succeeded; and also the strong support we received from Scott Vesper, Lester Reagan, and Jon Dittmer.

Special thanks go to our in-house editors, Len Estrin and Pennie Walters, for their efforts in making our writing appear acceptable, Barbara White and Suzanne Couturiaux for making our work presentable, Shelia Rosenthal for helping us with the bibliography, Peter Gordon from Addison-Wesley for keeping the effort on target, and the Addison-Wesley production team, including Elizabeth Ryan, John Fuller, and Karin Hansen, and Evelyn Pyle and Rob Mauhar.

We are also grateful to the reviewers, whose insightful comments are reflected throughout our work: Thomas Soller, Ed Morris, Steven Seacord, Edward Neubecker, and Peter Bye. We also happily acknowledge the contributions of members not already mentioned of the Software Engineering Institute (SEI) COTS-Based Systems initiative. Last, we are indebted to Steve Cross, the director of the SEI, for providing an environment in which software engineering theory can be hardened in practice and promoted in public.

1

The Legacy Crisis

The significant problems we face cannot be solved at the same level of thinking we were at when we created them.
—Attributed to Albert Einstein

From the moment a software product is released, the race against time and aging begins. The cliché that "legacy code is code written yesterday" is increasingly true. As the pace of technology development increases, so too does the pace of technology obsolescence. Software modernization attempts to evolve a legacy system, or elements of the system, when conventional evolutionary practices, such as maintenance and enhancement, can no longer achieve the desired system properties.

Software modernization is more challenging than most software engineers, including seasoned veterans, suspect. Many modernization efforts fail. The Standish Group research shows that 23 percent of projects are canceled before completion, while only 28 percent finish on time and budget with expected functionality [Standish 01].

1.1 Modernization Challenges

Legacy system modernization efforts fail for a variety of reasons that, in our experience, reduce to a handful of factors: complexity, software technology and engineering processes, risk, commercial components, and business objectives.

COMPLEXITY

Because of the size and inherent inscrutability of most legacy systems, it is critical to reduce complexity where possible and to manage complexity where it cannot be eliminated. More than anything else, complexity is the greatest limiter in legacy system modernization. This complexity stems from a need to

- Consider a diverse set of modernization options, each of which may involve significant trade-offs
- Perform analysis and interact with experts to compensate for a lack of up-to-date legacy system requirements/design documentation
- Resolve the uncertainties about the implementation of a legacy system, including its functionality, integrity, and quality attributes
- Obtain extensive quantitative and qualitative data on which to base decisions
- Explore the impact of modernization from the perspective of multiple stake-holders and resolve conflicts stemming from multiple viewpoints
- Accommodate organizational and project constraints and coalesce decision making across the organization.

SOFTWARE TECHNOLOGY AND ENGINEERING PROCESSES

Software engineering processes and software technology are often separated by a large chasm. Technologists often look on software engineering as irrelevant. Software engineers, on the other hand, often fail to recognize that even the most advanced processes do not guarantee success if the product is not competitive. To succeed in building an enterprise system, it is necessary to understand the theory behind engineering processes, the "bits and bytes" of software technology, and the business requirements. However, the intersection of these concepts is a no-man's-land where programmer, software engineer, or manager dare not tread. Communication among these splintered groups is sporadic and ineffective, and successes are often the result of accidents and individual heroics. Although mastering the range of concepts and techniques required may be daunting, the alternative—backing into success while avoiding the many pitfalls—should be frightening.

RISK

Unfortunately, many organizations are unable or unwilling to properly manage risk. This may stem from a misbelief that "what I don't know can't hurt me" or a lack of time, usually stemming from an unwillingness to properly manage past risk. It may also stem from an insufficient understanding of risk management and risk mitigation techniques, such as contingency planning.

Of course, not all software modernization risks are bad risks; accepting some risk is essential if we are to accomplish anything meaningful. However, much advantage can be gained by simply identifying risks early in the project, maintaining and monitoring these risks, and asking, "How will this activity help mitigate risk identified in my modernization effort?"

COMMERCIAL COMPONENTS

The use of commercial components in a modernization effort is a practical necessity but is not without problems. Almost all software systems show signs of aging even before they are released. This is especially true for those developed with a large number of commercial components, because new component versions are released regularly. Software development efforts are often confronted with the problem of when to adopt and when to ignore these new releases. Many times, products are adopted when they fix an existing problem, less often when they provide a new capability, unless this new capability solves an existing problem. If the system is already well into the test phase, the configuration management board will be unlikely to accept the introduction of new versions of commercial software products, because the risk of introducing instabilities in the system is too great. As a result, it is likely that the released software contains old or obsolete component versions.

BUSINESS OBJECTIVES

When asked, many software engineering professionals tell you that they are in the business of making software; in reality, however, they are in the business of making money. As information technology (IT) is often considered overhead, this typically translates to increased efficiencies to accomplish the same or additional functions at lower costs. Legacy system modernization is an important tool in accomplishing this goal but must be performed within this context. Any modernization effort that falls outside business objectives, as management understands them, is headed for cancellation.

1.2 How Did We Get Here?

We've already looked at some of the challenges of modernization, but what are its root causes? One is *software size*. The amount of legacy code is immense and growing. This became evident in the late 1990s, when organizations hired legions of COBOL programmers and consultants to fix Y2K-related problems. In 1990, an estimated 120 billion lines of source code—primarily COBOL and FORTRAN—were being maintained [Ulrich 90]. Since 1990, there has been a huge increase in computers for business process support. One estimate is that roughly 250 billion lines of source code are now being maintained and that this number is increasing all the time [Sommerville 01].

Information systems tend to expand with time, as efforts to remove unused code are seldom funded. The average Fortune 100 company, for example, maintains 35 million lines of code and adds 10 percent each year only in enhancements, updates, and other maintenance. As a result, the amount of code maintained by these companies doubles in size every seven years [Müller 94].

So what is the problem with having all this software? Succinctly stated, more software means having more software to evolve and maintain. For example, companies modify software in response to changing business practices, to correct errors, or to improve performance, maintainability, or other quality attributes. This is all in accordance to Lehman's first law: "A large program that is used undergoes continuing change or becomes progressively less useful." [Lehman 85, p. 250]

Reasons for software change fall into the following four categories:

1. **Perfective.** These changes are made to improve the product, such as adding new user requirements, or to enhance performance, usability, or other system attributes. These types of changes are also called *enhancements*.

2. **Corrective.** These changes are made to repair defects in the system.

3. **Adaptive.** These changes are made to keep pace with changing environments, such as new operating systems, language compilers and tools, database management systems and other commercial components.

4. **Preventive.** These changes are made to improve the future maintainability and reliability of a system. Unlike the preceding three reactive reasons for change, preventive changes proactively seek to simplify future evolution.

Figure 1-1 shows the average distribution of software maintenance activities. In particular, more than 75 percent of maintenance costs are for providing

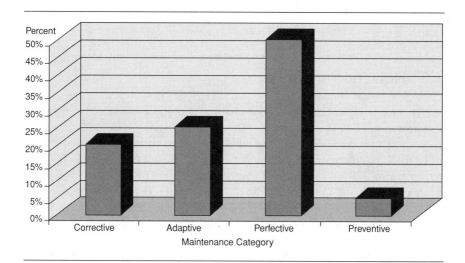

Figure 1-1   Distribution of maintenance by categories [Martin 83]

Is COBOL Dead?

Indicators suggest that COBOL remains ubiquitous.

- The Giga Information Group (GIG) has compiled data revealing that 70 percent or more of the world's active business applications are written in COBOL and that 16,000 large enterprises worldwide still use COBOL.
- The Gartner Group estimates that some 10,000 mainframe computers worldwide contain 200 billion lines of COBOL code.

Unfortunately, COBOL careers have little perceived growth. Most companies do not use COBOL for new development. COBOL code is being converted or replaced everywhere, limiting legacy COBOL programmers to maintenance tasks and data crunching. Young programmers do not want to learn COBOL because they do not want to be stuck doing maintenance. In fact, most universities don't teach COBOL anymore.

So how much longer will COBOL last? The answer is, until those 200 billion lines of COBOL are gone. That could be a long time.

—Grace

enhancements in the form of adaptive and perfective maintenance. This data is based on information collected more than 20 years ago [Martin 83]. Nonetheless, recent studies indicate that the distribution remains largely unchanged [Nosek 90, van Vliet 00].

Cumulative code changes over many years often leads to less maintainable code. Lehman's second law describes the effects of change on a system: "As a large program is continuously changed, its complexity, which reflects deteriorating structure, increases unless work is done to maintain or reduce it." [Lehman 85, p. 253]

Increased complexity means that the system becomes increasingly brittle because there is a greater chance of side effects with every change that is made. In turn, software maintenance becomes increasingly difficult, requiring more and better-trained software engineers.

The total cost of these types of modifications, which are considered maintenance or evolution activities, tend to exceed the initial development costs over the software's life cycle. As shown in Figure 1-2, the relative cost for maintaining and evolving the software has been steadily increasing and now represents more than 90 percent of the total cost [Moad 90, Erlikh 00]. Thus, most of the life-cycle costs for software occur after the initial delivery [Grady 87].

Therefore, *software change*, which leads to more code and more complex code, is another root cause of modernization. In the next section, we discuss how software size and software change have led to a legacy crisis.

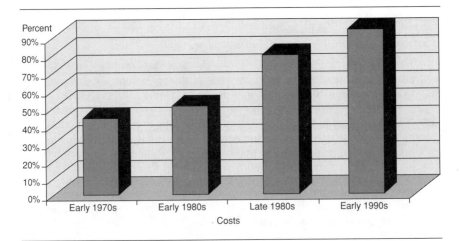

Figure 1-2   Software costs devoted to system evolution

1.3   The Legacy Crisis

Concern is growing that the development of new software is outpacing our ability to maintain it. With large portions of software budgets being devoted to maintenance, few resources remain for new development. Decreasing evolutionary costs significantly appears plausible but is difficult to achieve because many maintenance activities are unavoidable. If these trends continue, eventually no resources will be left to develop new systems, and we will enter the Middle Ages of the information age. In the remainder of this book, we refer to this as the *legacy crisis*.

We hope that the legacy crisis *can* be counteracted, but which forces are likely to reverse the trends? Possible counterforces include

- **Evolvable software development.** Maintainability is the ease with which a software system or component can be modified to correct faults, improve performance or other attributes, or adapt to a changed environment [IEEE 90]. As they become aware of the costs associated with maintaining legacy systems, management will increase the up-front investment necessary to develop evolvable systems. Organizations will spend the additional time and resources to keep these systems current and maintainable.

- **Software reengineering and modernization.** Concerned with increasing maintenance costs on existing legacy systems, organizations will attempt to reengineer or modernize these systems to reduce ongoing maintenance costs.

- **Use of commercial components.** Replacing custom code with commercial-off-the-shelf (COTS) software components reduces the amount of code an organization must maintain and costs are reduced because the cost of maintaining the COTS component is shared among multiple organizations. This task could involve replacing portions of a system or the whole system, as in the case of enterprise resource planning (ERP) systems.

- **Hardware improvements.** Increasingly powerful computing platforms allow maintenance organizations to reevaluate their approach to doing business.

- **Web and Internet.** The Web and the Internet have created a new model for building and using distributed systems. The move to e-business models, although not strictly a counterforce to the legacy crisis, is also driving legacy system modernization efforts. Many companies want on-line ordering, Web portals, and on-line services, not to mention a simple Web presence. Before they can implement enhanced Internet capabilities and services, companies must modernize their legacy systems to accommodate them.

- **Advanced programming languages and tools.** Programming languages and tools are becoming increasingly powerful and expressive. Modern programming languages allow the same amount of logic to be represented more succinctly, often reducing the amount of source code that must be supported. If used properly, object-oriented techniques, supported by many modern programming languages, also help to improve the maintainability of legacy software.

None of these counterforces alone is sufficient to prevent or to reverse the legacy crisis, but together they may reduce the overall effort required to maintain the ever-increasing amount of legacy software code.

1.4   Evolving Legacy Systems

System evolution covers a continuum of development activities, from adding a field in a database to completely reimplementing a system. System evolution activities can be divided into three categories: maintenance, modernization, and replacement [Weiderman 97]. Figure 1-3 illustrates how various evolution activities are applied at different phases of the system life cycle. The dotted line represents growing business needs. The solid lines represent the functionality provided by the information systems. Repeated system maintenance supports the business needs sufficiently for a time, but as the system ages, maintenance falls behind business needs. Eventually, a modernization effort that demands more time and effort than the maintenance activity is required. Finally, when the old system can no longer be evolved, it must be replaced.

Determining the evolutionary activity that is most appropriate at different points in the life cycle is a daunting challenge. Should we continue maintaining the system or modernize it? Should we completely replace the system? Enterprises that rely on legacy information systems, with limited budget, must obtain the best return on their investment. To make the correct decision, organizations

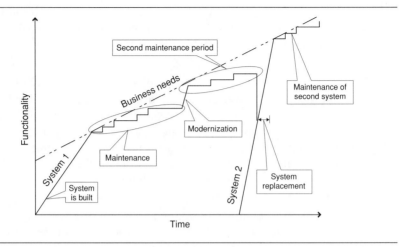

Figure 1-3   Information system life cycle

must realistically assess their legacy systems, determine an appropriate evolution strategy, and analyze the implications of each action. The result of the initial assessment must be based on an assessment of the value of the system to the organization and the system itself [Warren 98].

The remainder of this section examines the differences among maintenance, modernization, and replacement.

MAINTENANCE

Maintenance is an incremental and iterative process in which small changes are made to a system. These changes are often bug fixes or small functional enhancements that do not involve major structural changes. Maintenance is required to support the evolution of any system but has limitations. These limitations include the following.

- The competitive advantage derived from adopting new technologies is seriously constrained because enhancements, such as implementing a distributed architecture or a graphical user interface, are not typically considered maintenance operations.

- Maintenance costs for legacy systems can increase with time. Finding expertise in older technologies becomes increasingly difficult and expensive. Although it is relatively inexpensive to provide in-house training, engineers must be receptive to receiving this training.

- Modifying a legacy system to adapt it to new business needs becomes increasingly difficult, as the impact of many small changes can be greater than their sum.

MODERNIZATION

Modernization involves more extensive changes than maintenance but conserves a significant portion of the existing system. These changes often include restructuring the system, enhancing functionality, or modifying software attributes. Modernization is used when a legacy system requires more pervasive changes than those possible during maintenance, but it still has business value that must be preserved. Reasons for modernization usually stem from legacy system brittleness, inflexibility, isolation, nonextensibility, and lack of openness [Bisbal 99].

System modernization can be distinguished by the level of system understanding required to support the modernization effort [Weiderman 97]. *White-box* modernization requires knowledge of the internals of a legacy system. *Black-box* modernization requires knowledge only of the external interfaces of a legacy system.

White-Box Modernization. White-box modernization requires an understanding of legacy system internals. If this knowledge is unavailable, an initial process called *program understanding* [Chikofsky 90] is required. Program understanding involves modeling the domain, extracting information from the code, and creating abstractions that describe the underlying system structure [Tilley 95]. Although some advances have been made in program understanding, it is still a risky and work-intensive task [von Mayrhauser 94, Haft 95]. We discuss program understanding at length in Chapter 5.

After the code is analyzed and understood, white-box modernization can often include system or code restructuring. Software restructuring can be defined as "the transformation from one representation form to another at the same relative abstraction level, while preserving the subject system's external behavior (functionality and semantics)" [Chikofsky 90, p. 15]. This transformation is typically used to augment a quality attribute of the system, such as maintainability or performance.

Black-Box Modernization. Black-box modernization involves examining the inputs and outputs of a legacy system, within an operating context, to understand the system interfaces. This is usually not as difficult as white-box modernization.

Black-box modernization is often based on *wrapping*—surrounding the legacy system with a software layer that hides the unwanted complexity of the old system and exports a modern interface. Wrapping removes mismatches between the interface exported by a software artifact and the interfaces required by current integration practices [Wallnau 97, Shaw 95]. Ideally, wrapping is a black-box reengineering task because only the legacy interface is analyzed, and the legacy system internals are ignored. Unfortunately, this solution is not always practical and often requires understanding the software module's internals, using white-box techniques [Plakosh 99].

REPLACEMENT

Replacement requires rebuilding the system from scratch and is resource intensive. Replacement is appropriate when legacy systems cannot keep pace with business needs and when modernization is not possible or cost-effective [Bisbal 97]. Replacement may be the only option when white-box and black-box modernization approaches cannot be cost justified.

Systems can be replaced either all at once by using a "big-bang" approach or incrementally. When replacing a system incrementally, it helps if the system has some degree of modularization or cohesion. Often, the legacy system is reengineered as a preparatory step before beginning an incremental replacement effort.

Replacement has the following risks that should be evaluated before selecting this technique.

- IT personnel performing maintenance tasks may not be familiar with the new technologies.
- Replacement requires extensive testing of the new system. Legacy systems are usually well tested and tuned and encapsulate considerable business expertise. There is no guarantee that the new system will be as robust or functional as the old one (shown in Figure 1-3). This may cause a period of degraded system functionality.

1.5   Software Reengineering

Software reengineering is a form of modernization that improves capabilities and/or maintainability of a legacy system by introducing modern technologies and practices. Software reengineering offers a disciplined approach to migrating a legacy system toward an evolvable system. The process applies engineering principles to an existing system to meet new requirements. In the mid-1990s, the SEI developed a definition of reengineering: Reengineering is the systematic transformation of an existing system into a new form to realize quality improvements in operation, system capability, functionality, performance, or evolvability at a lower cost, schedule, or risk to the customer [Tilley 95, p. 3]. This definition emphasizes that the focus of reengineering is on improving existing systems with a greater return on investment (ROI) than could be obtained through a new development effort.

Reengineering is both more expensive than simple maintenance and less attractive—from a technical perspective—than replacing a legacy system. But even though reengineering may not be the cheapest or the most attractive option, it is often the most pragmatic. Because so many legacy systems exist, complete replacement is financially inconceivable for most organizations. Reengineering offers a cost-effective way to extend their useful lifetimes. The key advantages of reengineering over replacement are reduced risk and reduced cost.

Reengineering takes numerous forms: retargeting, revamping, use of commercial components, source code translation, code reduction, and functional transformation. All are intended to improve on a quality or set of qualities of the legacy system.

RETARGETING

Retargeting is the migration of a legacy system to a new hardware platform. Retargeting is often motivated by the gain of increasingly powerful hardware platforms and the pain of increasingly expensive maintenance cost of legacy platforms. The trend to retargeting is evidenced by the steadily contracting market share of traditional proprietary environments, such as Compaq/Tandem's Non-Stop, Unisys' MCP and OS 2200, Fujitsu Siemens' BS Series mainframes, Stratus's VOS, and Groupe Bull's GCOS. Migrating to a modern hardware platform often reduces operational and maintenance costs, allows the introduction of higher-performance computers, and provides an evolvable platform to other modernization efforts.

REVAMPING

The user interface (UI) is the most visible part of a system. Replacing only the UI is a common form of software reengineering often referred to as *revamping*. These days, organizations often "Web enable" their "green-screen" systems in response to pressures for Web presence and, from a technical standpoint, the ease of using a standard browser as interface to a system. Revamping the UI should improve usability and is always noticed by the end users of a system. On the other hand, Web enablement may require the purchase of additional hardware for the clients and may be slower than the legacy green screens.

A common black-box technique for revamping is *screen scraping* [Carr 98]. As shown in Figure 1-4, screen scraping consists of wrapping old, text-based interfaces with new, graphical interfaces. The old interface typically consists of a set of text screens running in a terminal. In contrast, the new interface can be a PC-based graphical user interface (GUI) or even a Hypertext Markup Language (HTML) client running in a Web browser. This technique can be extended easily, enabling one new UI to wrap one or more legacy systems. The new graphical interface communicates with the old one through a specialized commercial tool.[1] These tools often generate the new GUI automatically from the original screens.

---

[1] For example, OC://WebConnect Enterprise Integration Server from Open-Connect Systems or QuickApp from Attachmate.

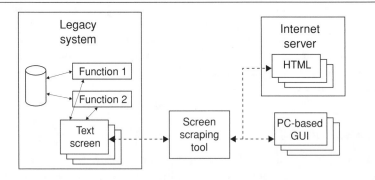

Figure 1-4 Legacy system wrapping using screen scraping.

From the perspective of the legacy system, the new graphical interface is indistinguishable from an end user entering text in a screen. From the end user's point of view, the modernization has been successful. The new system now provides a modern, usable graphical interface. However, from the IT department's perspective, the "new" system remains inflexible and difficult to maintain because it is still dependent on the legacy system. With screen scraping, it is still not possible to add, modify, or recompose functions and screens. Its detractors call this approach "whipped cream on road kill." Screen scraping can, however, be effective for stable systems for which the principal objective is to improve usability.[2]

Screen scraping can also be used to generate application program interfaces (APIs) from legacy user interfaces. This technique was applied in a large government program integrating an ERP system with other systems. In this case, screen scraping was used to extract data from the ERP, reversing the normal use of this wrapping technique, because the ERP did not provide a callable API.

COMMERCIAL COMPONENTS

Software reengineering projects may replace existing legacy code with commercial-off-the-shelf (COTS) components. Although replacing code that you own with components that you license may seem counterintuitive, there are numerous reasons to attempt it. Replacing legacy code with commercial components typically reduces the amount of source code that must be maintained. When building a business case for this type of reengineering project, it is important to consider not only the savings of not having to maintain code but also the cost of extracting the legacy code, the amount of glue code that must be developed and maintained, and any additional licensing and training costs.

---

[2] Imagine using on-screen buttons and other navigational tools instead of awkward combinations of function keys.

Commercial components may be categorized as *infrastructure* or *functional* components. Examples of infrastructure components are database managers, HTTP servers, ORBs, application servers, and middleware products. Financial systems, human resource systems, and ERP systems are examples of functional components.

Replacing legacy code with commercial *infrastructure* components is done for many reasons. These components are often more robust, more secure, have better performance, are more scalable, or are more usable. In addition, commercial infrastructure components often implement industry-standard interfaces, providing integration opportunities in future reengineering projects. Unfortunately, these components often touch many portions of the system, making the infrastructure difficult to extract and replace. Still, replacing legacy code with infrastructure components may well be worth the cost in many cases.

Replacing *functional* components may also provide additional capabilities and improve on such attributes of system quality as robustness or performance. Replacing functional components can be quite difficult. New components often support business processes that differ from existing ones. This often means undergoing some level of business process reengineering, which can be a time-consuming, expensive exercise.

SOURCE CODE TRANSLATION

Another common reengineering project is source code translation—converting from an old programming language to a more modern language. Source code translation may be performed along with moving a system off a legacy platform if, for example, the current language is not available on the target platform. These projects are somewhat risky because benefits are often overestimated and costs underestimated. To be cost-effective, these efforts require automated translation tools. Automatic translation offers consistency; however, it cannot significantly change the structure of the code. For example, automatically translating COBOL to Java often results in code that looks like COBOL written in the Java programming language. For this and other reasons, transformed code is often difficult to maintain: in this case, for either a COBOL or a Java programmer.

Transforming legacy source code to a newer version of the same language can help keep the legacy system current with the evolving environment. However, the risk of source code translation increases as the differences between the legacy and target languages increase. For example, converting from COBOL 68 to COBOL 74 or from COBOL 74 to COBOL 85 should be less risky than converting directly from COBOL 68 to COBOL 85. Likewise, converting from one object-oriented language, such as C++, to another, such as Java, might be fairly straightforward, whereas converting from a procedural language, such as COBOL, to an object-oriented language, such as Java, may be risky. For example, a straightforward translation from COBOL to Java might translate programs

A Tale of Automatic Translation

At the SEI, we are often asked to evaluate software engineering tools, methods, and processes. Recently, we evaluated the results of an automated translation of COBOL to C++. The characteristics of the resulting code follow.

1. The generated C++ is a relatively straightforward translation from COBOL to C++. Thus, the code looks like COBOL written in the C++ programming language.
2. The code contains large class structures, with many nested classes defined within these classes.
3. The class hierarchy is not well organized or designed.
4. All variables within a class are declared as public.
5. All methods within a class are declared as public.
6. Many of the class constructors have a huge number of initializers and are basically unreadable.
7. A large number of the methods do not have any parameter values or return values. Therefore, most of the generated C++ methods perform operations on data via side effects, using global variables.
8. The generated C++ uses GOTOs in an unacceptable manner for a structured programming language such as C++.
9. Many of the generated class and variable names are not meaningful to a developer or a maintainer.
10. The generated code contains few comments. Even comments from the original COBOL source code were lost.
11. The code does not separate application logic from the user interface in a way that the application logic could be reused in a modernized system.

—Dan

directly into classes regardless of object-oriented principles. The sidebar above, "A Tale of Automatic Translation" provides other examples of the consequences of automated translation.

CODE REDUCTION

Code reduction is conceptually simple even if its execution may be difficult. The idea is analogous to moving: It is better to throw out stuff before you move rather than move and then throw it out. In this case, unnecessary code is eliminated before porting the remaining code to another platform or language. The benefit of code reduction is especially apparent when using a third party to port the code. Many of the organizations providing this service charge from $6 to $20 per line of code ported [Singh-Rangar 00]. Therefore, eliminating unnecessary code can provide an easily measured cost savings.

Identifying functionality that is no longer required can account for large reductions in source code. This includes functionality that was originally required but is now unnecessary. You must make sure that there are no hidden or unknown dependencies with other software modules before removing this code.

Numerous tools exist to identify redundant blocks of code.[3] These tools are often included with software products designed to identify and extract business rules. Although their ability to differentiate business rules from garbage code is arguable, these tools can usually identify similar code segments, using pattern matching. These code segments can often be converted into subroutines through a manual programming effort.[4] Although this approach to code reduction is effective, it has risks. Because developing reusable subroutines is largely a manual process, it is easy to introduce defects, especially as the degree of similarity between the code segments decreases.

One approach to managing such an effort is to eliminate code segments with the highest degree of matching code and gradually proceed to less similar code segments. It is possible to track the cost of removing each line of code; when the cost of porting each line of code is well known, it is a simple matter to determine when the process should be terminated. Of course, this process must also account for any delay in the schedule resulting from the code reduction, as well as any "lost opportunities" as a result of using staff in this manner.

FUNCTIONAL TRANSFORMATION

Functional transformation includes *program structure improvement, program modularization*, and *data reengineering*. Program structure improvement can come in the form of replacing GOTOs with structured code or simplifying complex condition statements. Generally, improvements in program structure start by identifying the structural flaw that is repeated throughout the system. Correcting it involves choosing an alternative structure and converting from the old structure to the new one. The modification of the source code may be performed automatically or manually.

Program modularization collects related parts of a program into common modules. Modularization makes it easier to identify and to eliminate redundant code, optimize interactions between modules, and simplify interactions with the remainder of the system. Program modularization is often a preliminary step in an incremental modernization effort because well-defined modules are easier to replace with new components.

---

[3] For example, McCabe Reengineer and Semantic Designs CloneDR.

[4] *Authors' note:* In 1982, I worked with a programmer whose programs consisted of large blocks of similar code, each with only minor variations. When I asked why he used this unusual coding style, he told me that he had had a bad experience with subroutines and no longer trusted them. This is an example of how poor coding practices can lead to redundant code and increased maintenance costs. —rCs

Data reengineering involves modifying the storage, organization, and format of data processed by the legacy system. Data reengineering is often necessary because of data degradation or because data has been recorded inconsistently at the multiple locations from where it was consolidated.

1.6   Incremental Development and Deployment

The major case study in this book involves incrementally replacing a system through a series of white-box modernizations. Each of the counterforces introduced in this chapter was applied at various times to the overall effort.

Incremental development reduces overall program risks by allowing both users and developers to gradually understand the new system. Lessons learned from each increment can be applied to prevent mistakes in later increments. Smaller steps are typically easier to manage and to evaluate. Smaller increments can also result in a more focused effort.

Theoretically, building a system in a single increment minimizes development and deployment costs because it is necessary to test and deploy only a single system. The costs of system testing and deployment are fixed costs that are largely independent of the size of the increment, and are incurred for each increment. In practice, a single development/deployment cycle does not typically lower development costs, because of the complexity of completing the entire project at one time.

Incremental development is also likely to influence the target architecture toward resembling the legacy architecture. This occurs when the legacy system is separated into functional increments along lines dictated by the legacy architecture. As the number of increments increases and the corresponding size of each increment decreases, legacy and modernized architectures tend to converge.

A componentization strategy that defines new components and how they interact with legacy components to maintain existing functionality during the development period is also part of the overall strategy. Certain componentization strategies may require the database to be iteratively restructured. Restructuring the database has implied costs, including rework and the need to migrate the "new" legacy data after each increment.

To be successful, this strategy must consider the future of the programmers who have maintained these legacy systems for years. These programmers must be involved as stakeholders in defining the strategy. There should be a plan to enable them to come up to speed in the new technology while they are maintaining the legacy system. Legacy system programmers will more willingly collaborate if they have a clear role in the new system.

1.7 Summary

Software modernization requires carefully analyzing candidate modernization options and strategies that affect the interests of many stakeholders. As a result, software modernization requires making nontrivial and nonobvious trade-offs. These trade-offs are multifaceted and include technical, programmatic, and organizational considerations that may strain an organization's decision-making abilities.

As a result, development teams approach large modernization efforts either with trepidation and misgivings or with unwarranted self-confidence. Unfortunately, the former group is usually the one with the most experience.

Fortunately, there is a middle road, which is to approach the modernization with respect for the magnitude of the effort and a *plan*. This plan must demonstrate an understanding of the legacy system and modern information system technologies, as well as an understanding of the *as-built* and *as-desired* architectures. Most important, this plan must manage risk throughout the modernization effort.

1.8 For Further Reading

- Brodie and Stonebraker describe various replacement techniques [Brodie 95]. Seng and Tsai illustrate a complete replacement process [Seng 99].

- The book, *The Renaissance of Legacy Systems* [Warren 99] describes method support for software system evolution. This is part of the RENAISSANCE project—an ESPRIT-funded research project in software reengineering and software evolution.

- Ransom et al. describe an assessment technique for determining whether a legacy system should be replaced, modernized, or maintained [Ransom 98].

- Lakhotia and Deprez describe a semiautomatic restructuring technique to improve the cohesion of legacy procedures [Lakhotia 98].

2

The Beast

The remainder of this book is built around a modernization case study, affectionately nicknamed "The Beast." This case study combines elements from numerous modernization efforts we have participated in. The need to do so is straightforward: Large modernization efforts often take many years. By the time the final system is deployed, the methods and techniques used in the requirements phase have likely faded into obscurity. This case study is referenced throughout the remainder of this book to explain our approach to legacy system modernization.

The Beast involves the modernization of a large supply-chain system that we refer to as the Retail Supply System (RSS). Written primarily in COBOL, RSS has evolved over 30 years. When asked if anyone understood the design of this system, one of the lead engineers quipped, "Yes, but they are all dead now." As a result of this unstructured evolution, the system has become extremely brittle and difficult to maintain. RSS operates at more than 90 sites. Although the application is the same, the data stored is specific to each location. Because of the size and complexity of the system, a big-bang replacement was infeasible. The system is being modernized in a series of efforts, each of which replaces and retains significant portions of the legacy system.

Working with a large, complex system has presented the development team with many challenges, not the least of which is the information infrastructure of the enterprise. This infrastructure consists of a patchwork of mainframe, minicomputer, and desktop applications—both centralized and distributed—under dispersed control. These systems are separated by geography and variations in policies, cultures, and customs among various groups in the organization. Additionally, many of these systems are being modernized at the same time. Therefore, the composition of enterprise systems interfacing with the modernized RSS is schedule driven and time dependent. For example, if the RSS replacement system is deployed in 3 years, it will need to be integrated with the legacy financial system. However, if it slips 1 year, the RSS must be integrated with the replacement financial system unless the schedule for that system has slipped as well. Needless to say, this has created a rather dynamic planning environment. Despite these problems, all these legacy systems are critical and cannot be discarded without their capabilities being provided elsewhere.

The principal goal of the development effort was to create a modernized system that could be supported and easily maintained. The RSS management felt that this could be best achieved by developing a modern architecture based on software components that could be easily deployed at various geographical locations yet maintain the ability to communicate with the remainder of the system. These large-grained software components, or *business objects*, should also support industry-standard interfaces. This allows the use of commercial products—if not now, then as they become available.

Additionally, the modernized system was required to comply with the organization's proprietary Standard Retail Framework (SRF). The SRF is based on existing industry standards from the Open Applications Group, Sun Microsystems, and other industry groups. This constraint required that business objects be implemented by smaller-grained components, such as Enterprise JavaBeans (EJB), Java servlets, and CORBA servers. These small-grained components are conceptually closer to the components definition provided by Szyperski in his book on component software [Szyperski 98]. The process of creating a modern architecture along these lines is referred to as *componentization*. Although it is more appropriate to refer to this as business objectification, this phrase is too cumbersome.

2.1   The Retail Supply System

Before a modernization effort can begin, it is necessary to understand how the legacy system is used and how it is constructed. RSS has the following characteristics.

- The legacy RSS is deployed on a Unisys Clearpath server running the OS 2200 operating system.

- RSS is operated at more than 90 locations and supports 25,000 users at 350 locations, many of which are remote.

- A typical RSS transaction completes in 3 to 5 seconds.

- The RSS is coded in Unisys COBOL 85 and uses the Unisys Data Management System (DMS) 2200 network database.

- The system consists of approximately 1.8 million lines of code, including batch processing, reports, and on-line high-volume transaction processing (HVTIP) transactions.

- The user interface is implemented using the Display Processing System (DPS) with screens generated by the DPS FORMGEN tool.

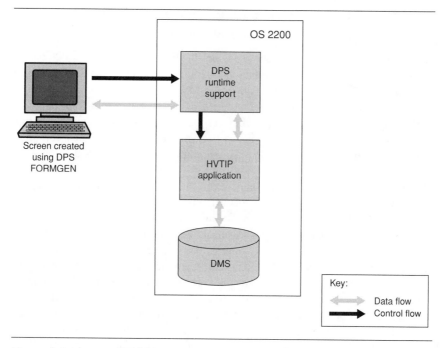

Figure 2-1   Legacy RSS high-level architecture

- The RSS consists of approximately 900 program elements, each containing about 2,000 lines of COBOL 85 code. In total, there are more than 13,000 CALL, COPY, and PERFORM dependencies between program elements.

Figure 2-1 provides a high-level architecture of the legacy RSS. The following sections describe additional details about the database, user interface, and transaction processing subsystems.

DATABASE

As already mentioned, the RSS maintains data in the Unisys DMS 2200 network database. The DMS is a logical data manager based on the specifications recommended by the CODASYL committees for network database processing. The DMS 2200 includes a variety of database storage structures, high-level language interfaces, and a selection of data-accessing techniques, as well as several levels of database recovery and security.

Program elements interact with the DMS by using the following operations:

- STORE: stores a new record in the database
- FETCH: combined FIND and GET that establishes a specific record in the database as the current record of the run unit

- MODIFY: changes the contents of specified data items in a database record
- DELETE: logically removes a record from a mass storage file

The RSS references 700 database tables in slightly fewer than 11,000 operations. Figure 2-2 illustrates both data flow and control flow in the RSS. Program elements typically fetch records from the DMS database into common storage. These data records may then be completely or partly transferred from common storage to working storage, where they can be accessed by application program elements. Modified data may be placed back in common storage and control is passed between program elements, using common storage to pass data between program elements.[1]

Eventually, data is written from working storage back to common storage. A program element may perform a STORE operation to create a new database record or a MODIFY operation to update an existing record.

Figure 2-2 is a fairly straightforward illustration of data and control flow in the RSS. However, many internal complications make it difficult to understand, much less depict, legacy data flows. Foremost among these is poor data encapsulation. Any program element can read and write to a database record. Many of these relationships can be identified easily by searching for STORE, FETCH, MODIFY, and DELETE operations in the source code. However, program elements can indirectly affect data stored in the database by modifying information in common storage that is then written to the database by a different program element.

Other complications include the use of FILLER space to hold data and the REDEFINES clause that allows the same common storage area to be accessed using different names. Both of these complications can make it difficult to identify and manage data flow in the legacy system.

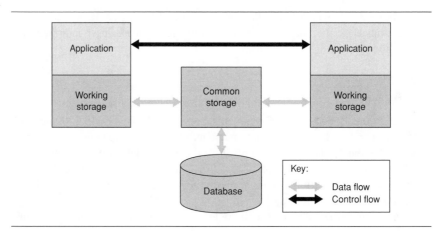

Figure 2-2 Data and control flow in RSS

[1] This is similar to the use of shared memory in System V UNIX.

USER INTERFACE

The RSS uses the Unisys Display Processing System (DPS 2200) to provide the user interface. The DPS 2200 enables a programmer to define forms—screens—and incorporate them into application programs. Forms are created by using the FORMGEN program and are then transferred to working storage.

At runtime, application programs read the screen data from working storage and display the screens to the end users. The DPS runtime handler transfers data between the form and the application program during program execution.

TRANSACTIONS

OS 2200 transaction processing (TIP) is a modular extension of the OS 2200 operating system. TIP is the basis for a high-performance system in which an end user at a remote terminal inputs a message that executes an application program. The high-volume transaction processing environment (HVTIP) passes transactions through an arbitrary sequence of subprograms to maintain high throughput.

The RSS relies on HVTIP to maintain data integrity during transaction processing. A typical RSS transaction invokes between 20 and 40 program elements, most of which range in size from 3K lines of code (KLOC) to 7K lines of code. The RSS also uses the Unisys message control bank (MCB) to interface with the transaction programs for message recovery and transaction scheduling.

2.2 Recent History

In this section, we describe some modifications to RSS that occurred prior to the modernization effort.

WEB ENABLEMENT

Before beginning the effort to replace the RSS, the project managers decided to comply with a corporate mandate to Web enable all legacy data systems. As the RSS replacement effort would result in a Web-enabled system, an argument could be made to defer Web enablement until a later stage in the process. Because this was primarily a political decision, however, arguing the merits of one approach over the other was somewhat irrelevant in this case.

Politically motivated decisions are part of any engineering and development effort, and responding to them in an appropriate manner should be routinely taught in any undergraduate software engineering course. In this case, the most appropriate action was to satisfy the request with minimal disruption and delay.

The user interface of the legacy RSS is implemented using the DPS, a screen-management system for creating and supporting "green screens." Unisys provides the Web Transaction Server (WebTS), a product that can revamp user interfaces developed in this manner. WebTS supports Web pages and transactions and can deliver Web-style HTML documents. It can also invoke transactions based on user actions, such as completing an input form or clicking a hyperlink. Transaction results are returned to the user as a standard HTML page [Unisys 00].

WebTS can deliver both *static* and *dynamic* pages. Static pages are prefabricated and may contain various types of data, such as text, VBScript, JavaScript, graphics—for example, JPEG and GIF—video, and audio. In addition to static data, dynamic pages can also include data that is retrieved at runtime and formatted by transaction programs.

When the user invokes a static page, the text, graphics, and other static content are read by the WebTS directly from the file system and referred to the Web browser for display. If the user calls a dynamic page, WebTS must start the targeted transaction, process the data, and generate an output message formatted in HTML.

WebTS implements dynamic pages by using traditional-style HVTIP/TIP transactions, as shown in Table 2-1. The use of Open/DTP transactions via a special OLTPTx transaction is not a viable option for the RSS that relies on HVTIP/TIP transactions. The two remaining mechanisms for invoking transactions are both viable options.

The Web Enabler for the DPS uses a Java applet that is downloaded to the client's browser. This applet accepts user input and makes the appropriate transaction calls. The transaction-processing application does not need to be modified to allow access from the Web.

TIP and HVTIP transactions can also be called using the WebTS interface based on the CGI. This approach requires modifying the existing code, but eliminates the dependency on the DPS.

To call a transaction, WebTS performs minimal processing to determine where to send the message. WebTS calls the HVTIP application, which initiates the transaction. All other processing is performed by the transaction itself.

The goal of this preliminary effort was to Web enable the RSS as quickly as possible. The Web Enabler for the DPS product was used to minimize the effort and consequent disruption to the RSS replacement schedule. Figure 2-3 shows the RSS architecture after Web enablement.

Table 2-1 Mechanisms for Invoking Transactions

Technique	Description
Web Enabler for the DPS	Existing DPS-based transaction applications can be called via WebTS without change.
CGI for C/COBOL	UCS C and UCS COBOL transactions can be called via WebTS, using a high-level, Web-compatible interface. Existing HVTIP/TIP transactions require at least some modification.
OLTPTx	Existing Open/DTP transaction applications can be called via WebTS with little or no change.

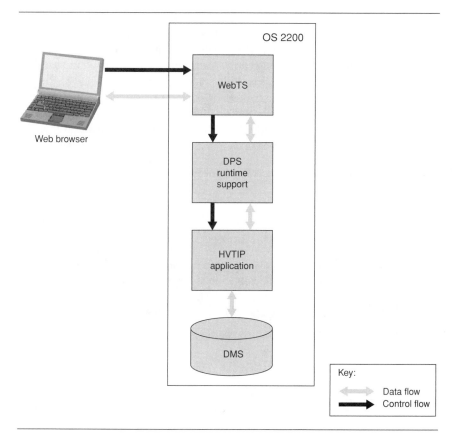

Figure 2-3   The RSS after Web enablement with the Web Enabler

REPORTS

RSS provides reports to management for decision making. As in any organization, management continually requested new reports, new data aggregations, and
new ways to look at data. The ability for the maintenance organization to provide
these new reports was hampered by a restriction from changing the database
schema—imposed because of the ensuing system instability—and the dispersal
of the data over 90 locations. These new requests usually resulted in manually
exporting raw data, importing it into another tool, such as Microsoft Excel, using
the tool to perform calculations on the data, aggregating the information from
various files, and, finally, formatting the data. Depending on the nature of the
request, this process could take anywhere from several hours to several days and
was not adequately responsive to management needs.

    After analyzing the existing database structure and the nature of the most
common requests, an Oracle database was created that aggregates data from the

90 DMS databases. Data is transferred from the DMS to the Oracle database once every 24 hours. Developers could create reports by using such tools as Oracle Discoverer or any other COTS-reporting tools that work with Oracle.

In addition to satisfying the needs of management during the modernization effort, migrating reports to Oracle at this stage had several advantages. Implemented reports using Oracle Discoverer or other COTS-reporting tool made it unnecessary to maintain and migrate COBOL report modules. The software maintenance staff also became more familiar with their future database environment early in the modernization effort.

2.3   Summary

Modernizing the RSS was, and continues to be, a complicated task with technical, process, and managerial issues. As a huge amalgamation of antiquated code implementing an obscure and undecipherable design, it is in every way a highly representative example of a legacy system! The complexity in the RSS is derived primarily from the system's size and inscrutability—making an ad hoc approach to modernization inherently risky.

3

Risk-Managed Modernization

First ponder, then dare.
—Helmuth von Moltke (1800–1891)

We are prepared to take risks, but intelligent risks. The policy of being too cautious is the greatest risk of all.
—Jawaharlal Nehru,
Speech to Parliament
New Delhi, 18 February 1953

The modernization approach described in this book integrates software engineering concepts with an organized understanding of the information systems technologies that both constrain and define the solution space. The objective of this approach is effective risk management and mitigation leading to the development of a modernization plan that minimizes the risk of the modernization effort.

This chapter introduces the *risk-managed modernization (RMM)* approach. This chapter briefly reviews the topic of risk management, recommends the use of portfolio analysis to select candidate systems for modernization, and introduces the activities involved in risk-managed modernization. The rest of the book expands on these activities and uses the case study introduced in Chapter 2 to illustrate this approach.

3.1 Risk Management

Risk management is a software engineering practice that continuously assesses what can go wrong (risks) determines what risks are important, and implements strategies to deal with those risks. Risk management is not a new idea; it is an integral element of the spiral development process developed by Barry Boehm

[Boehm 88] and is documented in a large body of work [Boehm 91, Karolak 96, Higuera 96, Hall 98].

Figure 3-1 illustrates a UML activity diagram of the RMM approach. Ovals in the diagram represent activities. Arrows represent transition between activities. The horizontal *synchronization* bars require completion of the previous activities before starting new ones. The process starts with a modernization project that has been selected using portfolio analysis. The end state for the process is an integrated modernization plan.

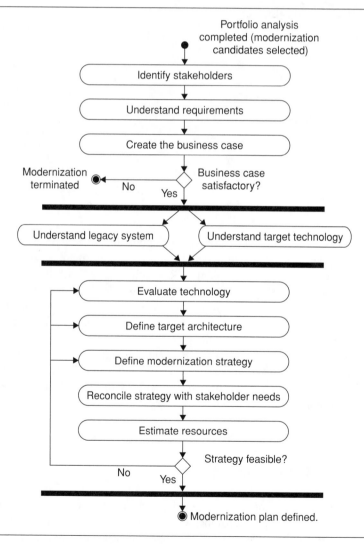

Figure 3-1   Risk-managed modernization approach

PORTFOLIO ANALYSIS

The portfolio analysis establishes measures of technical quality and business value for a set of systems and evaluates this set against the measures [Warren 99].

Technical quality is the measure of goodness of an application or system against a defined set of technical criteria. Example criteria for technical quality include frequency of new releases, ease of making changes, hardware and software reliability, organizational infrastructure, system performance, accuracy, ease of operation, availability of training, and number of vendor related tools and hardware.

Business value is a measure of importance of the system or application to the organization. Example criteria for business value include contribution to profit, level of usage, number of business goals satisfied, system value, user satisfaction and the value of the information that the system or application stores.

Legacy systems are evaluated against these measures and positioned on a portfolio analysis graph, such as the one shown in Figure 3-2. Positioning a system in one of these quadrants requires the establishment of criteria to measure technical quality as well as business value. The quadrant each system appears in can suggest an appropriate evolution strategy.

- **Quadrant 1:** Systems having low business value and poor technical quality are logical candidates for replacement with commercial packages, for two reasons. First, because they have low technical quality, they need to be improved or replaced. Second, because they have low business value, they do not provide any critical services or support any core competencies. These systems may be used for payroll, human resources, or similar services that are not specific to the company's core business.

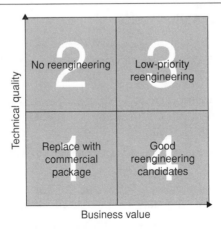

Figure 3-2 Portfolio analysis graph

- **Quadrant 2:** Systems with high technical quality and low business value should not require reengineering, modernization, or replacement efforts.
- **Quadrant 3:** High-quality systems with high business value should be actively evolved, using the evolutionary development practices discussed in Chapter 1.
- **Quadrant 4:** Systems with high business value and low technical quality are the best candidates for modernization or replacement.

After completing the preliminary *portfolio analysis*, you must take into account any organizational or resource issues. These issues can significantly increase risk to a modernization effort. Typical issues include politics, cost, schedule, available staff, technical skills required to perform the modernization effort, development staff, end user training, training personnel to use the modernized system, and user acceptance of the modernized system. Once you have performed the *portfolio analysis* and identified modernization issues, you can select and prioritize candidate systems and develop your overall modernization strategy.

IDENTIFY STAKEHOLDERS

Developers, testers, maintainers, system administrator, customers, vendors, sponsors, end users, architects, and representatives of interacting systems are stakeholders: people who have a vested interest in a project. These people will ultimately judge the outcome and impact of the modernization project. As a result, it is important to obtain their agreement and support. This can often be a challenge because stakeholders from different groups have different interests and view risks in different ways.

UNDERSTAND REQUIREMENTS

Requirements definition may be the most difficult task in software development and modernization. In general, requirements can be divided into the following four categories:

1. **User.** User requirements are capabilities that must be provided by the system. These requirements are often expressed as tasks or activities that must be supported by the system.
2. **System.** System requirements describe the capabilities of the system and the system itself.
3. **Constraints.** Constraints include decisions that have already been made, such as interactions with other systems, development standards, and cost.
4. **Nonfunctional.** Nonfunctional requirements include behavioral properties, such as performance, usability, and security, that the system must have.

Accurate software requirements clarify what is expected of the system, therefore reducing risk. Many software projects fail because of lack of rigor in the requirements process or an inadequate definition of requirements. As in any software project, requirements must be complete, consistent, understood, and valid. Using stakeholders to verify and validate requirements helps ensure that the system will ultimately perform as expected.

CREATE THE BUSINESS CASE

A business case is a document that supports decision making and planning. Because software modernization projects require substantial labor and financial resources, a business case can help convince management that the project is financially viable. Therefore, it is often key in obtaining project funding and approval.

As an essential part of the management decision process, a business case should not be viewed simply as a way to justify a particular effort. Rather, it should help the decision maker decide which approaches, if any, should be evaluated further. Therefore, a good business case considers several modernization approaches and contingencies, along with the technical and economical justification for selecting a particular approach. In general, a good business case should provide information about the project purpose and objectives, a description of the current system and current business process, a description of the future system and future business process, a cost estimate, a cost-benefit analysis, a risk assessment, a change analysis, and measures of performance. Change analysis includes changes to personnel, equipment, software, hardware, and support. Measures of performance are used to assess achievements, effectiveness, and efficiency.

It is crucial to understand stakeholder requirements to build an accurate business case. Chapter 4 provides more details on identifying stakeholders, understanding requirements, and creating the business case.

UNDERSTAND THE LEGACY SYSTEM

Understanding both the legacy system and its context are essential to the success of any modernization effort. The challenge is developing this competency in an efficient, cost-effective, and timely manner. Techniques available to meet this challenge include reverse engineering, program understanding, and architecture reconstruction. Chapter 5 describes these techniques in detail.

Reverse engineering and program understanding were briefly introduced in Chapter 1. Architecture reconstruction is the process of determining the as-built architecture of an implemented legacy system [Kazman 01]. This is done through a detailed analysis of the system, often using tool support. The tools extract information about the system and help build and aggregate successive levels of abstraction. If successful, the end result is an architectural representation that helps reason about the system.

When the Best and the Brightest Fail

Several years ago, we were involved in a legacy system modernization effort at a trucking company. The project was initially attempted by the internal IT department, which failed because of the team's lack of knowledge of the target J2EE technologies and because of organizational problems. Wishing to avoid repeating this failure, the trucking company hired professional services from one of the companies instrumental in developing the J2EE technologies being used. In fact, nothing negative could be said about this organization's understanding of J2EE technology and its ability to apply the technology in the construction of software systems.

Surprising many, this second effort also failed. The root cause of this failure was a lack of understanding by the professional services organization of the legacy system. Of course, what we mean by "legacy system" here goes well beyond simply understanding the source code and the hardware platforms. In this case, the professional services organizations had failed to

- Understand the organization of the trucking company
- Properly identify the stakeholders and quantify stakeholder needs
- Understand the operating policies and procedures of the trucking company
- Understand the modernization goals
- Properly elicit, understand, and negotiate system requirements

Despite the fact that this professional service organization consisted of intelligent, highly qualified software engineers, it was not able to succeed in this modernization effort. The cause was a failure to understand the legacy system.

—rCs

Architecture reconstruction introduces a second major theme of our modernization approach: "architecture driven." Architecture is necessary both to identify a desired end state and to guide you there.

Many excellent texts have been written on software architecture, in particular *Software Architecture in Practice* [Bass 98]. It is unnecessary to reproduce these efforts here. We have, however, included a chapter on architectural representation (Chapter 6) written in collaboration with Len Bass, Felix Bachmann, Paul Clements, David Garlan, James Ivers, Reed Little, Robert Nord, and Judith Stafford. This material is derived from their book *Documenting Software Architectures: Views and Beyond* [Clements 02]. Because the practice in this area is ad hoc, we felt it useful to include a summary of that work in this book.

UNDERSTAND EXISTING SOFTWARE TECHNOLOGIES

Software practitioners trying to modernize a legacy system often complain that the available software engineering techniques, methods, and processes are disconnected from reality. The reality of these practitioners is like reality anywhere: It is messy and lacks identifiable features that can be abstracted into a repeatable process. Instead of evaluating similar software development efforts and looking for common features, many software engineers simply create idealized processes that maximize one variable, such as quality, while ignoring numerous other variables, such as cost, schedule, and technology.

Of these variables, only technology is fixed; cost, quality, and schedule can be traded off. As a result, it is important to understand both the technologies used in the legacy system development and those that can be used in the modernization effort. The reason for this is simple: It is necessary to understand the fixed constraints in the problem space before considering how to bind values to the variables.[1]

In general, three classes of information system technology are of interest in legacy system modernization:

1. Technologies used to construct the legacy systems, including the languages and database systems.

2. Modern technologies, which often represent nirvana to those mired in decades-old technology and which hold (the often unfulfilled) promise of powerful, effective, easily maintained enterprise information systems.

3. Technologies offered by the legacy system vendors. These technologies provide an upgrade path for those too timid or wise to jump head-first into the latest wave of IT offerings. Legacy system vendors offer these technologies for one simple reason: to provide an upgrade path for system modernization that does not necessitate leaving the comfort of the "mainframe womb." Although these technologies can provide a smoother road toward a modern system, they often result in an *acceptable* solution that falls short of the ideal.

This book discusses all three classes of information system technologies. In Chapter 7, we describe the COBOL and Java programming languages, which figure prominently in the case study. We also discuss various forms of data repositories, including database management systems (DBMS) and data warehouses. Finally, Chapter 7 includes a discussion of data representations for information exchange, including electronic data interchange (EDI) and the eXtensible Markup Language (XML).

We further explore information system technologies relevant to our case study in Chapters 8 and 9. Chapter 8 discusses distributed transactions, providing background information on both distributed communication and transaction technologies. Chapter 9 describes middleware technologies and standards that may be used to develop a modernized enterprise information system (EIS) including Enterprise JavaBeans (EJB), message-oriented middleware (MOM), Java 2 Enterprise Edition (J2EE), and XML Messaging. We also identify products that implement these technologies, particularly in the Unisys ClearPath 2200 and Sun Solaris

---

[1] The same rationale applies to understanding the legacy system, as it is another fixed constraint in the equation.

operating system environments, because these two environments primarily frame the case study.

EVALUATE TECHNOLOGY

Once we understand available technologies and their capabilities, we can compare and contrast them. If their capabilities overlap, we must see whether these technologies solve the same problem with a different quality of service (QoS). We might include multiple technologies that serve the same purpose but provide different QoS in a modernization effort, as long as boundary conditions for each of them are clearly understood and communicated.

Technology evaluation is one of the first steps of building a *component ensemble*. An ensemble defines the collection of components that evolve into the architecture for the system. The book *Building Systems from Commercial Components* [Wallnau 01] describes the use of component ensembles, model problems, and other techniques for generating just-in-time competencies in components and component integration. For now, we will simply state that this evaluation is necessary to formulate the eventual architecture and design of the system.

In Chapter 10, we evaluate the feasibility of transactions that span over legacy and modernized components, on two different platforms, by constructing a model problem. In Chapter 11, we evaluate, contrast, and compare two approaches for component integration: a synchronous approach based on J2EE technologies and an asynchronous approach based on a business-to-business integration model. Each approach offers advantages over the other in particular areas. An understanding of the advantages and disadvantages of each approach is crucial in defining the target architecture.

DEFINE TARGET ARCHITECTURE

A target architecture represents the as-desired architecture of the system, providing the technical vision for a modernization effort. Thus, the target architecture must be described in a manner that supports adequate communication among the stakeholders. This usually requires descriptions using different views with different levels of granularity and specificity.

In an incremental modernization effort, the target architecture will likely evolve as the boundaries, constraints, and functionality of the legacy system become better understood and the underlying technology used to build the modernized system matures. Therefore, it is important to reevaluate and update the target architecture throughout the modernization effort.

In Chapter 12, we describe a generic enterprise information system architecture for a data-driven system as a collection of architectural patterns. Each of these architectural patterns illustrates common operations and how they are implemented in a compliant system.

DEFINE MODERNIZATION STRATEGY

Legacy system modernization is often a large, multiyear project. Because these legacy systems are often critical in the operations of most enterprises, deploying the modernized system all at once introduces an unacceptable level of operational risk. As a result, legacy systems are typically modernized incrementally. Initially, the system consists completely of legacy code. As each increment is completed, the percentage of legacy code decreases. Eventually, the system is completely modernized. A migration strategy must ensure that the system remains fully functional during the modernization effort.

An effective strategy defines the transformation from the legacy system architecture to the modernized system architecture. During the modernization effort, technologies may change, additional knowledge about the existing system may be acquired, and user requirements may change. A modernization strategy must accommodate these changes. In addition to meeting these requirements, a modernization strategy should minimize development and deployment costs, support an aggressive yet predictable schedule, maintain quality of interim and final products, minimize risk, meet system performance expectations, and maintain complexity at a manageable level.

Development of a modernization strategy is described in Chapters 13, 14, and 15. Chapter 13 describes getting from the as-built architecture to the as-desired architecture. This architectural transformation strategy includes code migration, database migration, and deployment approach. In our case study, this architectural transformation process is referred to as componentization because we are moving from a largely unstructured legacy system to a modern, component-based architecture. Chapter 13 also describes the use of data and logic adapters to support incremental development and deployment.

System preparation is an optional, potentially beneficial but often risky step that is implemented before architectural transformation. In system preparation, we evolve the legacy system to where it will be easier to perform the desired architectural transformation. The benefit is a reduction in overall modernization costs. The risk is that the system preparation does not go as planned and that the development team gets mired in the legacy code. Chapter 14 describes the analysis of alternatives that was performed as part of the system preparation work for RSS.

Chapter 15 describes the refinement of the selected modernization strategy. Refinement includes the development of a code migration plan and a data migration plan, so that the cost of the effort can be estimated and the strategy implemented effectively.

RECONCILE MODERNIZATION STRATEGY WITH STAKEHOLDERS

In modernizing any legacy system, stakeholders will have varying opinions on what is important and what is the best way to proceed. It is necessary to develop consensus before implementing a modernization plan.

In our modernization approach, the development team is responsible for producing the detailed modernization plan, primarily because that team will be responsible for implementing it. Also, the modernization plan is designed to minimize development costs and schedules while remaining technically feasible. This planning is best accomplished by the development team. Once this baseline modernization plan is in place, other business drivers can be reconciled with it.

Because the baseline plan seeks to minimize development costs, all other plans, in theory, will be more expensive to implement. However, the additional costs of implementing an alternative plan may be offset by other benefits to the business. Chapter 16 discusses a process for reconciling the modernization strategy with stakeholder needs.

ESTIMATE RESOURCES FOR MODERNIZATION STRATEGY

Estimating the costs of executing the modernization strategy is the final RMM step. Once this step is completed, you should have an understanding of the legacy system and modernization technologies, a target architecture, modernization strategy, cost estimate, and notional schedule. Based on this information, management must now determine whether the modernization strategy is feasible, given the available resources and constraints. If the strategy is adopted, the modernization plan is finalized and executed. If the strategy is not feasible, the question, Why not? must be answered.

Depending on the response to this answer, it may be necessary to repeat some RMM steps. For example, if the code migration plan does not result in functionality being deployed early enough in the schedule, you may need to revise the plan before the overall strategy is considered feasible. It is also possible that the target architecture was too ambitious and must be reconsidered or that the target technologies evaluated are too complex, expensive, or otherwise fail to satisfy the constraints of the modernization effort. In any of these cases, it is necessary to go back and revise the modernization strategy until a feasible approach can be identified or the modernization effort is determined to be infeasible, given current constraints, and terminated.

In many ways, application of the RMM approach described above can be thought of as a first-fit evaluation. We are developing and evaluating a modernization strategy to determine whether it is adequate and implementing the first plan that meets our minimum criteria. The RSS case study described in this book follows this approach. It is, however, also possible to apply RMM as a best-fit model. In this case, multiple modernization strategies—or contingencies in *Building Systems from Commercial Components* terminology—are evaluated simultaneously. Management can decide among these plans or, possibly, reject them all. In Chapter 17, we describe cost estimation approaches and how these can be applied in estimating costs for a legacy modernization effort.

3.2 Summary

The risk-managed modernization approach introduced in this chapter requires the application of a wide range of software engineering methods and techniques, as well as detailed understanding of legacy and modern technologies. Through the remainder of the book, we take you through this process in detail, using the RSS case study to illustrate each step. We also provide practical how-to guidance along the way and pointers to other processes and skills you may also need to accomplish your goal of system modernization.

4

Developing the
Business Case

*I think it is an immutable law in business that words are words,
explanations are explanations, promises are promises—but only
performance is reality.*
—Harold Geneen, Alvin Moscow
Managing, Garden City, NY:
Doubleday, 1984

A business case can determine whether a project is cost-effective. A business case is usually performed early in the project, normally after the portfolio analysis has prioritized the systems that should be considered for modernization. Because often more legacy systems are targeted for modernization than resources are available, a business case must be created for one or more of these projects. The business case must present a cost-benefit analysis, a financial advantage, or a competitive advantage to justify the modernization effort and associated implementation risks and must also reflect a believable and achievable story.

Even if resources are sufficient to modernize a legacy system, this does not mean that it should be done. Again, a legitimate business case must be made. Justifying a modernization effort is often more difficult than justifying a new application development effort, as modernization is often viewed as a last resort [Bisbal 99].

Portfolio analysis identified RSS as a system with high business value and low technical quality—an ideal candidate for modernization. RSS has high business value because of its ability to perform operations that are fundamental to the retailer business: place and fill orders, maintain appropriate inventory stocks, order and replenish inventory, and share inventory among retail locations. On the other hand, as explained in Chapter 2, the technical quality of the system has seriously deteriorated after years of neglect.[1]

---

[1] A related question that should also be considered is why the system was neglected and what in the organization has changed that will prevent the replacement system from suffering from the same neglect.

In this chapter, we describe how to develop a business case for a legacy system modernization effort. We also present aspects of the business case for RSS and discuss stakeholders, requirements, and goals for a modernization effort.

4.1 Where Are We?

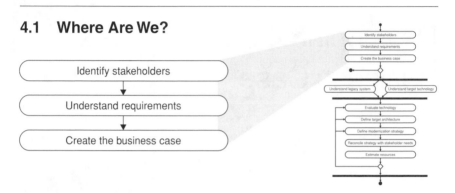

In this chapter, we begin executing the modernization process. A necessary precondition to this process is the selection of a modernization candidate through portfolio analysis. The process begins by identifying stakeholders, understanding system requirements, and creating a business case. Once the business case is completed, it must be evaluated by management. Management may decide to start the modernization effort, ask for the business case to be restated, or repeat the process for a different modernization candidate.

4.2 Identify Stakeholders

As mentioned briefly in Chapter 3, stakeholders are people with a vested interest in the system. They typically include developers, testers, maintainers, system administrators, customers, vendors, sponsors, end users, architects, and representatives of interacting systems.

RSS has five recognized groups of stakeholders:

1. **User groups:** individuals who represent the various classes of RSS system users. Most were once users themselves but have gone on to management positions. These user representatives are able to represent the views of system users; understand the user characteristics, such as average time on job and educational background; have an understanding of business needs; and understand the impact of proposed solutions on training. Using managers as user representatives is a risk because they may be too detached from day-to-day operations. Operational users may provide too narrow a view of business needs. The major risk, however, is in not including user representatives, which may lead to a system that is not accepted.

2. **Development team:** architects, designers, programmers, and testers. These people may or may not be familiar with the legacy system but are familiar with the modern technologies. Architects on the development team are responsible for the RSS-specific architecture. (By contrast, the architects on the architecture team are responsible for the corporatewide architecture.) The risk of not involving the development team is that its members may lack motivation to implement a plan they do not have confidence in.

3. **Architecture team:** responsible for the corporatewide architecture that the development team has to adhere to in designing the RSS-specific architecture. The architecture team reports through a different management structure than the team responsible for the modernization effort. This arrangement is not unusual. An architecture team typically directs multiple simultaneous projects within an organization. Not having the architecture team as stakeholders may lead to a system that is inconsistent with organizational goals and objectives.

4. **Legacy system maintainers:** programmers and engineers who have been maintaining the legacy system for more than 30 years. Their experience and knowledge are essential for the modernization effort; however, they can feel threatened by the eventual replacement of the system.

5. **Management:** a focal point for pressures from within the organization and, to a lesser degree, entities outside the organization. Management is concerned primarily with accomplishing business objectives within defined cost and schedule constraints. Not including management may produce a modernization strategy that falls outside of these constraints.

In general, stakeholders each bring their own unique perspectives, which are often at odds. For example, the architecture team is concerned primarily with corporatewide interoperability, cost reduction through sitewide licenses, and conformance to a standard architecture. The development team is concerned about the compatibility between specific products and the legacy system, modernizing the system within budget and schedule constraints, and achieving required system qualities. The perceived needs of the development team often conflict with the needs of the architecture team. For example, the development team may want to use a product that is compatible with the legacy software but not included in the corporate baseline required by the architecture group. The manner in which competing stakeholder interests are resolved depends on organizational structure, personalities, and so forth.

4.3   Understand Requirements

Once the stakeholders have been identified, expectations for the modernization effort must be established and requirements, as well as nonrequirements, agreed on among the stakeholders. Creating a steering committee or a working group consisting of stakeholders helps to identify win-win situations that will guide task definition and prioritization.

REQUIREMENTS

User, system, and nonfunctional requirements can come from the legacy system, business process reengineering, stakeholders, and technology advances.

Legacy System.   Most requirements in a modernization effort are derived from the legacy system itself, given that the decision to modernize acknowledges the existence of business rules and knowledge that must be preserved. To a large extent, the legacy system has fixed normative requirements. Thus, the modernization effort is typically geared toward improving system qualities, such as maintainability, ease of use, or performance. The risk of deriving requirements from the legacy system is that it may result in the recodification of obsolete or inefficient business practices.

Business Process Reengineering.   New requirements may also stem from business process reengineering (BPR). BPR attempts to realign the existing business processes with current needs to produce efficiencies. Business processes are codified in existing information systems, so it makes sense to perform BPR before beginning a legacy system modernization effort, to avoid recodifying obsolete or inefficient processes. This does not have to be a full BPR process. BPR raises the stakes in a legacy system modernization effort because business processes need to be reevaluated, revalidated, and revisited before any modernization work can begin. Required changes to legacy systems resulting from BPR can also affect multiple systems in an organization, making the effort difficult to scope.

Stakeholders.   Stakeholders generate new requirements, based on years of interaction with the legacy system. These requirements are often recorded in outstanding change requests. Many of these requirements are valid, but others may simply be user infatuations or have been made obsolete by technology. For example, a requirement to add hot keys to a menu-based system might be made obsolete by a decision to use a graphical user interface.

Technology Advances.   Stakeholders often want to include technical advances as requirements. The stakeholders may believe that advances in technology can address such problems as unacceptable performance, poor maintainability, or poor usability. Although this often is the case, new technologies can also bring new, unanticipated problems.

CONSTRAINTS

Constraints are decisions that have already been made and therefore place restrictions on the as-desired system or development processes. These constraints can be managerial, such as a predefined budget or schedule; architectural, such as a predefined corporatewide architecture; interface related, such as conformance to a specific standard or API; or process related, such as using an incremental development and deployment process.

4.4   RSS Requirements

In the case of RSS, specific requirements and constraints are separated into three categories: new functionality, architecture compliance, and process, with incremental development and deployment being the greatest process constraint.

NEW FUNCTIONALITY

The management team requires access to timely data. With the current system, for example, it is impossible to obtain the number of stock items available in real time. We refer to this requirement for access to corporatewide data as *total asset visibility*.

Management also needs timely reports based on consolidated data. This situation was partially resolved by the creation of the Oracle database that consolidates the data from the 90 DMS databases, as explained in Section 2.2. Nevertheless, it is far from being ideal. Data is not necessarily up-to-date, as the database is updated only once a day. Also, the Oracle database schema still more or less corresponds to the legacy database schema design, which makes it difficult to understand relationships between data elements and is not an efficient relational database design.

As in any other organization, user groups are dependent on RSS for their work. These groups are generally satisfied with the functionality of the system—in their words, "it is not optimal, but it works." Given this satisfaction, it is obvious that they want current functionality replicated in the new system. They do not want any gaps in its availability. On the other hand, they are continually faced with the difficulties of requests for improvements. Some users even have spreadsheets or small databases to help them cope with requirements that the system cannot satisfy. This is seen as overhead. The user group also wants adequate training, user's guides, reference manuals, and on-line help systems in place before fielding the system.

ARCHITECTURE COMPLIANCE

The retail organization modernizing RSS mandates the use of the Standard Retail Framework (SRF) in all modernization and development efforts. Developed by the architecture team, the SRF is a software architecture based on existing industry standards from the Open Applications Group, Sun Microsystems, and other industry groups. At a high level, the architecture requires defining and implementing large-grained business objects that represent chunks of functionality using Java and other open-systems technologies and communicating using asynchronous message passing.

SRF defines several constraints for RSS to promote interoperability and to allow for the reuse of products, code, and knowledge throughout the organization. Ideally, the use of industry standards in the SRF will also increase the likelihood of finding commercial-off-the-shelf (COTS) products that implement the various business objects.

Architectural compliance is a major concern for both the development and maintenance teams. The development team is concerned with the learning curve for the technologies incorporated in the SRF. The team is also concerned with its feasibility and compatibility with the legacy RSS system and requirements. The maintenance team is concerned with its unfamiliarity with the technologies mandated by the architecture team and lack of confidence that the architecture will perform adequately.

INCREMENTAL DEVELOPMENT AND DEPLOYMENT

Incremental development and deployment is a constraint imposed by management but is also supported by the development team as a viable approach. In general, this approach deploys new components before completing the entire system. To maintain existing functionality during incremental development, it is necessary to combine elements from the legacy system with the modernized components. The deployed system exists in this transitional stage—partly modernized and partly legacy—immediately following the initial deployment and until the final release. In a large modernization effort, this transitional period may last several years. Because the system must remain fully operational, it is necessary to achieve required system qualities in each deployment.

In this approach, funding is provided by increment. The results of each increment help justify funding for the next increment. If it is not demonstrating sufficient progress, the modernization effort may be terminated at the end of an increment. Many organizations, having failed in previous modernization efforts—our case study being no exception—mandate an incremental development and deployment to mitigate risks. In theory, incremental development and deployment is more expensive because of the need to verify and validate each deployment. In practice, however, these costs can be overshadowed by a catastrophic failure of a big-bang deployment.

Incremental deployment plans are driven primarily by complexity and technical feasibility. It is critical to ensure that the functionality, reliability, and performance of the system are not diminished after an incremental deployment, especially because the project could be terminated after any increment. Integrating legacy code alongside modern components requires careful planning and execution but can be an effective risk-reduction strategy.

MODERNIZATION GOALS

The modernization goals for RSS were defined with input from the stakeholders. These goals guide the development of the modernization plan.

Minimized Development and Deployment Costs.   Fielding modernized components alongside legacy code requires adapters, bridges, and other scaffolding code that will be discarded after the final increment. Scaffolding code represents an added expense, as this code must be designed, developed, tested, and maintained during the development period. Minimizing the development of scaffolding code helps minimize overall development costs.

Schedule.   The modernization strategy should seek to minimize the time needed to develop and deploy the modernized RSS. Additionally, the approach should allow the RSS to be developed on a predictable schedule.

Quality.   The two issues regarding quality are: (1) the quality of the final, end-state system once the RSS modernization effort has been completed, and (2) the interim quality of the system after each increment. The final system should be easy to maintain and implemented around technologies that are not already obsolete. Each interim release should also improve the overall quality of the system.

Given the length of time required to complete the modernization, there will be many opportunities for the modernization effort to lose funding, be redirected, or take on a new focus. It is important that each fielded increment improve the overall quality of the system, because there is always the possibility that each increment will be the last.

Minimized Risk.   Risks occur in many different forms, and some risk is acceptable if managed and mitigated properly. Because of the overall size and investment required to complete the RSS development, it is important that overall risk be kept low. To this end, the RSS componentization strategy should apply tried-and-proven techniques when possible and lower-risk approaches when some risk is necessary to achieve overall system goals.

System Performance.   Because the RSS is replacing an existing system, users have expectations about performance. Although RSS modernization includes modernizing hardware as well as software, it is easy to negate hardware performance gains with poorly designed software. Therefore, the componentization strategy must ensure that user performance expectations are met or exceeded. Proper planning of the modernization effort and early prototyping help minimize performance and response-time issues. As a first step, the development team must benchmark the legacy system to determine its performance and response times.

Minimized Complexity.   Depending on how lines of source code are counted, the RSS consists of up to 1.8 million lines of legacy COBOL code developed over 30 years. The size of the RSS by itself is a major source of complexity. It is therefore critical to minimize overall system and development complexity. Managing the complexity of the development effort may be the single largest factor affecting the viability of the overall RSS modernization effort.

4.5   Create a Business Case

A business case provides details on expected revenue, expected costs, technical and management plans, and data supporting the realism of the plan. In this section, we discuss both the general structure and the contents of a business case, as well as specific arguments that can be made to support the incremental modernization of a legacy system.

GENERAL STRUCTURE AND CONTENTS

A business case can take a variety of forms. At a minimum, it should include a problem statement, a proposed solution and the cost for its implementation, risks, and a forecast of the benefits that fully justify the costs. Elaboration on each of these business case elements follows.

- **Problem statement:** The problem statement describes the current environment and highlights the inadequacies, inefficiencies, and weaknesses of the current situation. For example, the director of the Federal Aviation Administration (FAA) could provide a compelling argument for replacing an existing aviation system by claiming that the existing system would result in the loss, on average, of one fuselage per week within 4 years.

- **Solution:** The business case must also describe the solution at a high level. For example, the solution is to migrate a legacy system from the legacy mainframe system to a modern hardware/software architecture in a series of incremental development and deployment efforts. The solution should also propose a schedule and a cost estimate.

- **Risks:** Risks are an overlooked but important element of the business case. Up until now, you have probably been exaggerating the scope of the problem—for example, losing a fuselage a week. The risks section allows you to gain credibility by enumerating things that could affect the effort and limit the resulting system. This also allows you to start setting expectations early, a crucial part of any successful modernization effort.
- **Benefits:** This element of the business case identifies and, ideally, quantifies the benefits of the proposed solution minus the costs, with an allowance for the risks. You may want to produce several scenarios: a pessimistic scenario, the anticipated scenario, and an optimistic scenario. The optimistic scenario might not be believed, but it will lend credence to the idea that the anticipated scenario is *not* the optimistic scenario.

A business case should also identify project assumptions. Project assumptions must be documented in case they later turn out to be incorrect or invalid. In either case, it may be necessary to reevaluate the business case. For example, a project assumption might be that the staff will remain the same or that a certain technology will be available by the time the project starts.

Understanding, recording, and presenting the business case for the modernization effort are essential. They are needed both to obtain funding for the effort and to defend that funding over the life of the project.

INCREMENTAL MODERNIZATION

In his book *Making the Software Business Case,* Donald Reifer presents four dimensions of improvement, each of which can justify a modernization initiative [Reifer 02]. These dimensions are increased productivity, reduced time to market, cost reduction/cost avoidance, and improved quality. Each is valid as long as it is consistent with corporate goals and strategies. Remaining competitive, achieving economic benefits, supporting new product needs, avoiding legal entaglements, and achieving efficiencies are also valid reasons that can be used to strengthen the business case for modernizing a legacy system.

The two ways to present cost benefits in a modernization business case are *cost reduction* and *cost avoidance.* Cost reduction refers to actions taken in the present to immediately decrease costs. Cost avoidance relates to actions taken in the present to decrease costs in the future. The initial cost of a modernization effort is high because of up-front investment in equipment, training, rearchitecture/redesign of the system, and hiring or retaining qualified staff. Therefore, it is helpful to include cost-avoidance benefits supported by a cost-benefit analysis. In this analysis, the cost of the modernization effort is compared to the long-term benefits. Examples of cost avoidance are a cost comparison between maintenance costs for the legacy system and the modernized system—hardware, software, infrastructure, and operations—or the elimination of costs because of inefficiencies.

Modernization Benefits. The RENAISSANCE[2] framework summarizes the benefits of modernization over a strict replacement effort [Warren 99]. In some cases, it might be possible to quantify these benefits.

- **Lower costs:** Evidence exists from several projects in the United States that modernizing an existing system can cost less than developing a new system.

- **Lower risks:** Incrementally modernizing a system means lower overall risk because each increment eliminates unknowns. It is less likely that the business will inherit a system that does not meet its real needs, and there is less need for rework.

- **Better use of existing staff:** Existing staff expertise can be used. Furthermore, staff members can develop their skills as the system is modernized. There is less need to bring in new staff from outside the company. A side effect is increased morale among legacy maintenance staff, who will feel part of the project.

- **Revelation of business rules:** As a system is modernized, business rules embedded in the software may become clear. This is particularly likely when these rules relate to code that was written to put out a fire and eventually becomes the way of doing things.

- **Availability:** Incremental modernization reduces the risks of extended down time associated with a big-bang deployment.

- **End-user satisfaction**: End users have time to adapt to changes and are not faced with a completely new system.

Incremental modernization increases planning accuracy, as each increment provides historical data that can be used in cost estimation models. Higher quality can also be achieved by using modern technologies and methodologies to improve the organization's software development practices.

Metrics. Building a business case requires forecasting the benefits that justify the planned expenditures. Benefits can be tangible, which can be expressed by cost avoidance, but they can also be intangible. This is the most difficult part of stating a case for modernization. For example, how do you quantify an increase in customer satisfaction or employee morale? Because management usually expects numbers for project justification, the project manager is challenged to find quantifiable benefits that can be measured. This requires the existence of a software metrics program to collect the data. Table 4-1 lists sample quantifiable benefit metrics, proposed by Tilley, that can serve as objective measures of project success [Tilley 95].

---

[2] The RENNAISSANCE project is partly funded by the European Commission under the Framework Initiative (ESPRIT 22010). The project is developing a systematic method to support the reengineering of legacy systems.

Table 4-1 Sample Quantifiable Benefit Metrics

Objective	Sample quantifiable benefit metrics
Lower maintenance costs	Average cycle time to close problem reports
	Average labor hours to close problem reports
	Total staff census
	Average problem-report backlog
	Postrelease fix rework hours
Add new functionary	Count of new functions added to the product
	Value added by, or revenue generated by, new functions
Increase performance	Number of delivered operations, such as transactions, per unit time
Replace old equipment	Net annualized cost of purchase and maintenance
Recode in different language	Number of modules in each programming language
Reuse of existing artifacts	Number of artifacts used in other products
Data rationalization	Number of redundant database objects removed
Integrate disjoint applications	Number of unified applications accessible to users
	Measures of usability and training time required for application suite

Other items that add credibility to the business case are cash flow, cost basis, cost-benefit analysis, estimate fidelity, net present value, profit and loss, risk analysis, source of funds, tax implications, and benefit investment ratio [Reifer 02, STSC 97].

It is important to remember that this may not be the final business case and that all numbers presented are estimates. The initial business case is used primarily to gain support from sponsors. After the modernization planning process has been completed, it might be necessary to present a higher-fidelity business case.

4.6   The RSS Business Case

The business case for RSS was presented to management, and a tentative funding plan was established. However, funds were released only for the initial modernization planning phase. Additional funding had to be obtained for later increments, based on the success of the initial phase.

In this section, we present highlights of the RSS business case. In particular, key arguments included the high maintenance and support costs for the Unisys mainframe, the lack of asset visibility, and the need for timely reports based on consolidated data.

PROBLEM STATEMENT

As discussed in previous chapters, RSS is a critical enterprise information system that cannot be easily replaced or eliminated. Unfortunately, RSS is also at the end of its life cycle, as years of minimal maintenance activity have left the system in a state such that it can no longer be effectively maintained.

In both understanding and communicating the problem, it is helpful to assess environmental as well as legacy application factors. Table 4-2 lists environmental factors contributing to problems with the existing system; Table 4-3 addresses system factors.

Table 4-2   RSS Environmental Factors

Factor	RSS Environment
Supplier stability	The Unisys mainframe market continues to contract each year.
Failure rate	Changes to the database schema have not been allowed for 5 years, because the system is too brittle to handle these changes.
Age	RSS has evolved over 30 years in a relatively uncontrolled manner.
Support requirements	Support costs for Unisys software continue to increase as the market for this software contracts.
Maintenance costs	The cost of maintaining the Unisys mainframe operational is high and increasing.
Interoperability	RSS lacks interoperability with wholesale and other systems that provide total asset visibility.

Table 4-3   RSS System Factors

Objective	Sample Quantifiable Benefit Metrics
Understandability	As a result of the moratorium on schema changes, the programming staff has been using FILLER fields to store data, adding to the overall lack of comprehensibility of the system.
Documentation	User documentation is adequate, but system architecture and design documentation is lacking. Some documentation of the existing database schema exists.
Data	The schema for the system has evolved over time, resulting in a large number of duplicate fields.
Performance	Performance of the existing system is adequate.
Programming language	Replacing COBOL programmers is difficult because COBOL is not a core course in colleges anymore, and students do not want to learn it, because jobs for COBOL are limited.
Configuration management	Software is under adequate configuration management control.
Test data	Testing of the system had been adequate, although test data is not preserved for use in regression testing, for example.
Personnel skills	Seventy percent of the programming staff are within 5 years of retirement.

SOLUTION

The solution is incrementally developing and deploying a modernized RSS system over a 7-year period. An overview of the RSS modernization schedule to the release of the first increment is presented in Figure 4-1. These tasks are organized by team and are described next. One of the goals of the modernization planning effort is to have a detailed schedule for each increment.

Architecture Team. As shown in Figure 4-1, the architecture team is responsible for the SRF corporatewide architecture. An initial version of the SRF is already defined at the start of the modernization effort. Two minor version upgrades are anticipated before modernization planning is finished. A major version upgrade is expected by the time the first increment is deployed. It is assumed that the RSS migration planning and increment 1 development will influence the architectural development and that changes to the architecture will conversely serve as a source of instability in the RSS development effort. However, the amount of influence exerted in each direction depends on other concurrent development efforts and their influence on the architecture, technology advances, marketplace product releases, and organization politics.

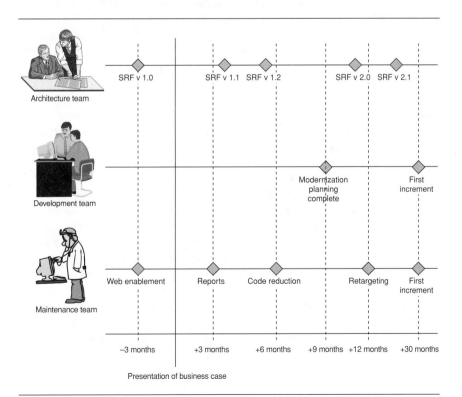

Figure 4-1 Modernization schedule for RSS

Development Team.   The development team is responsible for the modernization plan, the development of the RSS architecture in compliance with the SRF, and the development and deployment of modernized components. The maintenance team is in charge of creating adapters so that the modernized components can interact with the components of the legacy system that have not been modernized, as well as the usual maintenance tasks. Both the maintenance and development teams are synchronized for each increment because they are collaborating to deliver a system that consists of modernized and legacy components. The architecture team is not expected to be synchronized with the development and maintenance teams, because they are organizationally driven.

Maintenance Team.   The maintenance team has been in place for more than 30 years. Figure 4-1 shows the list of activities to be performed by this team before the first increment. At the start of the effort, the team completes work on a Web-enablement effort, which was explained in Chapter 2. Following the Web-enablement effort, the maintenance team begins a series of activities to simplify and support the overall modernization effort. The Reports activity refers to migrating data required for report generation to an Oracle database and using Oracle Discoverer to generate reports, as also explained in Chapter 2. This activity eliminates a large amount of report-generation code that otherwise might need to be ported. The Code Reduction activity eliminates code that is no longer required, so that this code does not need to be ported either. Following these activities, the maintenance team begins to work more closely with the development team to develop an initial increment that deploys both legacy and modernized components.

Cost Estimation.   The cost of modernizing RSS is estimated at approximately $108 million over a 7-year period. This includes development team and maintenance team activities but does not include the cost of the architecture team, which is covered elsewhere.

This rough order-of-magnitude estimate was created by project management as part of the business case preparation. To develop this rough estimate, the total lines of code (LOC) for the legacy system was converted to the equivalent LOC in the new implementation language and allocated evenly across the planned number of increments. Cost models were used to estimate the cost for requirements analysis and architecting for the whole system; the cost for designing, coding, and testing for each increment; and the cost of testing for the whole system, as each increment was going to be deployed. An estimate of 20 percent was added to the estimated cost to account for the effort in constructing adapters for each increment and for the one-time migration of the legacy database. Other costs presented were hardware equipment, network infrastructure, training, development tools, software licensing, support, and staff.

RISKS

Barry Boehm has stated that all software projects benefit from identifying risk elements during early stages [Boehm 91]. A risk evaluation involving the various stakeholder groups was performed for RSS. Risks were stated using the risk statement structure suggested by the Software Risk Evaluation (SRE) method developed at the SEI [Williams 99]: a condition—something that is true or accepted as true; a separator—an arrow, a semicolon, or a linking phrase; and a consequence—something that may occur as a result of the condition.

Twenty-six identified risks for incremental development and deployment for RSS were identified and prioritized according to impact on the project if the risk materializes. The top six risks identified follow.

1. In an incremental development and deployment, legacy and modernized components coexist, and adapters need to be built for communication between the two systems; the effort assigned to adapter construction may be underestimated, affecting cost and schedule.

2. RSS is a complex system that has grown over 30 years in an unorganized manner; coupling between the various modules in the system may be high, increasing the number of necessary adapters.

3. An incremental approach implies incremental funding; the funding may end before the modernization is complete.

4. Interactions between legacy and target software technologies are not well understood; target architectures and component ensembles may be infeasible.

5. Users have a perception of system performance given by the current legacy system; use of adapters for communicating between legacy and modernized performance might impact performance and cause user dissatisfaction.

6. The development team is not familiar with COBOL, and the maintenance team is not familiar with the new technologies; communication problems may occur, and assumptions may be made about each team's "knowns" and "unknowns."

Many of these risks are significant both in their probability and their potential impact on the modernization effort. These risks need to be considered as part of the business case.

BENEFITS

The business case for RSS presented both cost reduction and cost avoidance to justify the modernization, with an emphasis on cost benefit. The major cost-avoidance argument addressed the high and increasing maintenance costs for the Unisys platform. At the current growth rate, these costs would exceed 100 percent of the RSS maintenance budget within 4 years. Rising maintenance costs alone make a compelling argument for migrating RSS. However, the overall modernization goals are more ambitious and include rearchitecting the system.

The justification for rearchitecting the system derives largely from the inability to maintain the existing code. This is critical because the system must evolve to support changing business practices. The difficulty in maintaining the system is apparent in many of the metrics maintained in the defect-tracking database. For example, more than 60 percent of the maintenance effort on the legacy system is spent correcting defects caused by *earlier* defect fixes.

Additional benefits to RSS modernization that lend weight to the business case include

- **Improved functionality:** The RSS system will provide real-time visibility to all corporatewide data, including stock at all retail locations, warehouses, and in transit. "Total asset visibility" will improve decision making and lead to higher customer satisfaction and decreased operational costs.

- **Improved quality:** High-quality systems will result from the use of modern methodologies and technologies.

- **Improved maintainability:** The migration of each COBOL program will target code structure improvement and explicit interfaces. Eliminating dead code will also reduce the amount of code to maintain.

- **Evolvable system:** An evolvable system can adapt as business rules change and new functionality is required. With an evolvable architecture, it will also be easier to incorporate new technologies.

- **Increased productivity:** Staff will concentrate on evolving the system instead of working around the inflexibility of the current system.

- **Easier staffing:** It is easier to find qualified staff to work with the modern technologies.

4.7 Summary

In this chapter, we have established the need for a business case to justify a modernization effort and presented portions of the business case for modernizing RSS. Modernization efforts are often multiyear, multimillion dollar efforts competing with other efforts. As a result, a simple positive return on investment may be insufficient. It may be necessary to demonstrate a critical need that cannot be provided by the existing legacy system or a catastrophic flaw that will eventually result in dire consequences if not addressed. Most often, modernization dollars are spent on systems that are perceived as critical for the business to remain competitive, over less business-critical systems that may, from a strictly technical perspective, be in more dire need of modernization.

4.8   For Further Reading

- The book *Making the Software Business Case: Improvement by the Numbers* by Donald Reifer is a good source of information and examples of developing a business case [Reifer 02].

- Coleman et al. present several models for quantifying software maintainability, using software metrics such as the ones proposed by Tilley and described in this chapter [Coleman 94].

5

Understanding the Legacy System

with Dennis Smith and Liam O'Brien

> *It is quite true what Philosophy says: that Life must be understood backwards. But that makes one forget the other saying: that it must be lived forwards.*
> —Soren Kierkegaard (1813-1855),
> Journal entry, 1843.
> *The Diary of Soren Kierkegaard*, pt. 5, sct. 4, no. 136, ed. Peter Rohde (1960).

Studies estimate that between 50 percent and 90 percent of software maintenance involves developing an understanding of the software being maintained [Tilley 96]. Given these high costs, it makes sense to understand the processes used, the artifacts produced, and the level of understanding achieved.

Program understanding involves building mental models of the underlying software at various abstraction levels, ranging from models of the code to models of the underlying application domain. These models are then used to maintain, evolve, and reengineer the legacy system.

In this chapter, we discuss the context in which program understanding is applied, the forms of legacy system transformations that may be used, and the program comprehension techniques that support these transformations. We then describe architectural reconstruction in detail. We end this chapter by discussing how tools can support program understanding and common issues that may arise.

Dennis Smith and Liam O'Brien are senior members of the technical staff at the Software Engineering Institute at Carnegie Mellon University.

5.1   Where Are We?

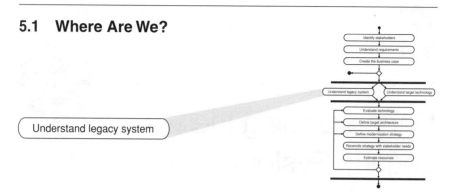

Understand legacy system

Once the business case has been defined and approved, we can begin two activities in parallel: understanding the legacy system and understanding the target technologies. These tasks necessarily contain some cross-loops, because the technologies used in the legacy system will influence, to a large extent, the technologies that are used in the modernization process and in the final system. Likewise, understanding of the target technologies will identify aspects of the legacy system that need to be studied in greater detail.

5.2   The Context for Program Understanding: The Horseshoe Model

A system modernization effort evolves an existing legacy system in a disciplined way. This effort consists of three basic processes:

1. *Reconstructing* one or more higher-level, logical descriptions of the system from existing artifacts

2. *Transforming* the logical descriptions into new, improved logical descriptions

3. *Refining* these new and improved logical descriptions to source-level code

The degree to which each of these processes is applied depends on the goals of the modernization effort. For example, a complete architectural transformation requires reconstructing the existing architecture, whereas a retargeting effort requires understanding only the code structure. Figure 5-1 illustrates a conceptual "horseshoe" that reconciles reengineering and architectural views of software analysis and evolution [Carriere 99, Woods 99, Kazman 98].

The three basic modernization processes—reconstruction, transformation, and refinement—form the basis of the horseshoe. Reconstruction goes up the left of the horseshoe, transformation goes across the top, and refinement goes down the right. The horseshoe model identifies three levels of abstraction that can be used for the logical descriptions, which can be as concrete and simple as the

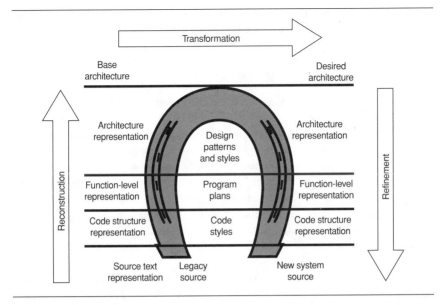

Figure 5-1   The horseshoe model

source code of the system or as abstract and complex as the system architecture. Taken as a whole, the visual metaphor integrates both the code-level and the architectural reengineering views of the world.

For example, the trip around the outside of the horseshoe represents a complete architectural transformation. However, code and functional transformations are also possible, depending on the goal of the modernization effort. These transformations are represented by two additional levels cross-cutting the horseshoe. In these cases, the reconstruction process does not result in a system architecture representation but rather in lower-level artifacts that may be closer to the source code. These paths across the horseshoe represent pragmatic choices based on the organizational or technological constraints, including the availability of reengineering tools. The three levels of abstraction and transformation are described in greater detail in the following sections.

CODE TRANSFORMATIONS

Code transformations are quick-and-dirty forms of software evolution, including such techniques as retargeting or source code translation. They are often associated more with maintenance activities than with reengineering activities. If the software is old and poorly structured and if none of the original designers is around to explain the structure of the code, this may be the best way to evolve the system. Code transformation does little to improve the structure of the legacy code and often results in code that is even more difficult to maintain. Retargeting is an important element of the RSS modernization effort. The specific use of retargeting in the case study is described in Section 14.2.

FUNCTIONAL TRANSFORMATIONS

Functional-level transformations are a medium-level approach to code transformations. These transformations are often associated with efforts to change technology while maintaining basic functionality. Functional transformations are often required, for example, when changing from a functional to an object-oriented paradigm, from client/server to object request broker, from off-line processing to electronic commerce, or from a hierarchical to a relational database. These changes tend to be concentrated in the system interfaces but may also be far reaching.

To make functional-level transformations, the structure of the system must be understood—at least at the interface level. When the internals are not well understood, it may be possible to *wrap* modules of functionality for use in another context.

Functional-level transformations can provide major benefits over code-level transformations. Mined and rehabilitated assets become better structured and provide clearly defined and better-documented interfaces.

ARCHITECTURAL TRANSFORMATIONS

The highest abstraction level in the horseshoe represents architectural transformation. In this case, the reconstruction process results in complete architectural recovery. Once this process is completed, it is possible to determine whether the as-built architecture conforms to the as-designed architecture—if it is available—and identify deviations. The discovered architecture can be analyzed with respect to performance, modifiability, security, reliability, or other quality attributes.

In the transformation process, the as-built recovered architecture is reengineered and then reevaluated against the system's quality goals. The refinement process transforms the architecture into a design and refines the design into source code.

The refinement process can be the same one used to develop custom code but may need to support the integration of existing code-level artifacts from the legacy system. This refinement process closely resembles processes for building systems from off-the-shelf components, such as the ones described in *Building Systems from Commercial Components* [Wallnau 01]. Specifically, the artifacts in the replacement system must be identified and their function in the new system clearly defined. Wrapping and interconnection strategies for integrating the legacy component must then be identified. However, unlike building systems from commercial components, the legacy system components may be modified to make them better fit for use in the new system.

5.3   Reconstruction

Reconstruction is closely related to program understanding. Program understanding allows the developer to form increasingly abstract descriptions of the system. Program-understanding techniques typically consider source code in increasingly abstract forms: raw text, preprocessed text, lexical tokens, syntax trees, control and data-flow graphs, program plans, architectural descriptions, and conceptual models. The more abstract forms entail additional syntactic and semantic analysis. This corresponds more to the meaning and behavior of the code and less to its form and structure. Different levels of analysis are necessary for different users and different reverse-engineering activities.

Reconstruction requires program-comprehension activities at each level of abstraction represented in the horseshoe model for architectural transformation. Knowledge discovered at each level of abstraction builds on knowledge gathered at the lower levels of abstraction. In architectural transformation, this process ends when a sufficiently accurate model of the architecture is developed. The following sections look at program-comprehension techniques at the code structure, functional, and architectural levels of abstraction.

CODE-STRUCTURE REPRESENTATION

Code-structure representation includes source code and artifacts, such as abstract syntax trees (ASTs) and flow graphs obtained through parsing and routine analytical operations. Recovering a system architecture begins with understanding source code and other existing artifacts. A number of activities can be applied in this process.

Manual Code Reading.   In this activity, the software engineer reads through source code in printed form or browses it on line. This activity is almost always applied in some form but it is not viable for very large systems. A good software engineer may be able to keep track of approximately 50,000 lines of code. If there is much more than that, the amount of information becomes unwieldy.

Artifact Extraction.   Artifact extraction involves discovering and documenting elements and relationships among elements in code-structure representations of the system. For example, Table 5-1 lists typical elements that might be extracted from a COBOL system and their relationships.

The specific set of extracted elements and relationships depend on the type of system. For example, if the system were written in Java, almost all the source element, relation, and target elements would change.

Static Analysis.   Static-analysis techniques commonly involve parsing the application's source code to generate a variety of reports, including call graphs,

Table 5-1   A Typical Set of Source Elements and Relationships

Source Element	Relationship	Target Element	Description
Program element	COPY	Program element	Includes another program element in the current program element
Paragraph or section	PERFORM	Paragraph or section	Transfers execution control, effectively invoking a subroutine
Data division	Declaration	Variable or file records	A declaration of a variable in a data division
Paragraph or section	CALL	Program element	Transfers control to another program in the executable image
Program element	FETCH	Record	Read access of a record
Program element	STORE	Record	Write access of a record
Program element	MODIFY	Record	Write access of a record
Program element	DELETE	Record	Write access of a record

data and control flows, structure charts, cross-reference information, and define/use analysis for data types and variable instances. Most reverse-engineering tools provide a variety of static-analysis capabilities.

In most cases, static analysis provides the necessary information to build abstractions. Static information can be obtained from the source code, design information, and compile-time artifacts, such as build and make files. However, relevant information may not be obtainable because of *late binding*. The use of polymorphism, function pointers, and runtime parameterization can all inhibit discovering source code structure by static analysis.

Another problem with static analysis is that the precise topology of a system may not be determined until runtime. For example, systems that use middleware, such as CORBA, Jini, or COM, frequently establish their topology dynamically, depending on the availability of system resources. Because the topology of such systems cannot be determined from their source artifacts, you cannot reverse engineer them using static extraction tools.

Dynamic Analysis.   Dynamic analysis observes a program executing in the operational environment or in a simulation of the operational environment. Dynamic analysis can help developers understand systems that use late binding and those that are configured dynamically. Examples of such systems include distributed, real-time, or client/server programs.

Dynamic-analysis techniques include *profiling*, *snooping*, and *code instrumentation*. *Profiling* gathers execution-time information, such as actual call sequences and data flow. Call sequences can show which system elements implement a particular feature. *Snooping* can provide insight into interactions between components by allowing you to observe communications between components or anywhere that data and control extend past a component boundary. *Code instrumentation* has a wide variety of uses for tracing code execution and changing data values.

Slicing.   Program slicing is a family of program-decomposition techniques. These techniques select statements relevant to a computation, even if the statements are scattered throughout the program [Lanubile 97]. A slice identifies all logic that affects the value of a particular set of variables at a given point in a program. Program slicing, as originally defined by Weiser, is based on static data-flow analysis on the flow graph of a program [Weiser 84]. Program slicing has been applied in program understanding and software maintenance, using conventional slicing, dynamic slicing [Agrawal 90, Korel 88], and other variants. Conventional program slicing has been also advocated in reverse engineering [Beck 93].

FUNCTION-LEVEL REPRESENTATION

Function-level representation describes the relationships among the program functions (calls, for example), data (function and data relationships), and files (groupings of functions and data).

Semantic and Behavioral Pattern Matching.   Semantic and behavioral pattern matching is similar to structural pattern matching but is used to discover dynamic behavior. Patterns are identified by discovering code components that share specific data-flow, control-flow, or dynamic—program-execution-related—relationships.

Redocumentation.   Redocumentation is one of the oldest forms of reverse engineering [Sneed 84]. It is the process of retroactively providing documentation for an existing software system. The reconstructed documentation is typically used to aid program understanding. This process can be thought of as a transformation from source code to pseudocode and/or prose, which is considered to be at a higher level of abstraction. The documentation produced is typically in-line text but can also take the form of linked documentation accessible via hypertext, cross-reference listings, or graphical views of the software system's artifacts and relationships [Tilley 91, 92].

Plan Recognition.   Program plans are abstractions of source code fragments. Comparison methods can recognize instances of programming plans in a subject system, using pattern matching at the programming language semantic level. Plan recognition can identify similar code fragments so that they may be consolidated.

Aggregation Hierarchies.   Aggregation hierarchies are artifacts created from legacy code by grouping elements together. This technique is used, for example, to aggregate objects into a common class hierarchy.

Refactoring.   Refactoring is the process of changing a software system so that it does not alter the external behavior of the code but instead improves its internal structure. Refactoring can also be viewed as cleaning up code in a disciplined way that minimizes the chance of introducing defects [Fowler 99].

ARCHITECTURAL-LEVEL REPRESENTATION

The architectural level of abstraction assembles clusters of function-level and code-level artifacts into subsystems of related components or concepts.

Structural Pattern Matching.   In structural pattern matching, existing libraries of design patterns are matched against code patterns that were mined using static-analysis techniques. Structural pattern matching can identify, for example, module dependencies that cannot be identified with a simple regular expression pattern-matching tool, such as grep.

Concept Assignment and Reasoning.   Concept assignment discovers human-oriented concepts within a specific program or its context and assigns them to their realizations [Biggerstaff 93]. One approach to concept assignment is for a maintenance engineer to designate relationships between textual cues and domain concepts and between domain concepts. These relationships form a simple domain model that can assign concepts to elements of the source code under analysis. These results can help the maintenance engineer understand the source code and reduce the cost of impact analysis.

Architecture and Structure Identification.   Architecture and structure identification involves uncovering the as-is architecture of the system. As this technique is of particular interest in our modernization approach, we discuss it in detail in the next section.

5.4   Architecture Reconstruction

Architecture reconstruction provides analysis at the highest level of abstraction. In this process, the as-built architecture of an implemented system is obtained from the existing legacy system by analyzing it, using tools to extract information and to build system models at various levels of abstraction.

   This process produces a representation of the system architecture and generates views of this architecture. These views aid in analyzing the system and serve as a means of communication among stakeholders. In some cases, such as legacy systems without an original architectural design, the lack of system structure may make it impossible to generate a useful representation.

Architectural reconstruction is a complex task requiring a variety of activities and skills. Software engineers familiar with compiler construction techniques and data-mining tools and techniques are typically required to successfully complete the task. Although tool support is usually a requirement for architectural reconstruction, no single tool or set of tools supports all reconstruction activities.

Architecture reconstruction is not a straightforward process. Architectural constructs are not explicitly represented in the source code; they are realized by diverse mechanisms in an implementation. Usually, these mechanisms are a collection of functions, classes, files, objects, and so forth. When a system is initially developed, its high-level design/architectural elements are *mapped* to implementation elements. Therefore, when we reconstruct architectural elements, we need to inverse these mappings.

Architecture reconstruction is an interpretive, interactive, and iterative process, requiring the skills and attention of both the reverse engineer and the architect or someone who has substantial knowledge of the architecture. The reverse engineer can build queries based on the architectural patterns that the architecture expert expects to find in the system. These queries result in new aggregations that show abstractions or clustering of the lower-level elements, which may be source artifacts or may themselves be abstractions. By interpreting these views and actively analyzing them, it is possible to refine the queries and aggregations to produce several hypothesized architectural views of the system under analysis. These views can be interpreted, further refined, or rejected. The process is complete when the architectural representation is sufficient to support user needs.

The software architecture reconstruction process can be divided into three distinct phases: *view extraction, visualization and interaction,* and *pattern definition and recognition.*

1. **View extraction:** View extraction constructs models of a system from the knowledge base. These views can be *simple*—displaying some of the data that has been collected—or they can be *fused* views that reconcile and establish connections between collected data. Fused views are often necessary to depict a system completely. For example, in the case of late binding of function calls, it may be impossible to identify through static analysis what functions are actually called. On the other hand, dynamic analysis can identify the functions that are called during execution of the system for a given set of inputs. Fusing the static- and dynamic-view information provides a more complete and accurate view than either view can provide alone.

2. **Visualization and interaction:** Visualization and interaction allows users to explore and manipulate views. Views are usually presented as a hierarchically decomposed graph. Most reconstruction tools provide a set of options for exploring and manipulating views. These options include the ability to

produce different layouts or to filter views based on different types of nodes or edges.

3. **Pattern definition and recognition:** Pattern definition and recognition provides facilities for architectural reconstruction. These facilities allow users to construct abstract views from detailed ones by identifying aggregations of elements and applying patterns to the underlying information. Patterns are queries on the information in the database. Most tools allow users to select a set of nodes in the view and to group them into an architectural entity.

5.5   Issues

In this section, we describe several issues you may face in reverse engineering and architectural reconstruction.

TOOL SUPPORT VERSUS MANUAL EFFORT

Architecture reconstruction and reverse engineering can be completely manual or tool supported but are not yet a completely automated activity. For example, manual code reading is an essential part of architectural reconstruction. Performing these tasks manually has the advantage of being a hands-on activity. Developers spend time directly evaluating legacy system artifacts instead of relying on tools to do this job. However, given the large amount of code in some systems and the amount of data to be extracted and analyzed, tool support is often a practical necessity. Tools are more exhaustive in their evaluation, but manual evaluation may discover information, such as source code comments, that might not be evaluated in an automated approach. As a result, most reengineering efforts will use some combination of manual and tool-supported activities.

DECOMPILATION/DISASSEMBLY

In some circumstances, legacy source code may not be available. If the system is being reengineered through code transformation, the source code—or at least a higher-level language representation—must be recovered from the available executable or object code. Recovering source code can be accomplished through *disassembly* and *decompilation*. Disassembly translates an executable program into its equivalent assembly representation. Decompilation translates an executable file into a higher-level language.

Companies providing these types of services focus mainly on mainframe applications written in COBOL and RPG. For example, these services were used extensively to fix Y2K bugs in older applications. More recent applications of disassembly and decompilation include the *javap* program included with the Sun

JDK for disassembling Java bytecodes and various decompilers, including *Deja Vu*, *Jad*, and *Mocha*.

Decompilation is not a straightforward process, and there are difficulties in trying to do it. The main problems are separating data and code—that is, obtaining a complete disassembly of the program—reconstructing control structures, and recovering high-level data types. To achieve a greater percentage of the decompilation/disassembly automatically, you can use decompilers that apply knowledge about the specific compilers and libraries used in the original compilation.

5.6 Summary

Understanding the legacy system is one of the major challenges involved in modernizing legacy systems. The level of understanding required, the appropriate techniques to apply, and the appropriate models to create depend largely on how the legacy system will be transformed.

The RSS modernization effort, for example, involves a complete architectural transformation requiring both static and dynamic analysis of the legacy system at all levels of abstraction. This required discovering and documenting the relationships between source-level elements in RSS, including call and create-read-update-delete (CRUD) data. The RSS architecture also had to be reconstructed to the degree required to map between program elements in the legacy system and the target architecture.

The RSS modernization effort required transforming the existing but largely uncharacterized legacy system architecture to the target architecture we define in Chapter 12. Chapter 6 discusses architectural representation and its application in legacy system modernization.

5.7 For Further Reading

Bowman et al. describe an approach to reconstructing the architecture of the Linux system by using the Portable Bookshelf [Bowman 99].

6

Architecture Representation

with Len Bass, Felix Bachmann, Paul Clements, David Garlan, James Ivers, Reed Little, Robert Nord, Judith Stafford

> *It is the mark of the educated man and proof of his culture that in every subject he looks for only so much precision as its nature permits.*
> —Aristotle, *Nicomachean Ethics, Book I,* Chapter 3

Architecture plays a key role in systems development, especially in the modernization of legacy systems. A typical modernization effort may use multiple architectures at any time, including representations of the as-built and as-desired architectures. The as-built architecture represents the state of the system at the start of the modernization process. If this architecture does not exist, it may need to be reconstructed as described in Chapter 5. The as-desired architecture represents the idealized end state of the system and provides the technical vision for the modernization effort. In most modernization efforts, this ideal architecture is never achieved, but that does not lessen its value.

An incremental modernization effort requires developing an architecture that defines the scope, structure, and design for each increment. Each increment, other than the last, includes elements of both the as-built and as-desired architectures. At the completion of each increment, the incremental release architecture, properly maintained and updated, defines the latest as-built architecture, and the previous as-built architecture is replaced.

Len Bass, Felix Bachmann, Paul Clements, and Reed Little are senior members of the technical staff at the Software Engineering Institute at Carnegie Mellon University. James Ivers is a member of the technical staff at the Software Engineering Institute at Carnegie Mellon University. David Garlan is an associate professor in the School of Computer Science at Carnegie Mellon University. Robert Nord is a member of the architecture group at Siemens Corporate Research in Princeton, New Jersey. Judith Stafford is a professor in the Department of Computer Science at Tufts University and a visiting scientist at the Software Engineering Institute at Carnegie Mellon University.

The as-desired architecture for the system also evolves during each increment. This evolution occurs for a variety of reasons: the boundaries, constraints, and functionality of the legacy system become better understood; the technology used to build the modernized system evolves; requirements for the modernized system change; and new modernization technologies are developed.

For these reasons, properly developing and maintaining architectural representations is extremely important. The remainder of this chapter explains why we should care about architecture representations, describes the requirements for architectural representation, presents architectural views, and discusses some additional considerations.

From this chapter to the end of the book, Unified Modeling Language (UML) notation [OMG 01] is used to represent architectures. This does not mean that UML is the only appropriate notation. The language, or notation, is simply the medium. What is important is what the notation is trying to represent. UML is not an architecture description language (ADL) and has limitations that are covered in this chapter. UML does, however, include constructs that are useful for representing architectures, is a familiar notation, and has had great industry acceptance since being adopted by the Object Management Group (OMG) as a standard in November 1997.[1]

6.1   Where Are We?

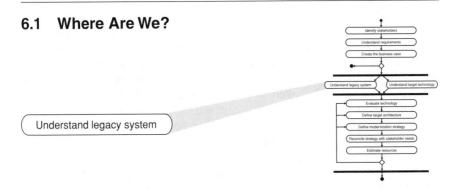

In the previous chapter, we discussed methods for understanding the legacy system—program comprehension and architectural reconstruction and transformation. In this chapter, we discuss how best to represent both the legacy system and the target *as-desired* architectures. In this chapter, we use examples from the legacy RSS system to illustrate the application of the various architectural representations.

---

[1] UML 2.0 is a work in progress, so it is not possible to foresee how UML 2.0 will solve the architecture representation problem, but the OMG working group on UML 2.0 is well aware of the limitations of UML as an ADL.

6.2   Purpose of Architecture Representation

Architecture is used for three purposes, and each places requirements on the representation.

1. **Architecture serves as a means of education.** Architecture representation communicates the architecture to those who are unfamiliar with it. For example, new members of the development team need to be educated about the system, its state, and their role in its development. An architecture representation can communicate what the system does, how the system interacts with its environment, the major components of the system, the portion on which the new team member will be working, and how this portion interacts with the other portions. Architecture representations also present design options. The use of patterns as software design elements has grown dramatically. Some of these patterns are most easily communicated through architectural representations.

2. **Architecture serves a primary role as a communication vehicle for stakeholders.** This communication can occur vertically through the development organization's management chain, laterally within the development organization, and between the development organization and external stakeholders.

3. **Architecture serves as the basis for system analysis.** Analysis can be preformed during all phases of a development effort. Because it is an early artifact that represents the system, the architecture plays a key role in all these analyses. When determining how the functional and quality requirements are going to be met, the system developers usually have only the architecture as an artifact. During testing, the architecture defines the units and the aggregates to be tested.

6.3   Architecture Representation Requirements

Architecture representation is difficult because architecture has various uses. The information necessary for deadlock analysis, for example, is different from the information necessary for a manager to generate work assignments. In this section, we discuss the relationships among various architecture representations and how they are used.

VIEWS OF THE SYSTEM

When constructing a house, the various tradespeople use differing views of the house to understand their tasks. The plumber's view differs from the electrician's view, which differs from the carpenter's view. Similarly, differing system views convey different information.

The most fundamental distinction is between views that show the static structure of the system before execution and those that show the system when it is executing. This distinction occurs when considering static classes and dynamic objects. It also occurs when considering threads and messages, which exist during the execution of the system but do not exist statically.

One requirement for representation, then, is that at least one view must represent the system's static structure and another the system during execution. Another requirement is that at least one view show how the software is mapped onto hardware, including processors, memory, and network connections. Mapping software to hardware is essential for understanding system cost and performance.

What's more, the mapping between the views must be clear. Because the various views portray the *same* system, it must be possible to map entities in one view to entities in another view. These mappings should be clearly identified— through either naming conventions or written documentation.

LEVELS OF GRANULARITY

Both managers and developers use architecture representation. These two groups clearly require different levels of granularity and specificity. A manager tracking progress, for example, should not care about the signature of an interface. A developer constructing a component, on the other hand, is greatly concerned with the signature.

Having different levels of granularity allows you to address these different requirements. In each case, you should be able to decompose a high-level representation into a collection of lower-level representations.

6.4   Architectural Views

In this section, we discuss a variety of views and explain how each is used. The three basic views correspond to the three ways an architect thinks about a system. These basic views include a static view based on modules, a dynamic view based on components and connectors, and a view that displays the mapping between software and hardware.

Each element in each view type has a collection of properties. For example, a potential property of a component is that it is a "client." Associated with "clients" are "servers." Associated with clients and servers are "protocols of interaction." These properties are usually associated with design decisions. To deal with these groups of associated properties, we identify specific subviews of one of the three basic view types.

The layered view is an example of a view type associated with design decisions. Here the properties of interest involve the relation *allowed-to-use*. Modules are allowed to use other modules only if the two modules satisfy a certain set of constraints. These constraints restrict the property values of the modules involved. The association with design decisions reflects the fact that not every system is layered. It makes sense to represent a system in a layered view only if it is, in fact, layered. This is true for all of the subviews that we discuss.

Our list of subviews is not exhaustive. Every cohesive set of design decisions, such as embodied in architectural styles [Shaw 96, Bass 98], leads to a view for representing those decisions. Because architects tend to think in terms of architectural styles and patterns, subviews are created for common architectural styles and patterns.

MODULE VIEWS

A module is a software implementation unit that provides a coherent unit of functionality. A module can be a class, a collection of classes, a layer, or any decomposition of the set of code. Every module has a collection of properties, such as *responsibilities*, *visibility information*, and *author*. Modules have relationships, such as *is-part-of* or *inherits-from*.

UML provides a variety of constructs that represent different kinds of modules. Figure 6-1 shows some examples of UML notation. Packages can be used to group functionality. The subsystem construct can be used if the specification of interfaces and behavior is required.

Figure 6-2 denotes important UML relations in the module view. From left to right, the diagrams read as follows: Module B is part of module A, module D depends on module C, and module F is a type of module E.

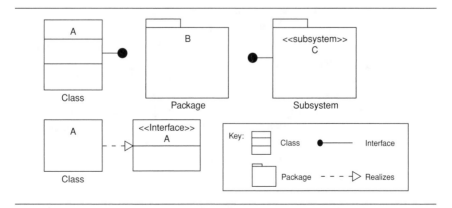

Figure 6-1 Examples of UML module notations

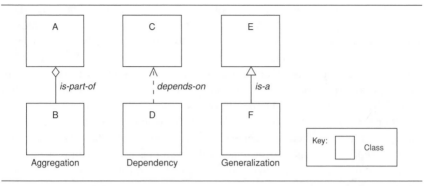

Figure 6-2   Examples of UML relation notations

Decomposition View.   This view represents the decomposition of the code into systems, subsystems, subsubsystems, and so forth. This view also represents a top-down view of the system. (The terms system and subsystem also have run-time interpretations and so need to be clarified in a particular context.)

The decomposition view gives an overall view of the system and its pieces. This view is particularly useful for education and manager-level communication and is often the basis of work assignments and completion measures.

In UML, the subsystem construct can represent modules that contain other modules. The class box is normally used for the leaves of the decomposition. Subsystems are both a package and a classifier. As a package, subsystems can be decomposed and hence are suitable for aggregating modules. As a classifier, sub-systems encapsulate their contents and can provide an explicit interface.

Aggregation is depicted in one of three ways in UML:

1. Modules may be nested inside one another, as in a package (see Figure 6-3A).

2. A succession of two, possibly linked, diagrams can be shown, with the second depicting the contents of a module shown in the first.

3. An arc denoting composition is drawn between the parent and the children (see Figure 6-3B). In UML, composition is a form of aggregation that implies strong ownership: Parts live and die with the whole. So if module A is composed of modules B and C, B or C cannot exist without the presence of A. If A is destroyed at runtime, so are B and C. Thus, UML's composition relation has implications beyond the structuring of the implementation units. The relation also endows the elements with a runtime property. As an architect, you should be comfortable with this property before using UML's composition relation.

Generalization View.   The generalization view shows how various code units relate to one another. Typically, this view represents the class hierarchy and inheritance structure.

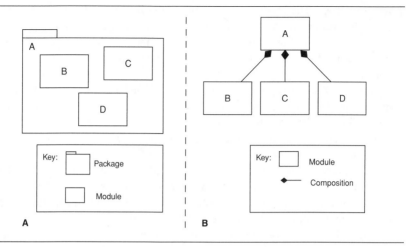

Figure 6-3   Decomposition in UML with (A) nesting and (B) arcs

This view is used mainly to express object-oriented designs. It can support a variety of forms of maintenance. Reuse is frequently based on classes. New functions are often added by modifying old functions.

Expressing generalization lies at the heart of UML. Modules are shown as classes, although they may also be shown as subsystems, as discussed in the decomposition style. Figure 6-4 shows the basic notation available in UML. UML provides two line styles to show generalization. These two diagrams are semantically identical. UML allows an ellipsis (...) in place of a submodule. This indicates that a module can have more children than shown and that additional ones are likely.

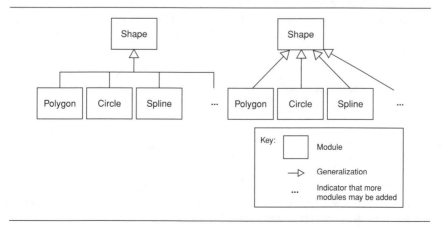

Figure 6-4   Documenting generalization in UML

Layered View.   The layered view organizes the code as disjoint layers. Code in the higher layers is allowed to use code in a lower layer according to predefined rules: for example, allowed to use code only in the next lower layer, allowed to use code in any lower layer, or allowed to use code in the lower layers or in a utility layer.

This view shows how the code is decomposed into levels of abstraction. Typically, the lowest layer involves those portions of the system close to the hardware, including the operating system. The next layer might involve database management, the layer above that might involve business logic, and the layer above that the user interface.

The layered view is used for education and to support reuse; code in lower layers is likely more flexible. This view can also support portability. Having hardware-dependent code localized in a single layer, for example, supports changing the hardware without affecting the rest of the system.

Sadly, UML has no built-in primitive corresponding to a layer. However, simple—nonsegmented—layers can be represented in UML by using *packages*, as shown in Figure 6-5. A package organizes elements into groups. UML has predefined kinds of packages for systems and subsystems. We can introduce an additional package for layers by defining it as a stereotype of package. The dependency between packages is *allowed-to-use*. Layers are designated by using the package notation with the stereotype name <<layer>> preceding the name of the layer or by introducing a new visual form, such as a shaded rectangle.

COMPONENT-AND-CONNECTOR VIEWS

Unlike static views, dynamic views are expressed as components that have some runtime presence, such as processes, objects, clients, servers, and data stores. Additionally, component-and-connector (C&C) views include connectors that also have a runtime presence and act as the pathways of interaction, such as communication links and protocols, information flows, and access to shared storage. Often, these interactions are carried out using a complex infrastructure, such as middleware frameworks, distributed communication channels, and process schedulers.

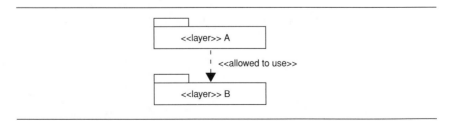

Figure 6-5   A simple representation of layers in UML

A C&C view depicts runtime entities in action. Within such a view, there may be many instances of the same component type. Drawing on an analogy from object-oriented systems, C&C views are similar to object, or collaboration, diagrams. One strategy for documenting C&C views using UML is to represent component types with UML classes and component instances with objects. Although there are several other strategies, and associated rationale for choosing among them, a complete explanation is too detailed for our purposes here. For a treatment of these strategies, see [Garlan 02].

Figure 6-6 shows a graphical representation of a component-and-connector view of a runtime client/server architecture for a simple bank.

This figure, backed up by its supporting documentation, presents a bird's-eye view of the system during runtime. The system contains a shared repository of customer accounts (`Account DB`) accessed by two servers (`Account Server-main` and `Account Server-backup`) and an administrative database application (`Admin`). A set of client tellers (`Client Teller 1 .. Client Teller N`) can interact with the account repository servers, embodying a client/server style. These client components communicate among themselves, publishing and subscribing to events. The two servers, we learn from the supporting documentation, enhance reliability: If the main server goes down, the backup takes over. Finally, the `Admin` component allows an administrator to access, and presumably maintain, the shared data store.

Each type of connector in this figure represents a different form of interaction among the connected parts. The client/server connector allows a set of concurrent clients to retrieve data synchronously via service requests. This variant of the client/server style supports transparent failover to a backup server. The database access connector supports authenticated administrative access for monitoring and maintaining the database. The publish/subscribe connector supports asynchronous announcement and notification of events.

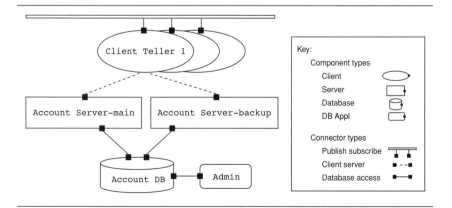

Figure 6-6   A simple C&C view

Each connector represents a complex form of interaction, requiring nontrivial implementation mechanisms. For example, the client/server connector type represents an interaction protocol that prescribes how clients start a client/server session, constraints on ordering of requests, how/when failover is achieved, and how sessions are terminated. Its implementation will probably involve runtime mechanisms to detect when a server has gone down, queue client requests, handle attachment and detachment of clients, and provide other client services. Connectors can involve more than two participants.

C&C diagrams may also make it possible to qualitatively and quantitatively analyze system properties, such as performance, reliability, and security. For instance, the design decision that causes the administrative interface to be the only way to change the database schema would have a positive impact on the security of the system. But it also might have implications on administratability or concurrency; for example, does the use of the administrative interface lock out the servers? Similarly, by knowing properties about the reliability of the individual servers, one could produce numeric estimates of the overall reliability of the system, using some form of reliability analysis.

Some things to notice about this figure follow.

- It acts as a key to the associated supporting documentation, which is not shown.

- It is simple enough to comprehend immediately.

- It is explicit about its vocabulary of component and connector types.

- It provides a key to discussions about the number and kinds of interfaces on its components and connectors.

- It uses abstractions for its components and for its connectors, concentrating on application functionality rather than on implementation mechanisms.

The documentation that contained the graphic shown in this figure elaborates on the elements shown. Supporting documentation should explain how `Account Server-backup` increases the reliability of the overall system. An expanded figure, not shown, might focus on the main account server, its backup, and the client/server connection.

Notation.   The class concept is perhaps the most natural candidate for representing component types in UML. The type/instance relationship in an architectural description is a close match to the class/object relationship in a UML model. Properties of architectural components can be represented as class attributes or with associations; behavior can be described with behavioral models.

Using the class concept in UML causes problems in representing connectors and systems. Problems result from the lack of a match with UML concepts and the requirement to be more precise about the type of connection between components.[2]

---

[2] Restrictions in using UML to represent components and connectors are partially driving UML 2.0, as mentioned in the introduction to this chapter.

Problems also arise in modeling systems. In UML, a package represents a set of elements that may be imported into another context but not a structure per se. In contrast, a system in an architecture design is a structure with defined subparts.

Several notations can be used for representing a portion of component and connector interactions. They include use case maps, sequence diagrams, collaboration diagrams, and message sequence charts.

Use Case Maps – Use case maps are used to visualize execution paths through a set of elements from a bird's-eye view [Buhr 96]. The fairly intuitive notation communicates how a system works—or is supposed to work—without too much detail.

Use case maps can be derived from informal requirements or from use cases, if they are available. Responsibilities need to be stated or inferred from these requirements. Separate use case maps can be created for individual system functions or even for individual scenarios. However, the notation's strength resides in integrating related scenarios. In such cases, use case maps can illustrate concurrency, such as resource consumption problems—multiple paths using one element—or possible deadlock situations—two paths in opposite directions through at least two of the same elements.

If you ever followed a discussion of developers trying to answer concurrency-related questions, such as, "Does an element need to be locked?" or "Is there potential for deadlock?" you may have seen them drawing a picture similar to the sketch shown in Figure 6-7. The circles denote system elements. Each line denotes a path of activity through the elements. This type of informal notation is useful in answering such questions and illustrates a need for the well-defined equivalent found in use case maps.

The basic idea behind use case maps is captured by the phrase *causal paths cutting across organizational structures*. An execution path in a use case map describes how elements are ordered according to their responsibilities. When it enters an element (a box), an execution path (a line) states that this element now does its part to achieve the system's functionality. A responsibility that is assigned to the path while within an element defines it as a responsibility of the element.

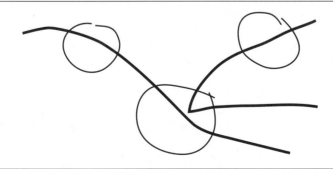

Figure 6-7   Informal notation for activity paths through system elements

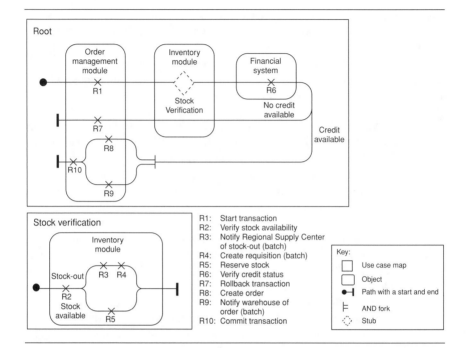

Figure 6-8 Use case map for order placement in RSS

The use case map notation includes many other symbols for such features as timers and timeouts; data containers; interactions between execution paths, such as aborting; and goals, which are useful when describing agent-oriented elements. An example of a use case map for an order placement in RSS is shown in Figure 6-8.

Sequence Diagrams – Sequence diagrams document a sequence of interactions over time. These diagrams present a collaboration of instances of elements, with interactions between them arranged in time sequence. In particular, a sequence diagram shows only the instances participating in the scenario being documented. A sequence diagram has two dimensions, with the vertical dimension representing time and the horizontal dimension representing instances. In a sequence diagram, relationships among the objects, such as those found in a module view, are not shown.

Sequence diagrams nicely support picturing dependent interactions: in other words, they show which stimulus follows another stimulus. However, they are not explicit in showing concurrency. Although a sequence diagram shows instances as concurrent units, no assumptions can be made about ordering, as for example, when a sequence diagram depicts an instance sending messages at the "same time" to different instances.

It might be intended that the interactions shown in various sequence dia-grams can be performed independently of one another. If this is the intention, it should be noted somewhere. It is not appropriate to document independent behaviors within the same sequence diagram.

Figure 6-9 shows a sequence diagram for order placement in RSS. A stimulus is shown as a horizontal arrow. For example, the arrow labeled `verifyStock()` depicts a message sent from the Order Management module to the Inventory module. The direction of the arrow defines the producer—start of the arrow—and the consumer—end of the arrow—of the stimulus. A stimulus usually has a name that describes the stimulus and usually maps to a resource in the interface of the consumer instance. A stimulus can be drawn as a dotted line to indicate that it describes a return of control to the sender.

UML's sequence chart notation supports more features than we have illus-trated. For example, interactions can be documented using various types of arrows to indicate more specific semantics for the communication, such as syn-chronous, asynchronous, periodic, and aperiodic types of communication. In addition, forms of flow control, such as decisions and iteration, can be depicted in various ways. For the sake of clarity, it is recommended to avoid too much logic in the diagram.

A constraint language, such as the UML's Object Constraint Language (OCL) can be used to add more information. OCL statements can be attached to the arrow and become recurrence values of the action attached to the stimulus.

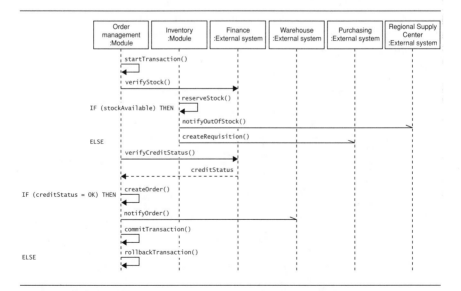

Figure 6-9   Sequence diagram for order placement in RSS

Collaboration Diagrams – A collaboration diagram shows ordered interactions among elements. Whereas a sequence diagram shows order using a time-line-like mechanism, a collaboration diagram shows a graph of interacting elements and annotates each interaction with a number denoting order.

Collaboration diagrams are useful when the task is to verify that an architecture can fulfill the functional requirements. Such diagrams are not useful for understanding concurrent actions, as in performance analysis.

Figure 6-10 shows a simple collaboration diagram for order placement in the current RSS, given that the product is out of stock but that funds are available. Interactions are labeled by arrows attached to links—lines—between the instances—boxes. The direction of the arrow identifies the sender and the receiver of each interaction. Special types of arrows, such as a half-headed arrow, depict different kinds of communication, including asynchronous, synchronous, and timeout.

Sequence numbers can be added to interactions to show order. Subnumbering shows nested stimuli and/or parallelism. For example, the interaction with a sequence number 2.1 is the first interaction sent as a result of receiving stimulus number 2. The letter *a* in interaction 4.a means that another stimulus, 4.b, can be performed in parallel. This numbering scheme may be useful for showing sequences and parallelism, but it tends to make a diagram unreadable.

A collaboration diagram also shows relationships, or links, among the elements. Links show relationships between structural instances. Links between the same instances in different collaboration diagrams can show different aspects of relationships between the same structural elements. Links between instances have no direction. A link states only that the connected instances can interact. If a more accurate definition is required, additional documentation, possibly a textual description, must be introduced.

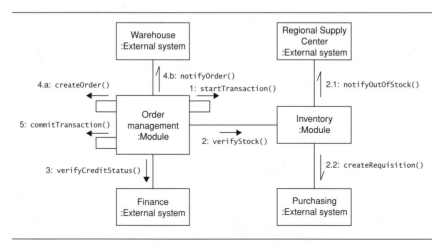

Figure 6-10   Collaboration diagram for order placement in RSS

Collaboration diagrams express similar information as sequence diagrams. Whereas sequence diagrams show time explicitly, collaboration diagrams use numbers to indicate time. Some users prefer collaboration diagrams because they show element relationships, whereas sequence diagrams do not show these relations if connected elements do not interact in the scenario depicted in the sequence diagram.

DEPLOYMENT VIEW

The deployment view incorporates hardware elements, including processing nodes, communication channels, memory stores, and data stores. The software elements in this view are usually processes. This view describes how processes are allocated to hardware and the resulting message traffic.

The deployment view is used to analyze performance, security, and reliability. This view also provides a basis for estimating the cost of deployment of a single node. Figure 6-11 illustrates a sample deployment diagram for RSS, showing that multiple instances of the RSS component can run on a single Unisys OS 2200 server. Each instance communicates with a different database to support one or more retail locations. Clients from each retail location communicate with the RSS instance responsible for supporting their location.

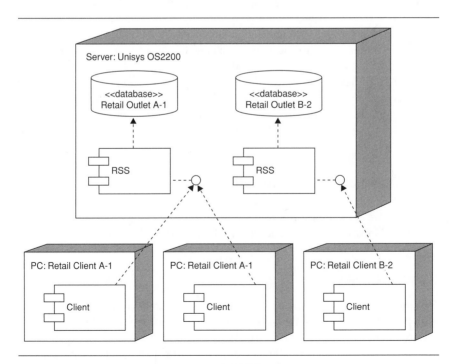

Figure 6-11   A UML deployment view for RSS

In UML, a deployment diagram is a graph of nodes connected by communication associations. Nodes may contain component instances, indicating that the component lives or runs on the node. Components may contain objects, indicating that the object is part of the component. Components are connected by dashed-arrow dependencies, possibly through interfaces. This shows that one component uses another component's services. A stereotype may be used to indicate the precise dependency, if needed. The deployment type diagram may also show which components run on which nodes, by using dashed arrows with the stereotype «supports».

A node is a runtime physical object that represents a processing resource. A node generally has at least a memory capability and often a processing capability. Nodes include not only computing devices but also human resources or mechanical processing resources. Nodes may be types or instances. Runtime computational instances, both objects and component instances, may reside on node instances. A node is shown as a figure that looks like a three-dimensional view of a cube. A node type has a type name. A node instance has a name and a type name. The node may have an underlined name string in it or below it.

Dashed-arrow dependencies show the capability of a node type to support a component type. A stereotype may be used to state the precise kind of dependency.

Component instances and objects may be contained within node instance symbols, indicating that the items reside on the node instances. Containment may also be shown by aggregation or composition association paths.

Nodes may be connected by associations to other nodes. An association between nodes shows a communication path between the nodes. The association may have a stereotype to indicate the nature of the communication path: for example, the kind of channel or network.

Symbols may be nested within the node symbol. Such nesting maps either into a composition association between a node class and constituent classes or into a composition link between a node object and constituent objects.

6.5   Additional Considerations

The views we have described provide the basis for generating an architecture representation. However, there are additional considerations, described in this section.

SYSTEM CONTEXT

Systems do not operate in a vacuum; they exist in an environment and interact with the elements in that environment. These interactions may consist of responding to inputs from users, other systems, or sensors; providing outputs to users, other systems, or actuators; or both, that is, interoperating with other systems.

Representing the software architecture of a system should also depict its interactions with its environment. Any of the views we have discussed can be used to represent these interactions. A *context diagram* represents the system and its environment within one of the base views.

A context diagram within a module view can represent what is inside and outside the system. For example, if the system is being constructed on top of commercial middleware, the context diagram would include the commercial middleware and indicate the services being used.

A context diagram within a component-and-connector view could represent the protocols that the system assumes for communicating with its environment. The diagram could also provide the performance-analysis information that depends on elements of the environment. For example, if the response time of a system depends on the load on a router in the network that is outside the system, this router would occur in a communicating-process context diagram.

Similarly, a context diagram for the allocation view could show hardware elements that are outside the system. Databases, for example, that are outside the system being constructed and that reside on distinct hardware could be shown on an allocation-view context diagram.

HYBRID VIEWS

A hybrid view is a combination of several existing views. Hybrids are a means of expressing relationships that can be very powerful or very confusing.

The power of hybrids comes from their ability to display different concepts in the same representation. Understanding the operation of a system, for example, may require knowing that multiple objects are instantiated from a single class. This can be represented through a hybrid. Understanding the performance of a system, for example, may require knowing both the protocol that is used to communicate between a client and its server and the load on a network connection from message traffic. All these can be represented using a hybrid view. The confusion comes from combining two views that do not belong together or for which the mapping from one view to another is not made explicit. When understanding the performance of a system, the sources of traffic on a network connection must be shown to draw inferences. If a source is not connected to the message traffic, the hybrid view does not convey the necessary information.

6.6 Summary

Architecture representation is crucial to a modernization effort. Each incremental release must have both an as-is and a to-be architecture that guide the development effort.

Architecture representation can be used for education, communication, and analysis. Each of these uses affects the selection of views and granularity. Specific guidance in the choice of views includes

- Understanding what uses will be made of your representation and choosing the views appropriately.

- Creating at least one module view, one component-and-connector view, one deployment view, and also context diagrams showing the interaction of the system with its environment.

- Creating behavioral models when runtime behavior is a key element in representing and analyzing the system architecture.

- Being clear about the mapping between views whenever constructing a hybrid view. To test for clarity, ask someone not involved in generating the hybrid view to explain all the mappings to you.

6.7 For Further Reading

- Material in this chapter is derived from the book *Documenting Software Architectures: Views and Beyond,* by Paul Clements, Felix Bachmann, Len Bass, David Garlan, James Ivers, Reed Little, Robert Nord, and Judith Stafford [Clements 02].

- A discussion of architectural styles is in the book *Software Architecture: Perspectives on an Emerging Discipline* [Shaw 96].

- The SEI Series book *Software Architecture in Practice* also provides additional information on architectural representation [Bass 98].

7

Languages and Data Management

with Lutz Wrage and Russ Bunting

> *Language can only deal meaningfully with a special, restricted segment*
> *of reality. The rest, and it is presumably the much larger part, is silence.*
> —George Steiner,
> "The Retreat from the Word,"
> *Language and Silence* (1967).

In this chapter, we begin our exploration of the information system technologies that constitute the design space for RSS modernization. Gaining competency in these technologies is a major issue in the modernization of legacy systems, as developers who understand both the legacy system and modern technologies are a rare commodity.

Competency can be gained through traditional techniques, such as reading and training. *Building Systems from Commercial Components* argues that competence in technology is best obtained *just in time* and *as needed* as part of the design process [Wallnau 01]. This is particularly true of modern technologies that are still rapidly evolving. Rather than repeat ideas from that book, here we provide some concise but rudimentary information about technologies that are relevant to our case study. This level of information should be sufficient to guide your understanding of the case study; however, we provide references throughout these chapters if you need additional information on a particular technology.

In the remainder of this chapter, we examine the main programming language used in RSS (COBOL) and the main language for the target system (Java). We also look at data repositories, including database management systems—past,

Lutz Wrage is a visiting scientist at the Software Engineering Institute at Carnegie Mellon University. Russ Bunting is a Member of the Technical Staff at the Software Engineering Institute at Carnegie Mellon University.

present, and future—and data warehouses. Finally, we look at standard data representations for information exchange, including electronic data interchange (EDI) and the eXtensible Markup Language (XML). If you are already familiar with these technologies, you may wish to proceed to the next chapter.

7.1 Where Are We?

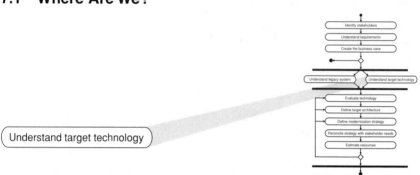

Understand target technology

In the "understanding" phase, we need to understand the technologies used in the legacy system, as well as the target, modernization technologies. This is the first of three chapters on the information system technologies that both populate and constrain the solution space for the RSS modernization effort. In this chapter we focus on programming languages, data repositories, and data representations for information exchange.

7.2 COBOL

As pointed out in Chapter 1, the majority of legacy systems are implemented in COBOL or FORTRAN. Because many programmers today don't know anything about COBOL, we provide a short overview of the language according to the COBOL 85 standard, highlighting some of the challenges of analyzing COBOL code.

HISTORY

The history of the COBOL programming language begins in 1960, when the Conference on Data Systems Languages (CODASYL) produced a report that described the common business-oriented language (COBOL 60). After some intermediary revisions—COBOL 61, COBOL 61 Extended, and COBOL 65—the American National Standards Institute (ANSI) gave formal definitions in 1968 and 1974. The latest major revision—ANSI COBOL 85—attempted to end "spaghetti coding" by introducing new language constructs that support a structured style of programming while remaining backward compatible. However, because these constructs were introduced to COBOL only in 1985, older programs are usually not well structured. In addition, other COBOL language constructs make it easy to produce spaghetti code. Thus, structured COBOL programming requires discipline and rigid guidelines.

Several compiler vendors have recently updated the language to include constructs for object orientation (OO COBOL). The International COBOL Committee (ISO WG4) is developing the next major revision of the language that includes support for internationalization, object-oriented programming, exception handling, better arithmetic, and other modern language capabilities.[1]

GENERAL STRUCTURE

A COBOL program consists of one or more files containing source code. A source code file that can be compiled is called a program element. Additional types of source files, such as source code fragments, can be copied into a program element during compilation—similar to include files in C or C++. A collection of these elements makes up the overall program. A program element can be invoked directly from the runtime environment or can be called from another program element.

COBOL program elements were designed to resemble natural-language documents to be understandable by nonprogrammers. This results in programs that are often wordier than those written in other programming languages. Compare, for example, the assignment x := 1 in Pascal to MOVE 1 TO X or, even worse, COMPUTE X = 1 END-COMPUTE in COBOL.

In general, a COBOL program consists of DIVISIONs that are composed of SECTIONs. A section can be divided into paragraphs consisting of sentences. These sentences are the statements of COBOL and are terminated by a period.

In the course of introducing some structure into COBOL, COBOL 85 allowed program sentences to consist of multiple statements to make nested statements possible.

In the following sample program, variables a and b are assigned values, the values are swapped, and the results are displayed on the screen:

```
IDENTIFICATION DIVISION.
   PROGRAM-ID. Example
DATA DIVISION.
   WORKING STORAGE SECTION.
      01 A PIC 9.
      01 B PIC 9.
      01 Temp PIC 9.
```

---

[1] For more details on the final text to ISO see http://www.sei.cmu.edu/cbs/mls/links.html#dkuug.

```
PROCEDURE DIVISION.
  MAIN SECTION.
    MOVE 1 TO a
    MOVE 2 TO b
    PERFORM swap
    DISPLAY a
    DISPLAY b.
  STOP RUN.
  swap SECTION.
    MOVE a TO Temp
    MOVE b TO a
    MOVE Temp TO b.
END PROGRAM.
```

In the following alternative formulation of the procedure division, the PERFORM statement is used to execute a sequence of paragraphs:

```
PROCEDURE DIVISION.
  MAIN SECTION.
    MOVE 1 TO a
    MOVE 2 TO b
    PERFORM moveA THRU moveTemp
    DISPLAY a
    DISPLAY b.
  STOP RUN.
  moveA.
    MOVE a TO Temp.
  moveB.
    MOVE b TO a.
  moveTemp.
    MOVE Temp TO b.
END PROGRAM.
```

The statements in the procedure division can be grouped into paragraphs. A paragraph starts with a paragraph name and ends before the next paragraph name or with the end of the section or procedure division. Paragraphs look like labels scattered throughout the source code. Not surprisingly, these labels can be used as destinations for GOTO statements.

Paragraphs themselves may be grouped into sections, which begin with a section name and the keyword SECTION. The end of a section is either the beginning of the next section or the end of the procedure division.

A procedure division can be composed of paragraphs without sections or of sections that may contain paragraphs. If the procedure division contains sections, every paragraph of this division must be contained in a section.

Sections, paragraphs, and sequences of paragraphs are executed by PERFORM statements. Control is transferred to the first statement in the called section or paragraph. Then all statements in the section or paragraphs are executed, and control returns to the next statement after the PERFORM statement. It is not possible to pass parameters with this mechanism.

ARITHMETIC

One of COBOL's built-in features is signed, fixed-point arithmetic with overflow/ underflow handling. Other programming languages must emulate this, so COBOL has an advantage here. COBOL's original arithmetic capabilities were extremely limited. Since then, many COBOL vendors have added floating-point extensions to handle the numeric applications found in computational finance, insurance, and other fields.

VARIABLES

In general, a COBOL program works on data records. Variables are called data items in COBOL. Simple data items are either alphanumeric with a fixed length or numeric in a fixed-point format. Combining simple data items forms compound data items. Combining simple and compound items forms even more complex, compound data items. This results in a tree structure with simple items as the leaves, similar to nested structures in C. Substructures of complex data items are referenced by qualified names. Parts of a compound data item may be redefined, resulting in a construct similar to unions in C.

Simple items are stored by default as a sequence of characters, even for numeric items. No type checking is required of the compiler. Therefore, it is possible to extract substrings from numbers, which is perfectly legal with some compilers, or to perform calculations with non-numeric items, which usually crashes the program. In addition, numeric values can be stored in binary format.

In COBOL, a variable declaration consists of a line in the DATA DIVISION that contains a level number; a data-name, or identifier; and a picture clause. The following example illustrates some variable declarations:

```
01 Person
   02 SSN PIC 9(9)
   02 Name
       03 FirstName PIC X(15)
       03 MiddleInitial PIC X(1)
       03 LastName PIC X(30)
   02 DateOfBirth
       03 Day PIC 99
       03 Month PIC 99
       03 Year PIC 9(4)
   02 dummy REDEFINES DateOfBirth.
       03 NumDate PIC 9(8)
```

The variable Person, at level 01, is composed of three variables at level 02: SSN, Name, and DateOfBirth. The REDEFINES clause applies a new name to a segment of memory already set aside. In this case, the data in DateOfBirth can also be accessed by using the name NumDate. SSN is a numeric variable of length 9, as specified by PIC 9(9). FirstName is an alphanumeric variable of

Table 7-1 Examples of Assignments in COBOL

Operation	Comment
`MOVE 22 TO Day OF DateOfBirth OF Person`	Complete qualification.
`MOVE 5 TO Month OF Person`	Incomplete qualification is permitted if unique.
`MOVE "22051965" TO DateOfBirth OF Person`	Now `Day` is `22`, `Month` is `5`, `Year` is `1965`, and `NumDate` is `22051965`, owing to the `REDEFINES` clause.
`MOVE "year" TO Year OF Person` `ADD 1 TO Year OF Person`	The add operation crashes with "Illegal decimal operand" or a similar message.

length 15 as specified by `PIC X(15)` and is a part of the variable `Name`. Some assignment examples based on these variable declarations are shown in Table 7-1.

Data items defined in a program element are, by default, visible only in this program element. Data items can also be specified as global to make them visible to other program elements. It is not possible to define variables that are local to a paragraph or a section.

CALLING AND PARAMETER PASSING

Program elements invoke other program elements by using the COBOL `CALL` statement. The `CALL` statement transfers control to another program in the executable image. The destination program name is specified as a string literal or a data item containing the string.

The `CALL` statement can pass data items as parameters to the called program element with the `USING` clause. Parameters are passed by reference—the default— or by value. The called program element specifies the names of its formal parameters in the `PROCEDURE DIVISION` header with a `USING` clause as well. The structure of the parameter items is specified in the `LINKAGE SECTION` of the `DATA DIVISION` that precedes the `PROCEDURE DIVISION`.

In a program element `PE0815`, for example, we can call `PE4711` as follows:

```
CALL "PE4711" USING Data-1, Data-2
```

The subroutine in `PE4711` is declared as follows:

```
DATA DIVISION.
    LINKAGE SECTION.
        01 Para-1.
            02 Parm-1
            02 Parm-2
        01 Para-2.
            02 Parm-3
            02 Parm-4
    PROCEDURE DIVISION USING Para-1, Para-2.
```

One weakness is that no type checking is performed on the parameters by the compiler. Analyzing call hierarchies in COBOL programs is especially difficult if a variable rather than a string literal is used for the name of the called program. A called program element can also return a data item as the result of the call.

COBOL 85 introduced nested program elements that contain multiple procedure divisions with local data divisions. This makes COBOL a block-structured language; unfortunately, however, this feature is not in widespread use.

COMPOSING SOURCE FILES

COBOL includes a mechanism to compose program elements from various source files at compilation time. The programmer can include arbitrary fragments of COBOL source into a program element by using the COPY statement. In addition to including another file, the COPY statement can also apply textual modifications to the included source (COPY REPLACING). For example, you can put a lengthy variable declaration into a separate file and include this into every program element that uses this data item. COPY REPLACING is a useful aspect of COBOL for producing multilingual applications.

OBSOLETE LANGUAGE FEATURES

Some COBOL features are no longer found in programming languages but rather in libraries or separate tools. These features include file access for sequential, random, and indexed files; report generation; and screen descriptions of forms for input/output (I/O) on a text terminal. In a system modernization, these functions are usually completely redesigned.

STANDARDS

COBOL X3.23-1968.   This is the American National Standards Committee on Computers and Information Processing (X3) standard, based on the original COBOL specification. The standard defines COBOL as a nucleus and eight functional modules: Table Handling, Sequential I/O, Random I/O, Random Processing, Sort, Report Writer, Segmentation, and Library.

COBOL X3.23-1974.   This standard revises and expands the functional modules from eight to eleven. Random I/O and Random Processing are replaced by the new modules Relative I/O, Indexed I/O, Debug, Inter-program Communication, and Communication.

ANSI COBOL X3.23-1985.   This standard introduces a revised core language to support structured programming by changing COBOL into a block-structured language.

PRODUCTS

Because COBOL has a long history, many different COBOL compilers and runtime environments are available for various platforms. Our case study uses compiler environments on Solaris and Unisys platforms.

ASCII COBOL.   The COBOL source language implemented by the OS 2200 ASCII COBOL compiler system includes all the features of American National Standard COBOL X3.23-1974. In addition, ASCII COBOL includes numerous compatibility features for American National Standard COBOL X3.23-1968, as well as a random processing—multitasking—capability based on the work of the CODASYL COBOL committee [Unisys 98].

Universal Compiling System (UCS) COBOL.   The COBOL source language implemented by UCS COBOL, commonly known as UCOB, includes all the required features of ANSI COBOL X3.23-1985, as well as numerous compatibility features for migrating from ASCII COBOL to UCS COBOL [Unisys 99].

Object-Oriented COBOL.   The object-oriented COBOL environment is a member of the Unisys OS 2200 UCS family. The object-oriented COBOL compiler includes the features specified by the ANSI COBOL X3.23-1985, as well as object orientation and other features included in the emerging COBOL standard.

Micro Focus COBOL.   Micro Focus COBOL is part of the Server Express product for UNIX and MS Windows environments. Server Express includes the Micro Focus COBOL compiler, Animator for debugging, and File Handling.[2]

7.3   Java

The Java programming language is a common topic in legacy system modernization and in modern application development in general. The biggest selling point for Java is its platform independence. This means that Java code can run on any platform for which there is a Java Virtual Machine (JVM), as opposed to the platform-dependent code used by most legacy systems.

HISTORY

Java, an object-oriented programming language and runtime environment, was developed by a group headed by James Gosling at Sun Microsystems starting in

---

[2] A further description of the product can be found at: http://www.sei.cmu.edu/cbs/mls/links.html#microfocus.

1991 [Sun 97b]. Java was originally intended for programming electronic consumer devices. Later, in 1995, when the explosion of interest in the Internet began, it became clear that Java was a suitable programming language for Internet applications [van Hoff 96]. Java addresses issues of interoperability, security, portability, and trustworthiness.

GENERAL STRUCTURE

A Java program is essentially a *class*. A class defines the data (state) and methods (behavior) of the specific concrete objects that are subsequently constructed from that class. Figure 7-1 shows a simple class, called Point, that has two data elements, x and y, also called *attributes;* a *constructor,* Point(); and eight *methods:* setX(), getX(), setY(), getY(), moveRight(), moveLeft(), moveUp(), and moveDown().

A Java program uses the new statement to create an object, or instance, from the Point class as follows:

```
Point p = new Point();
```

When an instance of a class is created, its constructor is invoked, in this case Point(). The initial values for the Point object just created are x=0 and y=0, corresponding to the code inside the constructor.

Objects communicate with one another through *method calls*. A fragment of a program that creates an instance of the Point class, moves the point in several directions and uses elements of the Java API to display the values of X and Y follows:

```
Point p = new Point();

// Displays X=0, Y=0
System.out.println("X=" + p.getX() + ", Y=" + p.getY());

p.moveRight(5);

// Displays X=5, Y=0
System.out.println("X=" + p.getX() + ", Y=" + p.getY());

p.moveUp(10);

// Displays X=5, Y=10
System.out.println("X=" + p.getX() + ", Y=" + p.getY());
```

THE JAVA PLATFORM

The Java platform has two components: the Java Virtual Machine and the Java application programming interface.

```
class Point {

    private int x;
    private int y;

    public Point() {
      x=0;
      y=0;
    }

    public void setX(int value) {
      x = value;
    }

    public int getX() {
      return x;
    }

    public void setY(int value) {
      y = value;
    }

    public int getY() {
      return y;
    }

    public void moveRight(int value) {
      setX(x+value);
    }

    public void moveLeft(int value) {
      setX(x-value);
    }

    public void moveUp(int value) {
      setY(y+value);
    }

    public void moveDown(int value) {
      setY(y-value);
    }
}
```

Figure 7-1 Example of a Java class

Java Virtual Machine.   The JVM is what makes platform independence possible. A Java program is compiled into *bytecodes* on any platform that has a Java compiler. These bytecodes can then be run on any implementation of the JVM, be it a development tool, the command line version of the JVM, or a Web browser that can run applets. The JVM parses and runs each Java bytecode instruction. Compilation happens only once; interpretation occurs each time the program is executed. This means that as long as a computer has a JVM, the same program written in the Java programming language can run on it.

Java Application Programming Interface.   The Java API is a large collection of ready-made software components that provide many useful capabilities, such as graphical user interface (GUI) widgets. The Java API is grouped into *packages* of related classes and interfaces.

As a platform-independent environment, the Java platform can be slower than code that is compiled for a specific platform, that is, native code. However, there are mechanisms, such as just-in-time bytecode compilers, that convert bytecode to native code on the fly. These compilers can bring performance close to that of native code without threatening portability.

CHARACTERISTICS OF THE JAVA LANGUAGE

Besides platform independence, the Java language has several other attractive characteristics [Gosling 97].

Object Orientation.   Java is an object-oriented programming language. A well-designed application can benefit from inheritance, encapsulation, polymorphism, and dynamic binding—the claims to fame of object orientation.

Interpreted.   The JVM can be thought of as a bytecode interpreter. Code is compiled once and interpreted on the fly. Classes can be compiled individually, as opposed to the usual compile-link-load cycle that performs these operations for the whole application every time a change is made.

Portability.   In theory, applications will run without modification across multiple platforms because of the JVM. However, JVM versions must be compatible for guaranteed portability.

Memory Management.   The Java runtime environment (JRE) provides memory management and automatic garbage collection. Once memory is allocated for an object, the runtime system tracks the object's status and automatically reclaims memory when the object is no longer in use, freeing memory for future use. There is no explicit use of pointers.

Multithreading. The multithreading built into the Java programming language and runtime platform supports concurrent threads of activity.

Dynamic Loading and Binding. Classes are linked as required and can be downloaded from across networks. Incoming code goes through bytecode verification before being passed to the JVM for execution.

Security. The Java runtime environment provides security at multiple levels, from class file verification to access control mechanisms and algorithms [Gong 02].

TYPES OF JAVA PROGRAMS

The Java API contains packages that allow you to write several types of programs:

- **Applets.** An applet is a Java program that runs within a Java-enabled browser.
- **Applications.** An application is a stand-alone Java program that runs directly on the JRE.
- **Servlets.** A servlet can be thought of as an applet that runs on the server side. Instead of working within browsers, servlets run in a servlet engine and are accessed from browsers.
- **JavaBeans.** Beans are Java components written in conformance with the JavaBeans API. The JavaBeans API specifies naming patterns that allow variables and methods to be identified as specific bean features. These beans can then be exposed to builder tools for visual manipulation. The builder tool maintains the beans in a toolbox. These beans, in turn, can be combined into any of the previous types of programs [Sun 99b].
- **Enterprise JavaBeans.** This server-side component model is best suited for the development of business logic that must be both transactional and secure. Enterprise JavaBeans are discussed in detail in Section 9.2. The only thing that JavaBeans and Enterprise JavaBeans have in common is that components adhering to both models are specified in Java.

JAVA APPLICATION PROGRAMMING INTERFACES (APIS)

Java specifies a core set of application programming interfaces (APIs) required in all Java implementations, as well as an extended set of APIs covering much broader functionality. Some APIs of particular interest to the case study are the following.

Java Native Interface. The JNI allows Java code that runs within a JVM to operate with applications and libraries written in other languages, such as C and C++. In addition, the Invocation API allows you to embed the JVM into your native applications [Sun 99a].

Remote Method Invocation.   RMI enables the programmer to create distributed Java-to-Java applications. In these applications, the methods of remote Java objects can be invoked from other JVMs, possibly on different hosts. A Java program can make a call on a remote object after obtaining a reference to the remote object, either by looking up the remote object in the bootstrap naming service provided by RMI or by receiving the reference as an argument or a return value. A client can call a remote object in a server, and that server can also be a client of other remote objects [Sun 02a].

Object Request Broker.   An ORB has been integrated with the Java runtime environment since JDK v1.2. The Java 2 Platform, Standard Edition, v1.4, provides an ORB and two CORBA interface mechanisms—RMI-IIOP and Java IDL—that can use the Java CORBA ORB and Internet Inter-ORB Protocol (IIOP) [Sun 02b].

PRODUCTS

The virtual machine for the Java platform on OS 2200 is an implementation of the JDK v1.2.2 code, adapted to the 2200 Series architecture. The implementation of the Java runtime environment allows pure Java-server applications to run under OS 2200. Databases, such as DMS and relational data management system (RDMS), may be accessed by using Java database connectivity (JDBC). The Java Core Classes are included, as well as the virtual machine.

Unisys provides OS 2200 proprietary Java classes for interfacing to OS 2200 services. The JNI service allows existing OS 2200 applications, including COBOL programs, to call Java programs running in the JVM. JNI also allows Java application programmers to create wrappers to make use of other OS 2200 services, if required. RMI is supported, allowing the OS 2200 JVM to interwork with other JVMs. These facilities provide considerable scope for using off-the-shelf Java components in OS 2200 environments. The JVM also supports Java servlets, complying with the Java Servlet v2.2 specification and the JavaServer Pages v1.1 specification [Unisys 00].

7.4   Data Repositories

Most legacy systems use some form of data repository. Many have database management systems that predate the relational models now prevalent. Given the importance and quantity of legacy data, data warehousing is becoming a popular way to make this data available to modern applications. In this section, we discuss both database management systems and data warehouses. Database management systems support mainly on-line transaction processing (OLTP), whereas data warehouses support on-line analytical processing (OLAP).

DATABASE MANAGEMENT SYSTEMS

Most database management systems (DBMSs) in use today are based on the relational database model. In the past, systems were based on other database models, such as the hierarchical model and the network model.[3] The marketplace is slowly evolving toward object-oriented database models.[4]

Hierarchical Databases. Hierarchical databases are based on parent-child relationships, modeled as a tree. A database schema is represented as multiple occurrences of a single type of tree, as shown in Figure 7-2. The example contains four record types: DEPARTMENT, MANAGER, EMPLOYEE, and TASK. The database is represented by multiple occurrences of the *root* record type, DEPARTMENT, which is a parent record type for the MANAGER and EMPLOYEE record types. Likewise, TASK is a child record type of the EMPLOYEE record type.

In this model, a parent can have zero or more children, allowing one-to-one and one-to-many relationships. In the example, a department has one manager and many employees. Many-to-many relationships are not supported in this model, because a child can have only one parent. In the example, even though an employee can be assigned to many tasks, it is impossible—or at least difficult without some hacking—to assign the same task to more than one employee.

Network Databases. This model is an extension of the hierarchical model. In a hierarchical model, a child record can have only one parent, whereas in the network model, a child can have any number of parents. A database schema is represented by a set of records and a set of links. Each link type connects one parent record type with one child record type, as shown in Figure 7-3. This example shows three record types—DEPARTMENT, EMPLOYEE, and TASK—and three

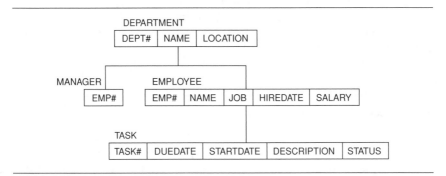

Figure 7-2 Example of a hierarchical database schema

[3] The inverted-list model is another common pre–relational database model.
[4] Relational databases that incorporate object-oriented concepts are referred to as object-relational databases.

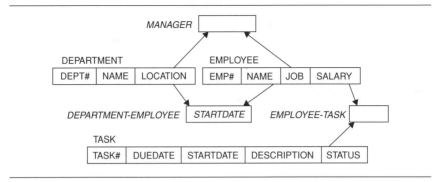

Figure 7-3   Example of a network database schema

link types—MANAGER, DEPARTMENT-EMPLOYEE, and EMPLOYEE-TASK. Link types can also contain information, as in the DEPARTMENT-EMPLOYEE link record.

Parents are usually connected to their child occurrences through a circular linked list that starts at the parent record, traverses all the child occurrences, and returns to the parent record. Many-to-many relationships are supported because a record can participate in any number of link types either as a child or as a parent. In the example, an employee can be linked to many tasks, and a task can be linked to many employees.

Relational Databases.   The majority of database systems today are relational. A relational database schema is composed of *tables*. The data elements describing data to be stored in the tables are called *columns*. Each entry in a table is called a *row*. *Primary keys* are unique identifiers for a row in a table, and *foreign keys* represent table data that is *related to* data in another table. Relational database schemas are usually represented in an entity-relationship (E-R) diagram, such as Figure 7-4.

The example shows four tables: EMPLOYEE, DEPARTMENT, TASK, and TASKASSIGNMENT. The primary key for each table is identified as PK. The foreign keys are identified as FK#. One-to-one relationships are represented by a column in a table acting as foreign key to another table. The DEPT# column in the EMPLOYEE table represents a one-to-one relationship between EMPLOYEE and DEPARTMENT. It signifies that an employee works in one department. One-to-many relationships and many-to-many relationships are represented by an additional table that maintains the relationship. The TASKASSIGNMENT table contains EMP# (the EMPLOYEE primary key) and TASK# (the TASK primary key) and stores the employees assigned to the different tasks.[5]

---

[5] Relational database design usually follows a *normalization* process to produce optimal table definitions.

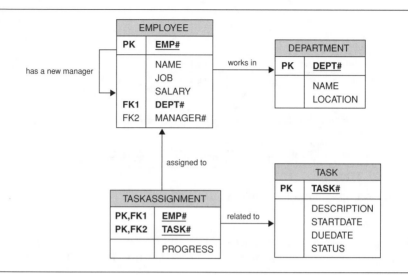

Figure 7-4   Example of a relational database schema

The most important aspect of relational databases is SQL support for defining, manipulating, and retrieving data without predefining access paths, as in the previous two models.

Object-Oriented Databases.   Object-oriented database management systems (ODBMSs or OODBMSs) integrate database and object-programming language capabilities. For the programming language, the OODB objects appear as programming language objects. The language itself is extended with libraries for database capabilities, such as queries, transparently persistent data,[6] concurrency control, and data recovery.

An object-oriented database schema is usually represented by a class diagram, as shown in Figure 7-5. Comparing the OO model to the relational model, we find that classes are similar to tables, object instances to rows, and attributes to columns. Data is retrieved from the database as persistent objects and manipulated directly by the object programming language, as if they were in-memory, nonpersistent objects. The data model at the application and database levels are the same. The OODBMS transparently synchronizes the persistent and nonpersistent data. There is no need for embedded SQL or JDBC to retrieve data from the database. The equivalent functionality is part of the object programming language. For all these characteristics, object-oriented databases are becoming popular for object-oriented applications that have high-performance and complex data

---

[6] Transparent persistence is the ability to directly manipulate data stored in a database, using an object-programming language.

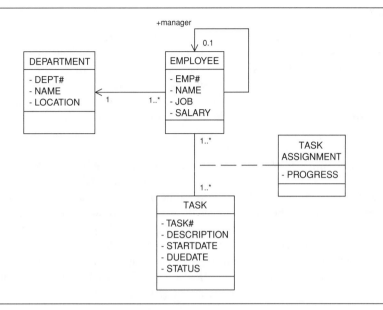

Figure 7-5   Example of an object-oriented database schema

requirements. OODBs are also being used as data staging areas for object-oriented applications written in C++, Java, or any object-oriented programming language.

Although object-oriented databases have many advantages, several factors have limited the acceptance of OODBMS.

- Organizations are wary about adopting OODBMS, owing to limited industry experience.

- Many RDBMS vendors have introduced object-oriented features to their core products, creating object-relational database management systems (ORDBMS).

- OODBMSs imply tight coupling between the application and the data, as the data model is the same both at the application and database levels. Owing to this lack of a data abstraction layer, moving to a different DBMS requires significant adaptation and testing.

- OODBMSs require different development and administration skills. Every DBMS product has its own proprietary extensions. Finding people with specific OODBM skills is more challenging than finding people with RDBMS skills, especially in the area of database administration.

- Ad hoc query support is still emerging in OODBMS products. Object-oriented databases are still weak at supporting queries that, for example, require extracting data from objects that do not share a relationship.

DATA WAREHOUSES

A data warehouse is a repository that supports management decision making at the enterprise or business-unit level. Data warehouses contain data that presents a coherent picture of business conditions at a single point in time. At the technical level, the development of a data warehouse includes developing systems to extract data from operational systems and installing a warehouse database system that provides flexible access to the data. At the business level, data warehouses often require modifying the decision-making processes so that they efficiently use this data.

The term *data warehousing* generally refers to combining many different databases across an entire enterprise. A data mart is a database, or collection of databases, that helps managers make strategic decisions about their business. Whereas a data warehouse combines databases across an entire enterprise, data marts are usually smaller and focus on a particular subject or department. Some data marts, called *dependent data marts,* are subsets of larger data warehouses. Data in a data mart is accessed using a business intelligence (BI) application. An example of data marts and data warehouses as defined by IBM in its Information Aggregation pattern is shown in Figure 7-6 [IBM 01].

STANDARDS

CODASYL (Conference on Data Systems Languages). CODASYL[7] was founded in 1957 by the U.S. Department of Defense to guide the development of a standard programming language that could be used on many computers. This effort led to the development of COBOL. In 1971, CODASYL's Database Task

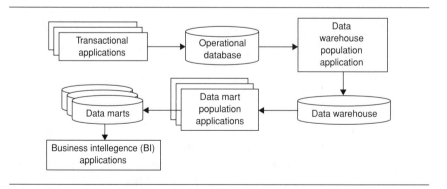

Figure 7-6 Data marts and data warehouses

---

[7] CODASYL is also referred to as Committee on Data Systems Languages because of the working group that was created after the conference to address the various issues and proposals.

Group (DBTG) proposed the network data model[8] as a standard for database definition and access. The DBTG report contained proposals for a data description language (DDL), a data manipulation language (DML), and the underlying network database structure.

SQL (Structured Query Language).   SQL is a database query language that was adopted as an industry standard in 1986. SQL statements are used to retrieve and update data in a database. SQL works with relational database systems, which usually have their own proprietary extensions to the language. This standard has continually evolved over the past 15 years.

- SQL-86: The first SQL standard provided basic language constructs for defining and manipulating tables of data.
- SQL-89: This version added language extensions for referential-integrity and generalized-integrity constraints.
- SQL-92: Also known as SQL2, this standard provided facilities for schema manipulation and data administration, as well as substantial enhancements for data definition and data manipulation.
- SQL:1999: Formerly known as SQL3, this standard specifies the SQL:1999 object model, which adds user-defined types to SQL.
- SQL:200n: This is the working document of the standard.

Open Database Connectivity.   ODBC is an Open Group standard API for accessing a database and was developed by Microsoft. An ODBC database driver links an application to a specific database. Both the application and the DBMS must be ODBC compliant. The application must issue ODBC commands, and the DBMS must respond to them.

ODBC allows programs to use SQL requests to access databases without knowing the proprietary interfaces. ODBC converts the SQL request into a request that the individual database system understands. The benefit of ODBC is that an application's source code does not need to be recompiled for each database it accesses.

Java Database Connectivity.   JDBC is an API that allows Java programs to send dynamic SQL statements to a database. JDBC is similar to ODBC but is designed specifically for Java programs. ODBC, by comparison, is language independent. The JDBC standard defines four types of JDBC drivers:

- **Type 1.** This is the JDBC-ODBC bridge that requires software to be installed on client systems.
- **Type 2.** This contains native methods calls (C or C++) and Java methods. It also requires software to be installed on the client.

---

[8] The network database model is also referred to the CODASYL data model.

- **Type 3.** These drivers use a networking protocol and middleware to communicate with a server. The server then translates the protocol to DBMS-specific function calls.

- **Type 4.** These drivers use Java to implement a DBMS vendor networking protocol, such as Oracle's SQL*Net or Ingres's Ingres/Net. Type 4 drivers are pure Java drivers.

Object Data Management Group.   ODMG is a standard produced by the Object Data Management Group for persistent object storage. The standard builds on existing database, object, and programming language standards, including those of the Object Management Group (OMG), to simplify object storage and ensure application portability [Barry 98].

Object Query Language.   OQL is the query language of the ODMG-93 standard. An SQL-like declarative language with support for objects, OQL can be used either as an embedded function in a programming language or as an ad hoc query language [ODMG 98].

OQL works with programming languages for which ODMG has defined bindings, such as C++, Java, and Smalltalk. The advantage gained by using OQL is that it returns objects matching types in the specific programming language so that these objects can be easily manipulated.

PRODUCTS

Data Management System 2200.   The DMS is a logical data manager based on the specifications recommended by the CODASYL committees for network database processing. DMS 2200 includes a variety of database storage structures, high-level language interfaces, and a selection of accessing techniques, as well as several levels of database recovery and security. DMS 2200 is a highly respected data manager for large, complex databases with demanding performance requirements.

Oracle Database.   Oracle is a relational database management system[9] designed to support data management, transaction processing, and data warehousing. The latest versions of the Oracle database provide built-in capabilities for Internet development and deployment—Web applications, portals, database distribution, replication, database management, and high availability. Oracle also includes application development capabilities, such as PL/SQL and Java programmatic interfaces for writing database triggers and stored procedures. Additional features of interest for this case study include a JVM with a native

---

[9] Oracle 9i, the latest version of the Oracle database, is considered to be an ORDBMS because it includes SQL with object-relational capabilities.

compiler, a CORBA v2.0 ORB, an EJB server, an embedded server-side JDBC driver, an SQLJ[10] translator, and XML support.

Oracle Discoverer.   This ad hoc query, reporting, analysis, and Web-publishing tool is used to access information from data marts, data warehouses, OLTP systems, and non-Oracle data sources. Data can be obtained from all these sources and stored in summary tables for on-the-fly analysis.

Relational Data Management System 2200.   RDMS 2200 is a relational database that uses SQL for data definition and manipulation. SQL statements can be embedded in COBOL, FORTRAN, and other programs. RDMS 2200 provides a self-organizing database. All data is presented in simple, two-dimensional tables of horizontal columns divided into rows. Relational tables are easy to access and update. New tables can be created by selecting and combining columns and rows from the same or different tables.

UniAccess for OS 2200.   UniAccess, a product from Applied Information Sciences (AIS), provides SQL access from clients to RDMS 2200 data. With UniAccess, RDMS data can be accessed with the same client tools and applications that are used to access data in SQL databases running on other platforms, such as Oracle and Sybase. UniAccess enables Java clients to access RDMS data by using a JDBC-to-ODBC bridge to link to the UniAccess ODBC driver.

Unisys Data Access.   This product provides an SQL interface to nonrelational data on Unisys mainframes, including DMS. The product accesses data stored in DMS through ODBC. Because ODBC works with relational databases and DMS is a network database, Data Access creates a relational view of DMS, allowing the ODBC functions to operate.

Universal Data Management System 2200.   UDS 2200 provides data management functions within the 2200 environment of ClearPath IX systems. UDS Control, the UDS on-line data manager, provides a common architecture and environment for all UDS data models, including RDMS 2200 and DMS 2200. Both data models can be used concurrently by the same program, and all programs use the same method to commit or roll back changes for all files. UDS Control allows users to share files, controls access to those files, and automatically and uniformly resolves access conflicts. It also allows users to designate recoverable files, regardless of the data management method used, and provides consistent file recovery.

---

[10] SQLJ enables programmers to embed static SQL operations in Java code.

7.5   Data Representations for Information Exchange

The creation of standard data formats that can be used to share information across system and platform boundaries is an important innovation in data management. In this section, we describe two data representations for information exchange: electronic data interchange (EDI) and the eXtensible Markup Language (XML).

EDI

EDI is the computer-to-computer exchange of business data in standard formats between trading partners. EDI was first developed for the shipping and transportation industry more than 25 years ago to reduce paperwork burdens. Traditionally, individual trading partners implement EDI-shared definitions of document formats, including purchase orders, invoices, and shipping orders. The trading partners interface EDI to their existing systems via translation software rather than at the application level. EDI has been accepted by many industries, including health care, financial services, and government procurement. Such standards as ANSI ASC (Accredited Standards Committee) X12 and UN/EDIFACT (United Nations/Electronic Data Interchange for Administration, Commerce and Transport) enable the adoption of EDI by describing an agreed-on message format. Even though these standards reduce confusion about message formats, challenges in mapping message content persist.

EDI enjoys wide industry acceptance: According to the International Data Corporation, more than three times as many B2B electronic transactions occurred via EDI in 2001 than over the Internet. Nonetheless, EDI is often criticized for its syntactic rigidity and its implementation costs. The rise of the document-centric Web and the notion of e-business have resulted in new avenues for exchanging data. Many EDI adopters have begun exploring new technologies to enhance systems relying on EDI technology. The leading technology is XML.

XML

XML is a *markup language* developed by the World Wide Web Consortium (W3C). XML is used to structure data to reduce ambiguity between applications sharing information. Structured data includes the content and the role the content plays.

A data object is an XML document if it is well formed, as defined in the XML specification. Being well formed requires that the elements are delimited by start tags and end tags and are nested properly. XML offers a universal syntax for describing and structuring data independent from application logic and is being used to define languages for specific industries and applications.

It is important to note that XML is not a programming language but rather a markup language similar to HTML. Its design, however, was influenced by principles of good programming language design, including extensibility—allowing the introduction of new tags without breaking the existing document structure—platform independence, and support for internationalization, as it is based on Unicode. In fact, XML and HTML share a common ancestry, as they are both descendants of the Standardized General Markup Language (SGML), a 1986 ISO standard for structuring data commonly used in large technical documentation projects. Since its inception in 1996, XML has refined and focused SGML concepts into a simplified subset that is appropriate for use on the Web.

As XML has matured, several related standards have emerged. XSL (eXtensible Style Language) is the advanced language for expressing style sheets. XSL is based on XSLT (eXtensible Style Language Transformation), a transformation language used for rearranging, adding, and deleting tags and attributes.

DTD.   Although an XML document is the data itself, the means to describe and validate the structure of the data is left to a document type definition (DTD). A DTD expresses constraints on XML documents by defining the allowable elements within a document and their content, order, and attributes. An XML document is valid if it has an associated DTD and complies with its constraints. In addition to validation, a DTD can define entities, define notations, and provide default values for attributes. The DTD enables heterogeneous applications to share data. Numerous specialized DTDs are used in specific industries and applications and have become standards.

XML Schemas.   Schemas address several limitations of the DTD by providing a richer semantic encoding and by providing advances in describing document object models. Schemas are written in XML-instance-document syntax, using tags, elements, and attributes. Schemas can assign data types, such as integer and date, to elements and validate documents, based on not only the element structure but also the contents of the elements. DTDs lack an effective means to extend types and combine types from multiple names spaces, both of which are addressed by schemas.

XML Parsers.   Because it is structured data in the form of plaintext with tags to delimit the data, XML can be manipulated simply. Programmatically, writing XML can be as simple as sending characters to a file output stream. On the other hand, reading XML is best accomplished via XML parsers, available as libraries from numerous vendors. Parsing simply is the process of reading an XML document and reporting its content to a client application while checking that the document is well formed.

The two common techniques for parsing XML are using the simple application programming interface for XML (Simple API for XML, or SAX) and using the document object model (DOM). SAX defines the API to read an XML file in

sequence, line by line. SAX is based on two interfaces: the *XML Reader* interface, which represents the parser, and the *Content Handler* interface, which is
implemented to receive data from the parser. Callbacks of the event-oriented
architecture of SAX are used to notify the parsing implementation when element
names and data are encountered. This technique is useful when processing large
XML files and streaming data. The DOM is a standard set of function calls for
manipulating XML and HTML files from a programming language in which the
manipulation is not sequential but rather tree based. The DOM is most useful for
programs needing to manipulate large portions of small documents.

STANDARDS

XML 1.0. Extensible Markup Language (XML) v1.0, a recommendation of the
World Wide Web Consortium (W3C) is in its second edition.[11]

XML Schema. There are three W3C recommendations for the XML Schema:
XML Schema Part 0: Primer; XML Schema Part 1: Structures; and XML Schema
Part 2: Datatypes. The Primer, a non-normative document providing a readable
description of the XML Schema facilities, is useful for quickly understanding
how to create schemas using the XML Schema language. XML Schema: Structures specifies the XML Schema definition language, which offers facilities for
describing the structure and constraining the contents of XML v1.0. XML
Schema Part 2: Datatypes defines facilities for defining datatypes to be used in
XML Schemas, as well as other XML specifications.[12]

SAX. The Simple API for XML, originally a Java-only API, was the first
widely adopted API for XML in Java and is a de facto standard. The current version is SAX v2.0, and there are versions for several programming language environments other than Java.[13]

PRODUCTS

Apache Xerces. The Xerces Java Parser supports the XML v1.0 recommendation and contains advanced parser functionality, such as support for the W3C's
XML Schema recommendation v1.0, DOM Level 2 v1.0, and SAX v2.0, in addition to supporting the industry-standard DOM Level 1 and SAX v1.0 APIs.[14]

---

[11] For the full text of the specification, go to http://www.sei.cmu.edu/
cbs/mls/links.html#w3xml2000.
[12] All three recommendations, along with additional information, can be found at
http://www.sei.cmu.edu/cbs/mls/links.html#w3-xml-schema.
[13] For more information, see http://www.sei.cmu.edu/cbs/mls/links.html#saxproject.
[14] More information can be found at http://www.sei.cmu.edu/cbs/mls/links.html#apache.

IBM XML4J. IBM's XML Parser for Java (XML4J) is a validating XML parser written in 100% Pure Java. XML4J incorporates support for the W3C XML Schema Recommendation v1.0, SAX v1.0 and SAX v2.0, DOM Level 1, DOM Level 2, some features of DOM Level 3 Core Working Draft, and JAXP v1.1 support. IBM is a major contributor to Apache's Xerces-J code base. Version 1.4.2 of Xerces-J forms the basis for XML4J v3.2.1.[15]

SUN JAXP. The Java API for XML Processing (JAXP) supports processing of XML documents using the DOM, SAX, and XSLT. JAXP enables applications to parse and transform XML documents independently of a particular XML processing implementation. Developers can swap between XML processors, such as high-performance versus memory-conservative parsers, without changing the application code. The JAXP reference implementation v1.1.3 includes a high-quality parser supporting both SAX and DOM and a transformation engine supporting XSLT.[16]

7.6 Summary

This chapter provides concise descriptions of technologies that are relevant to our case study. This level of information should be sufficient to guide your understanding of the case study, and provides pointers to additional resources. However, we believe that any knowledge derived from reading books and manuals or even attending training is limited and that the only way to fully understand how to apply these technologies is through direct experience. This type of competency can be gained through the use of "toys" or model problems—prototypes for which the primary purpose is learning. The philosophy inherent in this approach was well stated by Confucius (circa 551–479 BC): "I hear and I forget. I see and I remember. I do and I understand." In the next chapter, we continue our exploration of the design space by looking more closely at transaction technologies.

[15] For more information, see http://www.sei.cmu.edu/cbs/mls/links.html#alphaworks.
[16] More information can be found at http://www.sei.cmu.edu/cbs/mls/links.html#sun.

8

Transaction Technology

Why, a four-year-old child could understand this report. Run out and find
me a four-year-old child.
—Groucho Marx, *Duck Soup*, 1933

Today, programmers have access to various commercial technologies to build distributed, transactional applications. These technologies are typically based on either synchronous remote procedure calls (RPC) or message queues. RPC-based technologies or products are normally associated with a *distributed-transaction* model. Message queue–based technologies or products are more commonly associated with a *queued-transactions* model. Both of these models are described in detail later in this chapter.

It is often difficult to determine when a particular model is appropriate or inappropriate. The answer is not always intuitive and often requires careful examination. This chapter provides some answers and guidance for selecting the appropriate model. However, because the choice of model goes hand-in-hand with the choice of a technology that implements it, we must consider such qualities as the reliability, usability, and maintainability of the commercial products that support particular transaction models. For example, in an incremental modernization effort, such as RSS, transactions may span legacy and modernized components on two different platforms. Which is the best model and the set of technologies for this situation?

8.1   Where Are We?

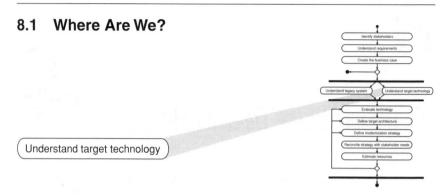

Understand target technology

In the "understanding" phase, we need to understand the technologies used in the legacy system, as well as the target, modernization technologies. This is the second of three chapters that examine the information system technologies that both populate and constrain the solution space. In this chapter, we focus on distributed communication and transaction technologies.

8.2   Distributed Communication

Distributed communication allows software running on different processors to interact and exchange information either directly or indirectly via a communication mechanism. Key attributes of distributed-communication technologies include support for *direct* or *indirect, connectionless* or *connection-oriented,* and *asynchronous* or *synchronous* communications. Several commonly used distributed communication technologies are presented in Table 8-1.

In models that provide synchronous communication, such as RPC (Figure 8-1), the calling application is blocked until a response is received from the remote application. Synchronous forms of communication typically work well in a local area network (LAN) environment, in which connectivity, network speed, and bandwidth are readily available. Synchronous forms of communication should be used with caution over slower networks or the Internet. Problems may arise from unexpected blocking time because of slow network performance, connectivity, or bandwidth availability.

In asynchronous communications, application processes are not blocked. Therefore, a message may be sent to a remote program, but the response from the remote application could be received at a later, possibly indeterminate time. This allows developers to build applications that interleave communications as well as perform additional processing.

As mentioned earlier, some communication technologies communicate directly with remote applications, whereas others communicate indirectly. Direct-communication technologies require a direct link to be established—and possibly

Table 8-1 Distributed Communication Technologies

Distributed Communication Technologies	Key Attributes					
	Direct Communications	Indirect Communications	Connection-Oriented Communications	Connectionless Communications	Synchronous Communications	Asynchronous Communications
Remote procedure call (RPC) (point to point)	✓		✓		✓	
Message passing (point to point)	✓		✓	✓	✓	✓
Message queuing		✓		✓		✓
Publish/subscribe (one to many)		✓		✓		✓

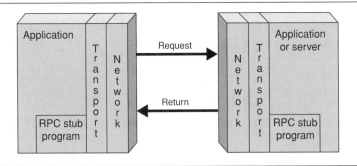

Figure 8-1 Remote procedure calls

maintained—between the two applications that participate in the information exchange. The receiving application must be available—running and reachable via the network under normal conditions—at the time of the request. Therefore, most direct-communication technologies are *connection oriented*. Once a connection is established between the two applications, the receiver binds to an instance of the requester, creating a connection context. In essence, the requester and the receiver share a state for the duration of the connection and can determine the exact context of both requests and responses.

By contrast, indirect-communication technologies, such as the message-queueing technology shown in Figure 8-2, do not require the receiving application to be available at the time of the request. The communication provider will usually queue messages for an application until it becomes available. Therefore, most indirect-communication technologies are *connectionless*. However, if the model does not queue messages through the use of an independent queue manager, as shown in the message-passing model in Figure 8-3, messages sent while the remote application is unavailable will result in a delivery failure or will be lost. Although the message-passing model itself is connectionless and asynchronous from the application's point of view, the process of sending a message is often implemented in a synchronous and connection-oriented manner. This means that the sender is blocked until either the message is delivered to the remote application's receive queue or the MESSAGE SEND operation times out and then fails because of an unreachable application.

Messages to a remote application are one-way and inherently asynchronous and stateless. Because this form of communication is stateless, all state information must be passed inside the message for the requester to determine the context of a particular response or request.

The publish/subscribe communication technology shown in Figure 8-4 is similar to the message-queuing model but is a one-to-many model. In this model, applications publish information on a network and subscribe to receive information of interest. Both the publisher, or producer, and the subscriber, or consumer, applications do not need to know about the existence, location, or state of the

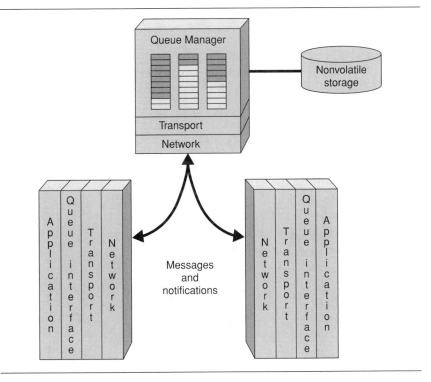

Figure 8-2   Message queues

information producers or consumers. Systems that use this model can be dynamically reconfigured with new publishers' or subscribers' programs without interruption.

Many middleware products are available to help developers implement these communication technologies. These products often provide features beyond the simple communication, such as object orientation, security, quality of service,

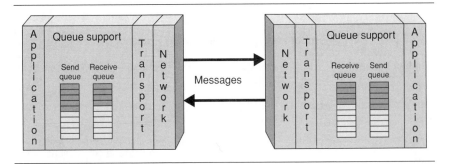

Figure 8-3   Message passing

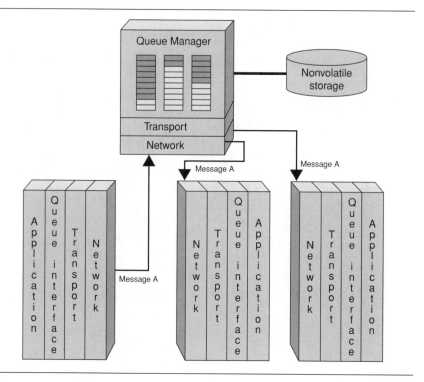

Figure 8-4 Publish/subscribe communications technology

and data marshaling. Table 8-2 presents some distributed communication middleware products, along with the communication technologies they implement.

The choice of a communication technology depends on the requirements of an application. This choice will strongly influence the system architecture, or design, and the manner in which an application performs transaction processing. Again, RPC or message-passing communication technologies are best suited for situations in which the distributed applications are expected to be available and

Table 8-2 Distributed Communication Middleware Products

Product Name	Vendor	Communication Technology
VisiBroker (CORBA)	Inprise	RPC (via IIOP)
BEA WebLogic (EJB Server)	BEA Systems	RPC (via RMI over IIOP)
MQSeries	IBM	Message queuing
Java Message Service (JMS)	Sun Microsystems	Message passing, message queuing, and publish/subscribe
MessageQ	BEA Systems	Message queuing

reachable under normal operating conditions and when an application requires a response from a remote application before continuing execution. Message queuing or publish/subscribe communication technologies are best suited to situations in which the remote application may not always be available and immediate responses are not required.

In general, distributed database applications typically use RPC or message queues for communication. The choice of a distributed communication technology has a large impact on transaction processing. Systems designed to use synchronous communication for distributed communications typically use a transaction-processing model called *distributed transactions* for database operations, whereas systems that use *message queues* for distributed communication use a model called *queued transactions*. In the sections that follow, we discuss the fundamentals of transactions and the differences between *distributed transactions* and *queued transactions*.

8.3 Transactions

Transactions are a part of everyday life. From a human perspective, a transaction is any exchange or transfer of goods, services, or funds. In a commercial transaction, either the consumer gets the goods and the seller gets the money, or the consumer does not get the goods and the seller does not get the money.

In the computing world, a transaction is a sequence of operations on a database. From the application developer's point of view, transactions are performed as an indivisible unit with a simple failure model. Transactions can have only one of two possible outcomes: success or failure. Transactions are guaranteed to have the following properties:

- **Atomicity.** The operations will be executed either completely or not at all.
- **Consistency.** The system moves from one self-consistent state to another.
- **Isolation.** The intermediate operations or states that occur during the transactions are not visible to other transactions that could be occurring simultaneously.
- **Durability.** The results of a transaction will not be lost in the event of a hardware or software failure.

These properties, often called ACID properties, ensure that transactions are complete, have consistent data, occur independently of concurrent transactions, and keep the results.

There are many types of transactions. The most common type is the flat transaction with or without save points. Other transaction types are not usually commercially supported and exist only in research products.

FLAT TRANSACTIONS

A *flat transaction*, the most basic type of transaction, is an atomic unit of work, managed by a single process. The transaction consists of one or more operations that can be performed by different processes or threads. These processes may be distributed across different platforms or servers. Once started, a flat transaction can only be committed or rolled back.

A simple example of a flat transaction is shown in Figure 8-5. In this example, issuing a `Begin Transaction` starts the transaction. Next, the necessary operations needed to complete the transaction are performed. Finally, if the operations were successful, the transaction is committed, using the `Commit Transaction` command; otherwise, the transaction is rolled back, using the `Rollback Transaction` command. Rollback means that the database is returned to its previous state, as if none of the operations within the transaction were executed. Figure 8-5 does not illustrate the results of possible failures.

Flat transactions can cause resources to be locked during the entire transaction. As a result, these transactions should be small and take minimal time to execute: typically, less than 2 to 3 seconds.

FLAT TRANSACTIONS WITH SAVE POINTS

Declared within the context of a transaction, *save points* are commands that save the progress of work, or operations performed, up to the location of the save point. If the transaction is aborted, it can be rolled back to the point of work performed just before the save point. Because save points allow a transaction to be broken up into smaller pieces, all operations between two save-point commands can be viewed as atomic. A common use of save points is to save work completed before beginning a set of operations, as shown in Figure 8-6. If a problem is detected during a transaction, the work can then be rolled back to the point just before the *save point* and retried in a different manner.

CHAINED TRANSACTIONS

Chained transactions are similar to *flat transactions* with *save points*. In this case, work is divided into a set of smaller transactions, using commit points—a chain operation—that specify the boundary of a subtransaction. A *commit point* is used to both commit the last subtransaction and start the next subtransaction. Figure 8-7 shows a chained transaction used within a loop. The `CommitPoint` commits the last transaction and starts a new transaction. As shown in the example, if a problem is encountered, a `Rollback` is issued. These commands will roll back only to the last commit point. Thus, commit points can be used as a restarting point in the event of a failure. When using this model, a program is always executing within the scope of a transaction.

```
Begin Transaction
 Operation 1
 Operation 2
 Operation 3

 ...
 Operation N
If (Success) Commit Transaction
Else Rollback Transaction
```

Figure 8-5   Flat transactions

```
Begin Transaction
 Operation 1
 Op1Save=SaveWork()
 Operation 2
 Op2Save=SaveWork()
 Operation 3
 If (Operation 3 Error) Rollback(Op2Save){
    Operation 4
    }
If (Operation 4 Error) Rollback Transaction
Else Commit Transaction
```

Figure 8-6   Flat transactions with save point

```
Set Chained Mode to true
While (HaveWorkToDo)
{
 Do Sub-Transaction
 If (Success) CommitPoint
 Else Rollback
}
Set Chained Mode to false
```

Figure 8-7   Chained transactions

CLOSED NESTED TRANSACTIONS

A *nested transaction* allows you to define subtransactions within other transactions by breaking the transaction into a tree hierarchy of subtransactions, as shown in Figure 8-8. This type of transaction is also called a closed nested transaction. The leaf nodes of the tree are always *flat transactions*, whereas subtree

```
Begin Transaction
 Begin Transaction
     Operation a1
     Operation a2
 Commit Transaction
 Begin Transaction
     Operation b1
     Operation b2
 Commit Transaction
Commit Transaction
```

Figure 8-8   Nested transactions

nodes—children—contain a nested subtransaction. This model allows subtrans-actions within the subtree node or a subtransaction in a leaf node to commit or roll back, but the *commit* will not take effect unless the root node of the tree com-mits. Before a subtransaction commits, its updated data is visible only to its sub-transactions. After a subtransaction commits, its updated data is made visible to other subtransactions that share the same parent. Rollbacks at a subtree node will cause any subtransactions under that node to also roll back.

This model supports top-level transactions with all the ACID properties. However, subtransactions in this model lack the *durability* property because of the behavior associated with rollbacks and commits with subtransactions. Sub-transactions are not actually committed until the parent transaction commits.

The concept of nested transactions has been around since the early 1980s, but this transaction model has little commercial support. However, it is possible to simulate nested transactions by using *save points*, as shown in Table 8-3. As in this example, *save points* are used to roll back nested transactions from a given point on without affecting the transactions nested under different save points. A major advantage of nested transactions is that they offer a higher degree of con-currency than do other transactional models.

OPEN NESTED TRANSACTIONS

Open nested transactions are similar to closed nested transactions except that a *commit* operation in a subtransaction takes effect immediately, making the updated data visible before the parent node or root node commits. Additionally, rollbacks must be handled using a *compensating transaction* or a *saga*. A com-pensating transaction is a group of operations, or a transaction, used to undo the effect of a previously committed transaction. A saga is the capability to automati-cally determine and start a compensating transaction for every committed trans-action in case a transactional failure occurs [Bernstein 97]. Sagas require an application programmer to write a compensating transaction for each transaction.

Table 8-3 Simulated Nested Transactions

Nested Transaction	Simulated Nested Transaction
| ```
Begin Transaction
Operation a1
  Operation a2
  Begin Transaction
    Operation b1
    Operation b2
    Begin Transaction
      Operation c1
      Operation c2
    Commit Transaction
  Commit Transaction
Commit Transaction
``` | ```
Begin Transaction
  Op1Save=SaveWork()
    Operation a1
    Operation a2
    Op2Save=SaveWork()
      Operation b1
      Operation b2
      Op3Save=SaveWork()
        Operation c1
        Operation c2
Commit Transaction
``` |

This model is useful only if the subtransactions are fairly independent and can be rolled back, using a compensating transaction or a saga.

As with closed nested transactions, this model has little commercial support. To date, the only commercial product that supports this transactional model is IBM Transarc's Encina TP monitor.

MULTILEVEL TRANSACTIONS

Multilevel transactions are similar to *open nested transactions* except that the tree of subtransactions must be balanced, that is, must all have the same depth. This balance allows the execution to be performed in layers. As with *open nested transactions*, a commit in subtransactions will take effect immediately, making the updated data visible, before the parent node or root node commits, and rollbacks must be accomplished by executing compensating subtransactions. The major advantages to this model are that it requires less locking and favors parallel execution.

DISTRIBUTED-ACCESS TRANSACTIONS

Distributed-access transactions are more an attribute of a transaction or a subtransaction than a type of transaction. A *distributed-access transaction* occurs when a distributed application performs a transaction on a single database server. In cases of distributed access, the distributed application must maintain a *transaction context,* or the logical grouping of all the data update operations performed as part of a transaction. The *transaction context* is used to track and determine the work that must be committed or rolled back. This context must be propagated to all threads and applications participating in the transaction. An underlying transaction manager usually maintains the transaction context transparently.

8.4 Distributed Transactional Operations

The occurrence of transactions in a distributed environment is quite common today. *Distributed transactional operations* are data updates to two or more databases by one or more applications or threads participating in the transaction. These types of transactions are usually implemented by using either a distributed-transaction model or the queued-transaction model.[1]

In this section, we describe both of these models and provide example architectures.

DISTRIBUTED-TRANSACTION MODEL

This model is typically implemented using remote procedure calls as a communication mechanism. Because RPCs are used for communication, requests are handled in a synchronous manner, and *all* participating applications or threads must be available at the time of the request. The *distributed-transaction* model assumes that a transaction will involve data updates to two or more databases by one or more applications or threads participating in the transaction. Typically, this model is implemented using a *flat* or *nested* transaction model with additional management for commit, rollback, resource locking, and access.

Commit and rollback functionalities are typically achieved using a *two-phase commit protocol*. This protocol ensures that the execution of data transactions is synchronized: All data updates are either committed or rolled back with respect to each of the distributed databases.

With this model, a *transaction context* is also maintained by the underlying transaction manager. It is this *transaction context* that ultimately defines a *global transaction*: a specific sequence of operations—that is, operations performed on all databases involved in the transaction—that conform to the ACID properties.

Given the complexity of building distributed-transaction applications, commercial components are available to help developers build these applications. Many of these commercial components conform to the Distributed Transaction Processing (DTP) reference architecture [OpenGroup 96] shown in Figure 8-9, which was developed by X/Open.[2] In reality, not all commercial solutions follow

---

[1] *Distributed-access transactions* are often viewed as *distributed transactional operations* even though only one database is involved in the transaction.

[2] X/Open merged with the Open Software Foundation in 1996 to form the Open Group. The X/Open DTP reference architecture is more correctly referred to as the Open Group DTP reference architecture. However, we use the more commonly recognized name throughout this book.

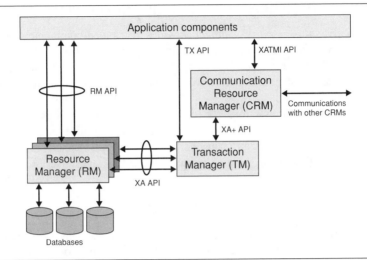

Figure 8-9   Distributed transaction architecture

the architecture described here. The architecture described is simply intended to provide a basic understanding of some of the commercial solutions available.

In the X/Open architecture, an application interacts with the transaction manager, resource manager, and communication resource manager through a set of transaction APIs that transparently support either local or distributed transactions. The functionality provided by each of these components is discussed in the following sections.

RESOURCE MANAGER COMPONENT

A *resource manager* provides access to shared resources, such as database servers and file servers. Additionally, it notifies the *transaction manager* of resources that will be used in transactions and participates in the commit and rollback procedures that the transaction manager controls. Communication with the *resource manager* is achieved through two sets of APIs: the transaction manager interface—XA (extended architecture) API—and an application component interface—RM (resource manager) API.

The transaction manager uses the XA API to communicate with the resource manager during commit and rollback procedures and to receive resource registrations. Additionally, it provides a two-phase commit capability.

Application components manipulate data by using the RM API. The format of the RM interface is resource-manager specific and is usually an SQL interface for database resource managers. It is not uncommon for an application program to communicate with more than one resource manager.

COMMUNICATION RESOURCE MANAGER COMPONENT

The *communication resource manager* provides distributed-communications services for the local transaction manager and application. Through the XATMI (extended architecture transaction manager interface) API, applications can communicate across system boundaries, using either a peer-to-peer or an RPC communication model.

For distributed transactions, the local transaction manager uses the communication resource manager XA+ API—an expanded version of the XA API—to communicate with transaction managers on other systems. Usually, this is done to coordinate activities, such as two-phase commits.

TRANSACTION MANAGER COMPONENT

The *transaction manager*—also called a transaction processing monitor, or TP monitor—coordinates the transactions for a distributed application. The TP monitor initiates transactions for applications, tracking all the resources participating in a transaction, establishing and propagating a transaction context, and conducting the two-phase commit and rollback procedures. The transaction manager coordinates with resource managers to ensure that all the subtransactions that make up the distributed transaction are committed or rolled back together. Thus, the transaction manager provides ACID properties to a distributed transaction without the use of any specialized code in the application components.

Applications communicate with the transaction manger through a *transaction manager* API called the TX (transaction) API. This API consists of approximately ten primitives that allow applications to inform it of a transaction's start, end, and disposition.

APPLICATION COMPONENTS

Application components implement transactions. The application component communicates with the transaction manager to start, commit, or roll back a transaction. To manipulate data, the application component communicates with the resource manager. Applications can communicate with another system's applications through the communication resource manager.

When it needs to perform a transaction, an application starts it by using the TX API. Then the application uses the RM API to update any local databases and, possibly, the XATMI API to call various remote applications to update their local databases. Next, the application uses the TX API to commit the transaction. This action causes the local transaction manager to contact all remote transaction managers via the communication resource manager, using the XA+ API, for approval to commit the transaction. Finally, if all transaction managers approve the transaction, all the database updates are made permanent; otherwise, the databases are returned to their original states before the transaction occurred.

QUEUED-TRANSACTION MODEL

The word *transactions* in the term *queued transactions* does not refer to database transactions. In this model, transaction requests—in this case, messages—are not dispatched for immediate processing as with the distributed-transaction model. Instead, the transaction requests are put in a transactional queue for processing by a server. Transactional queues are essentially message queues with the following enhancements.

- Messages are sent within the scope of a particular transaction.
- Messages sent to the same queue are delivered in the order in which they were sent.
- Support is included for transactional operations.

Once the server processes a transactional message, the result is written to a persistent queue—a response queue—for the application to retrieve. An example of this interaction is shown in Figure 8-10.

Message queuing and queued transactions guarantee that no messages will be lost. As a result, the server does not need to be available at the time of the request; it can process requests later.

This model is quite different from the *distributed-transaction* model discussed earlier. In the queued-transaction model, messages are sent and received in a transaction context and placed in the transactional queue. This transaction context relates only to the message, not to a database operation. However, this context can be programatically associated with the transaction context of a database operation. The transaction context for database operations may be included in the message content.

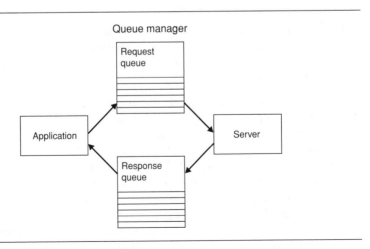

Figure 8-10   Queued-transaction model

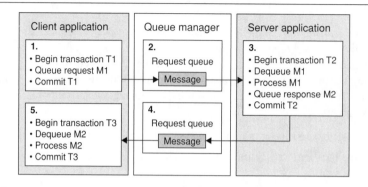

Figure 8-11 Queued-transaction example

Figure 8-11 illustrates queued transactions. In this example, the following operations occur:

1. The client starts transaction T1 and queues the request within the context of the message transaction. The queued request is not available to the server until transaction T1 is committed.

2. Next, the queue manager notifies the server of a pending request.

3. The server starts transaction T2, dequeues the request, and begins processing it. After the request is processed, the server sends a response back to the client and then finally commits transaction T2. If T2 is not committed, message M1 is not removed from the request queue, and message M2 is never placed in the response queue.

4. Next, the queue manager notifies the client of a pending response.

5. The client then starts transaction T3, dequeues the response, and begins processing it. After the response is processed, the client application commits transaction T3. If it is not committed, message M2 is not removed from the response queue.

This model has the benefit of decoupling the client and the server, but this benefit comes at a price. Each message exchange—application request to server and the server response—results in three separate message transactions, each with its own ACID properties. Therefore, it is impossible to wrap a multirequest database transaction in a single unit. Thus, under certain circumstances, it may be necessary to write a considerable amount of complex code to deal with rollbacks and other error states.

To illustrate this issue, suppose that operation 5 in the example fails. In this case, the system may want to roll back the server operations but cannot, because the server transactions are already committed. As stated earlier, this difficulty exists with queued transactions because there is no easy way to perform any type of nested or multirequest database transaction using transactional messages.

If the operations involve only one database, this problem can be solved easily by using a transaction context, as described in Section 8.3. Otherwise, resolving this problem may require complex logic to perform rollback processing, because the example violates the ACID property of *isolation*. The isolation problem of a multitransaction work flow usually requires application-specific solutions [Bernstein 97]. Extra processing, such as a *compensating transaction* or a *saga*, must be developed to perform rollback processing.

Another solution may be to use a *transaction manager* to manage the context of the *global transaction*. However, using such a manager may limit or eliminate the benefits of a queued-transaction model because of blocking. Note that in some cases, a rollback may not even be possible to implement without using a transaction manager.

The only other solution is to investigate changing the business logic so that a rollback is possible. This solution, however, requires reevaluating the business rules for the system.

8.5   Comparison of Transactional Models

Peter Houston provides an excellent comparison of transactional models [Houston 99]. Table 8-4 summarizes the advantages and disadvantages of distributed transactions; Table 8-5 provides the equivalent summary for queued transactions.

The major advantages of using distributed transactions are ease of implementing complex transactions and the ability to simplify error detection and correction. The major disadvantages of this model are blocking while waiting for a response, high availability requirements, and potential locking issues.

Queued transactions have the advantages of being able to asynchronously process requests, have reduced availability requirements, and have extensibility aspects. The major disadvantages of this model are the difficulties that can be associated with rollback processing/error correction. Some database transactions, particularly when using queued transactions without a TP monitor, can result in

Table 8-4   Evaluation of Distributed Transactions

Advantages	Disadvantages
Mature technology	Subject to locking conflicts that can be difficult to solve
Complex transactions possibly easier to implement.	
	Tight coupling between requester and server
Error detection and correction often easier to implement.	Requires high availability, so all parts of the system—applications, middleware, network, and platforms—must be available
	Requester is blocked while waiting for a response

Table 8-5 Evaluation of Queued Transactions

Advantages	Disadvantages
Less subject to locking conflicts	States can arise whereby requester is unsure of the fate of its messages
Less dependent on network and application availability	May be more difficult to implement complex transactions, such as
Usually easier to extend than distributed transactions (less coupling)	
Requester is *not* blocked while waiting for a response	Error detection and correction
Allows for more parallel processing to occur	Rollback processing
Possible to remove request from the queue and process based on priority	
Possible for the requester to determine the state of the request	

operations that cannot be undone or subtransactions that cannot be compensated using a compensating transaction or saga. Therefore, the rollback issues associated with transaction queuing should be a major concern when choosing a model.

Because both models have their own strengths and weaknesses, the choice depends on the context of the system being built. As a result, it is impossible to definitively state which model is best. However, some general guidance can be provided.

- The choice of a model goes hand-in-hand with the choice of the technology that implements it. Therefore, a major criterion in choosing a model is the availability of an implementation and its qualities, such as reliability, usability, and maintainability.

- If the client that starts a transaction must wait for a response from the server before proceeding, the *distributed-transactions* model is the better choice because *distributed transactions* can often be easier to implement than queued transactions. However, if a client starts a transaction, does not need to wait for a response, and can do other processing in the meantime, *queued transactions* may be a better choice [Chappell 98].

- If some server applications may not always be available, network availability may be intermittent, or network performance slow, consider using *queued transactions* [Chappell 98].

- If more than one server can handle a transaction, consider *queued transactions*. Load balancing can be implemented easily with *queued transactions*. A set of servers could be configured to read requests from a single transactional queue. It is important to note that some TP monitors and EJB servers automatically provide load balancing that is usually based on a simple round-robin model. With *queued transactions*, it is easier to implement more sophisticated and effective load-balancing techniques, such as the ability to prioritize transaction requests.

▪ If issues concerning rollbacks cannot be solved using compensating transactions, a saga, or a change to the business logic, seriously consider using *distributed transactions*.

8.6 Standards

OTS and JTS are two standard transaction-processing technologies based on the X/Open DTP model and mentioned in the case study.

Object Transaction Service. The OTS specification, by the Object Management Group (OMG), extends the CORBA model and defines a set of interfaces to perform transaction processing across multiple CORBA objects. OTS is based on the X/Open DTP model with the following enhancements. The OTS model replaces the functional XA and TX interfaces with CORBA IDL (Interface Definition Language) interfaces. The various objects in this model communicate via CORBA method calls over IIOP [Allamaraju 99].

Java Transaction API and Java Transaction Service. The JTA is a high-level, implementation-independent, protocol-independent API that allows applications and application servers to access transactions. The JTS specifies the implementation of a transaction manager that supports the JTA and implements the Java mapping of the OMG OTS specification at the level below the API. This allows JTA-compliant applications to interoperate with other OTS-compliant applications through the standard IIOP.

8.7 Products

Again, there are numerous transaction managers. Of primary interest to the case study are transaction managers that implement Java-based standards and transaction managers that run on the Unisys Clearpath 2200 platform.

BEA Tuxedo. BEA Tuxedo is a transaction server that provides distributed transaction management, dynamic workload balancing, transaction queuing, and event brokering.[3] BEA Tuxedo is compliant with the Open Group's X/Open standards, including support of the XA standard for two-phase commit processing.

---

[3] BEA Tuxedo is also a messaging middleware.

BEA Tuxedo also supports the CORBA specification for distributed application development.

IBM Transarc Encina. Transarc's Encina is a transaction-processing monitor (TP monitor) that implements the OTS specification, allowing multiple distributed objects on a single ORB to participate in atomic transactions. Two-phase commit coordination is provided, using either flat or nested transactions. Additional features include load balancing, scheduling, and fault tolerance across heterogeneous environments. Encina also complies with the X/Open standards and extends the Open Group's Distributed Computing Environment (DCE).

Open/DTP. Unisys originally implemented the full X/Open model but renamed the product the Open Distributed Transaction Processing (Open/DTP). The Unisys OS 2200 databases, including DMS and RDMS, as well as MQSeries message queues, are all XA compliant.

Figure 8-12 illustrates support for X/Open DTP in the OS 2200 environment. TM2200 implements the TM (transaction monitor) and CRM (communication resource manager) functions. Open Systems Interconnect Transaction Processing (OSI-TP) is used to communicate with other instances of the model.[4] The diagram shows an Open/DTP client accessing TM2200. The client invokes services

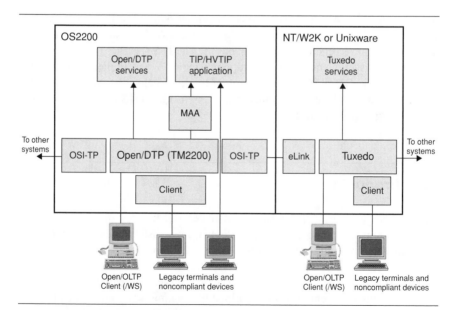

Figure 8-12 X/Open DTP in ClearPath IX systems

[4] OSI-TP is an interface between a communication resource manager and the OSI transaction-processing services.

by using XATMI (extended architecture transaction management interface) functions. The XATMI requests are passed to TM2200, which finds the service and invokes it. This may mean connecting to another system if that is where the service is located.

8.8 Summary

This chapter describes the models that are available to support distributed transactional operations. Additionally, we have provided some guidance for choosing a model.

The choice of a particular model depends on the system's requirements and its environment. The distributed-transaction model is particularly well suited to applications that require distributed resources to be available at all times. If distributed resources may not always be available and transactions can be easily rolled back, the queued-transaction model can be a good choice.

In designing a distributed system, keep in mind that a single model for distributed transactional operations may not suffice. It may be appropriate to use both models because each model has its own strengths and weaknesses.

9

Software Infrastructure

with Lutz Wrage

> *In people's handling of affairs they often ruin things when they are right*
> *at the point of completion. Therefore we say, "If you're as careful at the*
> *end as you were at the beginning you'll have no failures."*
> —Lao-Tzu, *Te-tao Ching*

> *The nice thing about standards is that there are so*
> *many of them to choose from.*
> —Andrew S. Tanenbaum, *Computer Networks,*
> 2nd ed. Englewood Cliffs, N.J.:
> Prentice-Hall, 1988, p. 254.

Software infrastructure consists of middleware and supporting services and standards that simplify the development of enterprise information systems. Middleware allows multiple processes running on one or more machines to interact. Middleware is essential for migrating mainframe applications to client/server applications and for communicating across heterogeneous platforms. This technology evolved during the 1990s to support three-tier architectures.

In this chapter, we discuss Enterprise JavaBeans, an emerging and important technology for enterprise information systems and an essential component of the target architecture for the RSS modernization effort. We then discuss message-oriented middleware and, in particular, the IBM MQSeries implementation of this model. Also covered in this chapter is the Java 2 Enterprise Edition architecture, which incorporates both of these technologies, as well as others. Finally, we discuss XML messaging technologies used in business-to-business and application-to-application integration—also an essential component of the RSS target architecture. If you are already familiar with these technologies, you may wish to proceed to the next chapter.

Lutz Wrage is a visiting scientist at the Software Engineering Institute at Carnegie Mellon University.

9.1 Where Are We?

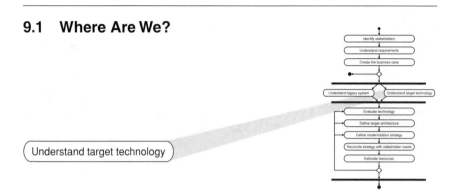

Understand target technology

In the "understanding" phase, we need to understand the technologies used in the legacy system, as well as the target, modernization technologies. This is the last of three chapters that explore the information system technologies that both populate and constrain the solution space for RSS. In this chapter, we consider Enterprise JavaBeans, message-oriented middleware, Java 2 Enterprise Edition, and XML messaging as elements of a software infrastructure solution for RSS.

9.2 Enterprise JavaBeans

The JavaSoft Enterprise JavaBeans (EJB) specification defines a component architecture for building distributed, object-oriented business applications in Java.[1] The EJB architecture addresses the development, deployment, and runtime aspects of an enterprise application's life cycle. Figure 9-1 depicts the EJB architecture.

EJBs encapsulate business logic. Each enterprise bean is deployed within a component framework, or container, that manages the details of security, transactions, connection management, and state management. An EJB container handles low-level details, such as automatic persistence, remote invocation, transaction boundary management, and distributed-transactions management. This allows the EJB developer to focus on the business problem. An EJB is, in essence, a transactional and secure object, some of whose runtime properties are specified at deployment, using XML documents called *deployment descriptors*.

---

[1] A link to the complete EJB specification is available at http://www.sei.cmu.edu/cbs/mls/links.html#javasoft.

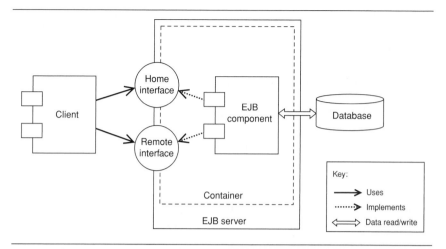

Figure 9-1   EJB architecture

ENTERPRISE JAVABEAN TYPES

The three kinds of EJBs are *entity beans*, *session beans*, and *message-driven beans*. Entity beans directly represent persistent business objects, such as an account or a purchase order, that can be shared among multiple clients. Entity beans are associated with a data store that keeps the persistent data between sessions, that is, across EJB server shutdowns or crashes. The data contained in an entity bean is most often stored in a relational database in one or more tables. However, the data can be stored anywhere, for example, in a legacy system.

Mapping EJB data to a persistent store can be implemented in the bean's methods, using bean-managed persistence (BMP), or can be delegated to the container, using container-managed persistence (CMP). CMP is applicable mostly in simple object-to-relational mappings, whereas BMP gives the bean developer detailed control over the storage of the bean's data fields. An advantage of using CMP is that the details of persistence can be configured during deployment— using tools supplied by the container vendor. These details do not depend on implementation decisions made by the bean developer. Thus, applying CMP increases the portability and reusability of entity beans.

Session beans come in two varieties: stateless beans and stateful beans. A stateless session bean does not keep any internal state between method invocations by a client. All the information that is necessary to execute a method must be included in the method parameters. Therefore, a stateless session bean can be shared among many clients, and a container can provide a pool of identical beans that service client requests. This makes an application that consists only of stateless beans easily scalable.

In contrast, stateful session beans maintain an internal state and are thus capable of not only providing simple services but also managing entire work flows.

The shopping cart in a Web site store is a good example of a stateful session bean. The contents of the shopping cart are captured in the bean's state, and this state is kept until the user completes the shopping session. The state in a session bean is not meant to be persistent; its lifetime is the length of a client session. Nevertheless, the session bean can read and update data in a database and take part in transactions. Each stateful session bean is bound to one particular client; it cannot be shared. This has drawbacks in scalability but can reduce network traffic because the session's state is kept on the server.

The newest bean type is the message-driven bean (MDB), introduced in the EJB v2.0 specification to integrate EJBs with the Java Message Service (JMS). An MDB is a stateless bean with a method that is invoked by the container when a JMS message arrives. This extends the EJB model to handle asynchronous events, which are not easily supported otherwise. In addition, MDBs enable the container to concurrently process a stream of messages by using a pool of bean instances.

Entity and session beans are accessible to clients, such as other EJBs or any Java program. A client can run locally in the same JVM as the accessed bean or remotely in any JVM. In addition, EJBs can be either be accessed only by local clients or by any remote client. Remotely accessible EJBs, such as a purchase order, are intended to be coarse-grained, whereas fine-grained components, such as purchase order line items or a delivery address, should be modeled as locally accessible enterprise beans or as dependent objects for efficiency.

MDBs are not directly visible to clients. The only way to access an MDB is for a client to send messages to the JMS destination for which the bean is registered as the message listener.

PERSISTENCE FOR ENTITY BEANS

As previously mentioned, the EJB specification gives the bean developer a choice. The developer can implement the bean's persistence directly in the bean by using BMP or can delegate the bean's persistence to the container by using CMP.

In BMP, the developer implements object persistence directly in the bean implementation code, including creation and finder methods. Creation methods must generate records in the persistent store from data passed in as arguments to the method. Finder methods must formulate the proper queries to locate the correct records in the persistent store and return a primary key or keys. In addition to writing creation and finder methods, the bean developer must specify methods to refresh the bean from the persistent store, store the bean in the persistent store, and remove the bean from the persistent store.

In CMP, the deployer uses the container provider's tools to generate all the code that moves data between the bean instance and a database or an existing application. The bean developer specifies either the container-managed fields (EJB v1.1 and EJB v2.0) or the abstract persistence schema (EJB v2.0 only).

SUPPORT FOR TRANSACTIONS

EJB servers must support distributed transactions to conform to the specification. This requires the container to support flat transactions that may span multiple servers or multiple database instances. The server must fulfill the role of a transaction manager that understands two-phase commits, as explained in Section 8.4.

Distributed transactions are carried out by the EJB server collaborating with JDBC drivers and databases. The database must support XA transactions to take part in the two-phase commit protocol. In addition, the JDBC driver must implement the XADataSource and XAConnection interfaces from the JDBC Optional Package, along with the JDBC v2.1 Core API. The EJB server itself has to contain an implementation of the JTS, which uses the JDBC driver's XADataSource and XAConnection interfaces to connect to the database [White 98].

Adding support for two-phase commits to a database driver is difficult and requires the cooperation of the database vendor. In most cases, developers rely on the vendor to provide the database drivers—for example, Oracle for an Oracle JDBC driver and Sybase for a Sybase JDBC driver. There are also independent providers of JDBC drivers. Merant, for example, offers a sophisticated JDBC driver package for Oracle, Microsoft SQL Server, and other databases.

The transaction boundaries can be controlled by the container or by the bean provider. In container-managed transactions, the EJB's deployment descriptors describe the transactional behavior of the bean's methods. When using bean-managed transactions, the bean developer includes code to start a transaction in the bean's implementation. Commits or rollbacks are handled by the container in both cases. For example, a transaction is rolled back if an exception occurs during the transaction or if the bean in a bean-managed transaction sets a rollback flag. Otherwise, the container tries to commit the transaction.

SECURITY

The EJB architecture shifts most of the burden of implementing security management from the bean to the EJB container and server. In particular, an enterprise bean's deployment descriptor features access control entries. These entries allow the container to perform runtime security management on behalf of the enterprise bean.

Security mechanisms fall into three categories: required by the EJB specification, EJB container and server specific, or hard-coded by the EJB developer [Jaworski 00]. The EJB specification describes a security infrastructure that addresses the authorization aspect of security. Authorization must be implemented by the container provider and regulates both the invocation of other beans and access to resources. Other security aspects include authentication, nonrepudiation, confidentiality, and security auditing. The EJB specification makes no provisions for these services other than the existing Java programming language security APIs. These APIs support only some of these security aspects. Support for nonrepudiation and security auditing is lacking. However, vendor-specific support for these services does exist in some products.

PRODUCTS

JBoss.   JBoss v2.4 is a free, open-source EJB server that includes full EJB v1.1 support, including all beans, all persistent types, and all transactional tags.[2] JBoss is supported on Windows 95/98/NT, Solaris Sparc, UNIX, OS/2 Warp, and other Java-enabled platforms. JBoss v3.0, the newest version, includes support for EJB v2.0 and runs on any platform with JVM 1.3.

WebLogic.   WebLogic, another commercial EJB server from BEA, complies with the EJB v2.0 specification, J2EE platform, and CORBA. BEA includes BEA Tuxedo transaction technology (T-Engine). WebLogic is supported on a broad range of platforms, including Windows NT, Windows 2000, Solaris, HP-UX, Red Hat and SuSE Linux, and IBM OS 390.

WebSphere.   WebSphere is a commercial EJB server from IBM. Version 4.0 complies with the EJB v1.1 specification, including Entity Beans support, servlets v2.2, JSP v1.1, XML/XSL support, distributed transactions, and CORBA interoperability—through Component Broker. When it is released, version 5.0 will support EJB v2.0. WebSphere is supported on JDK v1.3, AIX, Solaris, HP-UX, Linux, OS/400, Windows NT, and Windows 2000 platforms.

9.3   Message-Oriented Middleware

Message-oriented middleware (MOM) is an inherently loosely coupled, asynchronous technology. This means that the sender and the receiver of a message are not closely bound together, unlike synchronous middleware technologies, such as CORBA. Rather, the sender and the receiver stay independent and autonomous. The sender can send a message to a receiver and know that it will be delivered, even if the network link is down or the receiver is not available. MOM technologies also typically support one-to-many and many-to-many communications, using the publish/subscribe paradigm.

Different applications require different degrees of certainty about the delivery of a message. MOM technologies offer a different quality of service (QoS) for the messages they transport. Typically, this includes a fast, best-effort QoS, a slower but more reliable guaranteed QoS, and a transactional QoS that ensures

[2] A link to the server is available at http://www.sei.cmu.edu/cbs/mls/links.html#jboss.

complete delivery or failure of batches of messages, often in conjunction with database updates.

IBM MQSeries is a middleware product that provides distributed-communication services for application programs. (Although other products exist, such as Microsoft Message Queue and TIBCO Rendezvous, we will limit our discussion to MQSeries because it was selected by the corporate architecture team as part of the SRF.) Applications communicate with one another by using a communication model known as *message queuing*. In message queuing, applications send one another data in messages rather than calling one another directly, as with remote procedure calls (RPCs). Messages are not sent directly to the intended receiver but instead are sent to a message queue, which is a named *destination*. Messages accumulate on this queue until they are retrieved by the program that is designated to service the queue.

This communication model offers several advantages: providing reliable once-only delivery of messages, allowing applications to communicate in an asynchronous manner with no direct connection between them, and allowing applications to run independent of time. Because the sending and receiving application programs are decoupled, the sender can continue processing after sending a message without waiting for the receiver to acknowledge its receipt. Messages that are sent to target applications are queued independently of the application. Thus, the receiving application does not need to be available when the message is sent. Instead, it can retrieve its messages once it has been started or becomes available.

The basic architecture of MQSeries with application interaction is shown in Figure 9-2. The concepts used in MQSeries messaging are messages, message

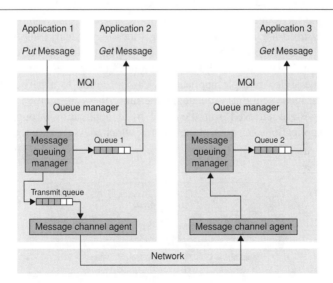

Figure 9-2 MQSeries architecture

queues, queue managers, triggers, and the message queue interface (MQI). Each of these concepts is described in turn in the following sections.

MESSAGES

As Figure 9-3 shows, MQSeries messages have two parts: a *message descriptor* and *application data*. The message descriptor is a header that identifies the message and contains control information understood by the queue manager. The control information includes such items as the type of message, target-queue name, length of user data, message priority, persistence, and reply-to queue name.

Each message has an attribute that determines whether it is persistent or nonpersistent. Persistent messages are written out to logs and queue data files. If restarted after a failure, a queue manager recovers these persistent messages as necessary from the logged data. Messages that are not persistent are discarded if a queue manager stops for any reason.

Application data can contain any sequence of bytes and is defined by the application. Therefore, this information is not understood by the queue manager but rather is private information between the two communicating applications.

MQSeries defines four types of messages:

1. **Datagram:** a simple message that does not require a reply

2. **Request:** a message that requires a reply

3. **Reply:** a response to a request message

4. **Report:** a message that describes an event, such as an error

As shown in Figure 9-4, coupling these message types with MQSeries messaging semantics produces three styles of messaging: *send-and-forget*, *request/response*, and *publish/subscribe*. In the send-and-forget message style, the application simply sends the message and assumes that it will be processed correctly. In the request/response style, the sending application waits for a response. In the publish/subscribe style, multiple applications can subscribe to a particular queue. When a message is sent to this queue, all the subscribers are notified.

Messages are retrieved from the queue by an application through the queue manager. Applications can control the order in which messages are retrieved from

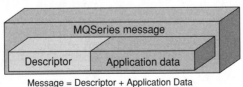

Message = Descriptor + Application Data

Figure 9-3   MQSeries message format

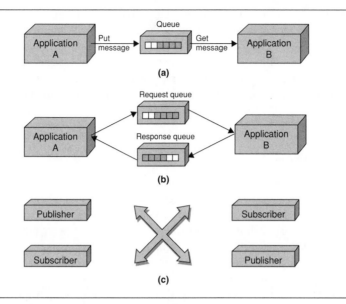

Figure 9-4   MQSeries messaging styles: (a) send-and-forget, (b) request/
response, (c) publish/subscribe

a queue. MQSeries provides the following options for message retrieval:

- **Priority.** Messages can be retrieved in the order of priority that was assigned to them by the receiving application. Messages of equal priority are stored in a queue in order of arrival, not the order in which they were committed.

- **FIFO.** First in, first out (FIFO) refers to the order in which the messages were received.

- **Identifiers.** The application can retrieve the first message that matches a specific identifier.

QUEUES

A message queue is a data structure that stores messages. Queues reside in and are managed by a queue manager. Messages accumulate in a queue until they are read by the receiving application. Each queue has a unique name for identification and exists independently of the applications that use it. Thus, a queue can serve as a named destination for messages. Queues usually exist in memory but can also be maintained on disk for recovery in the event of a system failure.

Each queue has set of attributes that determine which applications can retrieve messages from the queue, which applications can put messages on the queue, and whether access to the queue is exclusive to one application or shared among applications. Queue attributes can also set the maximum number of messages and the maximum length of messages that can be stored.

MQSeries queues can be either local or remote. A local queue is owned by the queue manager that is connected to the application. Remote queues are not owned by the queue manager that is connected to the application. Applications can put messages in local or remote queues but can get messages only from local queues. Applications send data to remote queues by using a *local definition of a remote queue*. This object holds the information necessary for the local queue manager to locate the remote queue.

QUEUE MANAGER

The queue manager allows applications to put messages in a queue and get messages from a queue. The queue manager can also generate events when special conditions, defined by the application, are satisfied. Queue managers also have an interface that allows administrators to create new queues, alter the properties of existing queues, and control the operation of the queue manager. An application must establish a connection to a queue manager to use its services. Several unrelated applications can use the queue manager at the same time.

As with queues, a queue manager can be local or remote. A queue manager is remote to an application if the application is not connected to that queue manager. Thus, the queue manager connected to an application is the local queue manager for that application.

Communication between the local queue manager and any remote queue managers requires defined message channels. A message channel provides a communication path between two queue managers on the same or different platforms. As shown in Figure 9-5, the message channel transmits messages from one queue manager to another and will transmit data only in one direction. Thus, two message channels are required for two-way communication between two queue managers. Because queue managers also route messages to other queue managers, it is not necessary to define a channel directly to the target queue manager. A queue manger will usually route messages to the appropriate queue manager by simply defining the next hop.

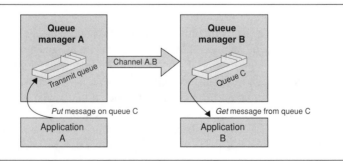

Figure 9-5 Channel communication

TRIGGERS

As stated earlier, the queue manager can generate events to an application when special conditions are satisfied, as defined by an application. At that time, as shown in Figure 9-6, the queue manager sends a trigger message to an initiation queue to indicate that a trigger event has occurred. The message contains information about the application that processed it.

The initiation queue is read by an application called a *trigger monitor*. The trigger monitor reads trigger messages and takes the appropriate action, such as starting an application to read and process messages from the appropriate queue. Trigger monitors are not really different from other MQSeries applications but read messages from the initiation queue.

MESSAGE QUEUE INTERFACE

MQI is an API used by applications to send and receive MQSeries messages. This interface is standard across all supported platforms and makes it easy to port applications from one platform to another.

TRANSACTION SUPPORT

MQSeries supports transactional messaging. It allows operations on messages to be grouped into units of work. A unit of work is either committed in its entirety or rolled back. When a group of operations is rolled back, it appears as if none of the operations took place. This functionality keeps the data shared by distributed applications in a consistent state.

For example, an application retrieves a message from a queue and processes the data in the message. In response to the received message, the application creates a set of messages to be sent to other applications, all within one unit of work. If

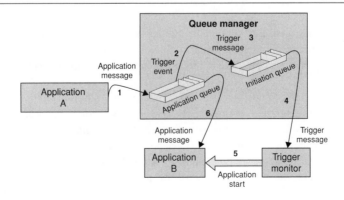

Figure 9-6   MQSeries triggers

the output queue for one of the messages to be sent is full, the application can roll back the entire unit of work so that the input message received from the queue is returned to the queue and the messages that were put into output queues are removed. After the rollback, everything is returned to the state it was in before the message was read from the application's input queue. It is as if the application had never processed the message in the first place. MQSeries can also coordinate units of messaging work with other transactional work, such as database updates, so that message data and database data remain synchronized.

MQSeries products are available for more than 35 platforms, including the Unisys ClearPath OS2200 and Sun Solaris. MQSeries supports multiple protocols, (SNA, TCP/IP, SPX, DECNet, NetBIOS) and a variety of programming languages, including Visual Basic, C, C++, Java, COBOL, and PL/I.

PRODUCTS

MQSeries for ClearPath OS 2200. MQSeries for ClearPath OS 2200 is based on IBM MQSeries v5.0 and was developed by Unisys under license from IBM. OS 2200 applications may use MQSeries to communicate with other MQSeries implementations. Language bindings are provided for UCS COBOL (UCOB) and UCS C (UC). Communication with other MQSeries implementations uses a TCP/IP infrastructure and COMAPI[3] as the interface.

WebSphere MQ. IBM MQSeries, already an important part of the WebSphere software platform for e-business, will have an even tighter association with WebSphere. MQSeries, responsible for dynamic integration, will be known as WebSphere MQ, reflecting the fundamental part it plays in dynamic e-business. MQSeries products will be renamed as part of the WebSphere family with each new release.

9.4   Java 2 Enterprise Edition

The Java 2 Enterprise Edition (J2EE) defines a standard for developing multitier enterprise services that are highly available, secure, reliable, and scalable. With the J2EE platform, it is possible to develop a large class of enterprise applications using only the J2EE APIs, ranging from a Java client accessing a database via JDBC to Web-based, multitier distributed enterprise systems.

The J2EE architecture includes EJBs and adds Web components and applet clients at the front end. At the back end, version 1.3 of the specification and later include the connector architecture to define transactional resource adapters. These allow plug-ins of legacy enterprise information systems (EISs) to any J2EE product. Figure 9-7 illustrates the architecture of a J2EE application [Sun 99a].

---

[3] The communications API (COMAPI) provides a simple socket interface for OS 2200 programs.

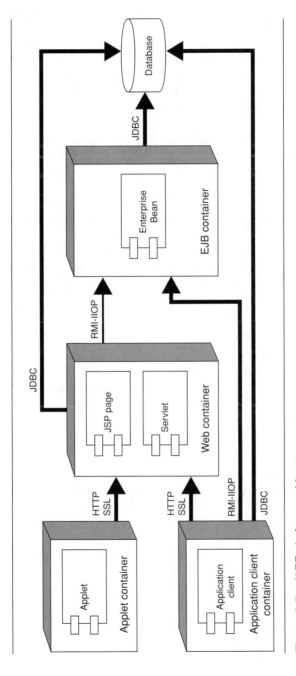

Figure 9-7 J2EE platform architecture

The various containers form runtime environments for their respective components. All components are built using the Java programming language. The arrows indicate access paths to other J2EE components.

Remote clients are implemented as stand-alone Java programs, as HTML pages, as applets, or as a combination of applets and HTML pages. The middle tier is split into an EJB tier containing the transactional business logic and a Web tier containing the software components that respond to HTTP requests. The persistence tier can be implemented in any database connected via JDBC or in a legacy EIS via connectors.

The deployed J2EE application components never interact directly. Instead, access is intercepted by the respective container. This allows the container to transparently provide services, such as declarative transaction management, access control, and others.

In addition, the containers manage security aspects, such as authorization (see Section 9.2), user authentication, and confidentiality. Users can authenticate by using HTTP basic authentication, HTTPS (HTTP, secure) client authentication, or form-based authentication. The Web container must support single sign-on by maintaining login sessions. Application client containers must also provide means to provide user authentication. The details are left to the J2EE product vendor.

J2EE SERVICES

The J2EE platform requires the containers to provide a set of standard services to be used by application components, including communication protocols, Java enterprise APIs, and Java runtime support. The complete list of services is enumerated in the Java 2 Platform Enterprise Edition specifications for each release.[4]

DEPLOYMENT

J2EE applications are packaged as enterprise archive files (.ear). These archives contain the components and other files. All references to other components and external resources are specified in deployment descriptors as XML documents. These references are bound at deployment time, using vendor-specific tools.

9.5   XML Messaging

XML messaging is the technology of choice for implementing business-to-business (B2B) and application-to-application (A2A) transactions and for connecting internal systems that previously operated as "stovepipes." The problem today is

---

[4] For more information, see http://java.sun.com/j2ee/j2ee-1_4-pfd-spec.pdf.

that so many companies and industry organizations are proposing standards for a common e-business language that it is difficult to differentiate among them or know which one to use. In this section, we look at the basic components of XML messaging, as well as several efforts to promote XML for standard communication among organizations and applications.

XML MESSAGING COMPONENTS

An XML messaging system contains

- A set of business processes and the XML content describing the constituent transactions
- A data dictionary description of the elements that make up the XML content
- A messaging service that specifies how the XML content is packaged, transferred, and routed

The transport mechanism itself is typically not specified as a component of XML messaging. Nevertheless, the messaging service must "wrap" the XML message, as required by the selected transport protocol. Examples of transport protocols used for XML messaging are HTTP, File Transfer Protocol (FTP), Simple Mail Transfer Protocol (SMTP), Microsoft Message Queue (MSMQ), MQSeries, and Electronic Data Interchange (EDI).

Another element is becoming an important part of XML messaging. That is an e-commerce registry and repository structure for looking up companies, discovering products and services they provide, and learning about the types of business relationships they support.

BIZTALK

BizTalk is an industry initiative headed by Microsoft to promote XML as the common data exchange language for e-commerce and application integration over the Internet. Although not a standards body per se, the group is fostering a common XML message-passing architecture to tie systems together.

BizTalk provides XML messaging services through the BizTalk Framework. Figure 9-8 presents a simple document exchange using the BizTalk Framework.

An application generates a business document—a well-formed XML document containing business data—adds any attachments, and submits it to the BizTalk Framework Compliant (BFC) server. Either the application or the BFC server can have responsibility for wrapping the business document in a BizTalk document. A BizTalk document is a Simple Object Access Protocol (SOAP) message. The body of the message contains the business document, and the header contains BizTalk-specific data. The BFC server processes the document and any attachments and constructs a BizTalk message as appropriate for the transport

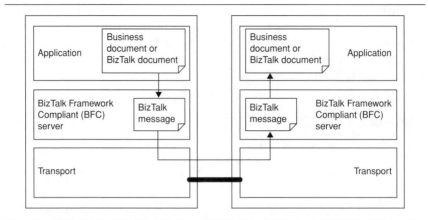

Figure 9-8 Document exchange using the BizTalk Framework

protocol. The BizTalk Framework does not prescribe transport protocols. Common protocols used for BizTalk are HTTP, SMTP, and MSMQ. The BizTalk Framework 2.0 documentation recommends using high-performance messaging middleware for reliable delivery and supports Secure Multipurpose Internet Mail Extensions (S/MIME) for securing BizTalk messages [Microsoft 00].

The BizTalk Framework does not prescribe the XML content or structure of the business documents being exchanged. The context and structure are defined by the organizations involved in the transaction. BizTalk.org provides an object library that can be queried and updated by its members.[5] This library is a set of sample schemas that members have used in their applications or schemas supported by members of the organization. These schemas can be used for communicating, but they are not a set of standard schemas that define business content to be transmitted inside a BizTalk message.

ELECTRONIC BUSINESS XML

Electronic Business XML (ebXML) is a project to standardize the secure exchange of business data, using XML.[6] The United Nations body for Trade Facilitation and Electronic Business Information Standards (UN/CEFACT) and the Organization for the Advancement of Structured Information Standards (OASIS) launched the ebXML project as a joint initiative. Its membership includes a wide variety of companies, ranging from major IT vendors to trade associations throughout the world.

---

[5] For more information, see http://www.sei.cmu.edu/cbs/mls/links.html#biztalk.
[6] For more information, see http://www.sei.cmu.edu/cbs/mls/links.html#ebxml.

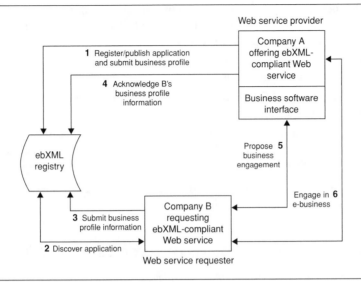

Figure 9-9   Typical ebXML usage scenario

Figure 9-9 illustrates a typical usage scenario for ebXML [Siddalingaiah 01].

1. Company A registers its ebXML-compliant application and business profile in the ebXML registry.

2. Company B discovers this application.

3. Company B submits its business profile to the registry.

4. Company A studies the information submitted by Company B and sends an acknowledgment to Company B, confirming whether their business scenarios are compatible.

5. Company B sends a proposed business arrangement automatically to company A, based on the information in the registry.

6. After company A accepts the business, the two companies are ready to engage in e-business, using ebXML messages.

To support this scenario, the ebXML Technical Architecture Specification defines the following elements [ebXML 01]:

- **Collaboration Protocol Profile (CPP).** A CPP is the standard for describing a company's business processes and message-exchange capabilities (business service interface).

- **Collaboration Protocol Agreement (CPA).** A CPA describes the exact requirements and mechanisms for the transactions between two companies. In essence, a CPA is a contract that can be derived automatically from two or more businesses' respective CPPs.

- **Business process and information modeling.** ebXML includes specifications for describing a business process in XML so it can be used in the CPP or to share business processes and information formats.

- **Core components.** The core components are the set of XML schemas that describe business transactions.

- **Messaging.** The SOAP-based ebXML messaging service provides security and reliable messaging.

- **Registry/repository.** The ebXML registry/repository stores CPPs, CPAs, core components, and any other ebXML documents that allow enterprises to find each other, agree to become trading partners, and conduct business.

Similar to the other standards, ebXML's messaging service is transport neutral. HTTP and SMTP are commonly used protocols.

OPEN APPLICATIONS GROUP INTEGRATION SPECIFICATION

The Open Applications Group (OAG) is a nonprofit consortium formed in February 1995 by a group of eight software vendors, including Oracle, SAP, and PeopleSoft.[7] The mission of OAG was to define and promote the adoption of a unifying standard for B2B and A2A interoperability, based on XML content. The result of this work is the Open Applications Group Integration Specification (OAGIS).

The OAGIS prescribes a content-based, business object model (Figure 9-10). To communicate with a business object in this model, events are communicated through the integration backbone in the form of an OAGIS-compliant, business object document (BOD) to a virtual object interface [OAG 99]. This virtual object interface is basically an OAGIS-compliant wrapper built around an application so it can exchange BODs with other applications. The integration backbone should provide at least the following services: request/reply, publish/subscribe, directory services, routing, queuing, and logging.

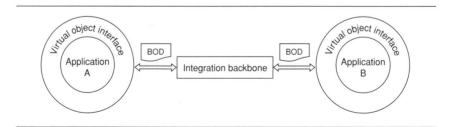

Figure 9-10   OAGIS virtual business object model

---

[7] For more information, see http://www.sei.cmu.edu/cbs/mls/links.html#openapplications-1.

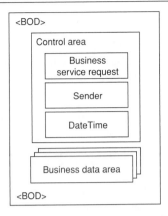

Figure 9-11   BOD structure

The BOD uses metadata, in the form of an XML schema. The BOD conveys two primary components: the business service request and the business data area. This BOD structure is shown in Figure 9-11.

Each business service request (BSR) contains a unique verb/noun combination, such as POST JOURNAL or SYNC ITEM, that drives the contents of the business data area (BDA). This combination of BSR and BDA corresponds to the object name, method, and arguments of a procedure call or method invocation model.

OAGIS does not contain a messaging infrastructure. It is strictly an XML content repository and a set of common integration scenarios. However, its scenarios do fit best with enterprise application integration middleware, such as MQSeries.

OAGIS is also responsible for OAMAS (Open Applications Middleware API Specification). OAMAS is a proposal to the middleware community for a common, higher-level middleware API so business applications can connect in a more standard way.

ROSETTANET

RosettaNet is a nonprofit organization that creates, implements, and promotes open e-business standards.[8] RosettaNet is defining a common parts dictionary so that companies can define the same product in the same way and is also defining up to 100 e-business transaction processes, mainly for supply chain integration. RosettaNet's members include Microsoft, Netscape, 3Com, Toshiba America, Compaq, CompUSA, Hewlett-Packard, IBM, and Intel.

---

[8] For more information, see http://www.sei.cmu.edu/cbs/mls/links.html#rosettanet.

The main standard components offered by RosettaNet are

- **RosettaNet Implementation Framework (RNIF):** Encapsulates business documents along with header components and other elements that must be exchanged between end points of a RosettaNet standard interaction into a RosettaNet message. RNIF covers the transport, routing, and packaging; security; signals; and trading partner agreements (TPAs).

- **RosettaNet business dictionary:** Provides properties for defining business transactions between trading partners.

- **RosettaNet technical dictionary:** Provides properties for defining products and services.

- **RosettaNet partner interface processes (PIPs):** Specifies specialized system-to-system XML-based dialogues that define business processes between trading partners.

A RosettaNet-enabled trading partner uses the RNIF and the dictionaries to set up its environment. Two RosettaNet-enabled partners must agree on a PIP to use and establish a TPA before any communication takes place. From then on, every time they need to communicate, they execute a PIP instance as a sequence of business messages and signals, such as the one shown in Figure 9-12 for order placement [RosettaNet 02].

RosettaNet business messages can be S/MIME packaged for security and can be transmitted using HTTP over SSL (HTTPS) or SMTP as protocols.

HOW THESE STANDARDS RELATE

BizTalk, ebXML, OAGIS, and RosettaNet compete and complement one another. In theory, any XML content conforming to the BizTalk, ebXML, RosettaNet, or OAGIS specifications can be transported using the BizTalk, ebXML, or RosettaNet infrastructures. OAGIS does not provide an infrastructure framework. In practice, it is not that simple. However, efforts are underway to make it happen. OAG

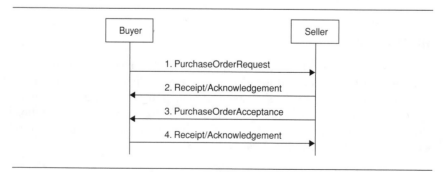

Figure 9-12   Sample PIP interaction sequence

has published several white papers on how to use OAGIS as the business content and BizTalk Framework, the RosettaNet Integration Framework, or the ebXML messaging service as part of the underlying messaging infrastructure. In addition, a product called BizTalk Accelerator for RosettaNet integrates these two products.

The process of packaging, routing, and transporting XML-based messages is not the main issue. Rather, the issue is that an implementation of XML messaging is useless if the parties involved do not agree on the semantics of the information being exchanged.

OAGIS is an XML content repository that represents common business transactions. RosettaNet and ebXML have some definitions of common content and also specifications for defining content and processes. In this case, the two parties must agree on their exchange in advance on an individual basis. The ebXML repository and the BizTalk object library try to make this agreement more automatic.

The bottom line is that XML messaging can aid data interoperability where shared semantics can be assumed. XML messaging does not guarantee semantic interoperability; nor does it solve the integration problem. But XML messaging does make solving the problem easier.

OTHER STANDARDS RELATED TO XML MESSAGING

Simple Object Access Protocol (SOAP).   SOAP is a platform-independent W3C protocol for applications to communicate with one another over the Internet. SOAP specifies exactly how to encode an HTTP header and an XML file so that a program in one computer can call a program in another computer and pass it information. SOAP also specifies how the called program can return a response. An advantage of SOAP is that program calls are much more likely to get through firewall servers because HTTP requests are usually allowed through. Other SOAP implementations include MSMQ, MQSeries, SMTP, and TCP/IP.[9]

Universal Description, Discovery, and Integration (UDDI).   UDDI is an XML-based distributed registry that enables businesses to list themselves on the Internet and to discover one another, similar to a traditional phone book's white, yellow, and blue pages. The ultimate goal of UDDI is to allow online transactions by enabling companies to find one another on the Web and to make their systems interoperable for e-commerce. UDDI allows businesses to list themselves by name, product, location, or the Web services they offer.

Web Services Description Language (WSDL).   WSDL is an XML-based language used by UDDI to describe the services a business offers and to provide access to those services electronically.

---

[9] The XML-RPC protocol, similar to SOAP and sometimes referred to as SOAP's younger sibling, is basically a remote procedure calling, using HTTP as the transport and XML as the encoding.

9.6 Summary

Software infrastructure simplifies the development of enterprise information systems by allowing developers to concentrate on implementing business processes and providing end user value. In particular, middleware is an essential technology in modernizing legacy systems. It defines an architecture and approach for implementing the modernized system, provides mechanisms for integrating legacy and modern components, and provides mechanisms for integrating disparate components in the modernized system, including commercial components and other existing assets.

This is the last chapter covered under understanding the target technology. In the next chapter, we begin to describe how situated evaluations can produce additional technology competency and start to formulate an architectural design solution for a modernization effort.

10

Maintaining Transactional Context

with Santiago Comella-Dorda

> *It is commonplace that a problem stated is well on its way to solution, for statement of the nature of a problem signifies that the underlying quality is being transformed into determinate distinctions of terms and relations or has become an object of articulate thought.*
> —John Dewey, (1859–1952)
> *The Symposium* (1930)

> *Any solution to a problem changes the problem.*
> —R. W. Johnson (b. 1916)
> *Washingtonian* (November 1979)

In an incremental modernization effort, transactions processed entirely in the legacy system may at some point be distributed across both legacy and modernized components. Identifying and validating a design solution to this problem is a prerequisite to the overall modernization effort.

Our approach to identifying and validating design solutions uses model problems—focused experimental prototypes that reveal technology/product capabilities, benefits, and limitations in well-bounded ways. Model problems reduce design risks. However, no amount of modeling can completely eliminate design risks. Therefore, the designer must be satisfied with reducing risk as much as possible. The use of model problems is a component-based software engineering technique described by Wallnau et al. [Wallnau 01].

Santiago Comella-Dorda is a business analyst with McKinsey & Company.

10.1   Where Are We?

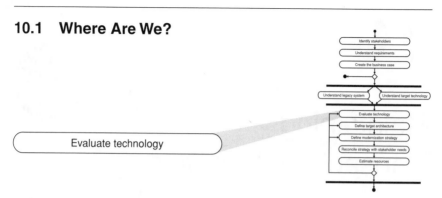

Now that we understand the legacy system and the target technologies, the next step is to perform a situated evaluation of these technologies and consider how they should be used in the modernization effort.

10.2   Model Problem: Retail Supply System

A model problem describes the design context. Two roles are involved in the description of the process: the architect and the engineer. The architect is the technical lead on the project and is responsible for overall design decisions. The engineer executes the model problem at the direction of the architect.

1. The architect and the engineer identify a design question. This question initiates the model problem and addresses an unknown that is expressed as a hypothesis.

2. The architect and the engineer define the starting evaluation criteria. These criteria will be used to determine whether the model solution will support or contradict the hypothesis.

3. The architect and the engineer define the implementation constraints. These constraints specify the fixed, or inflexible, part of the design context. They may include platform requirements, component versions, and business rules.

4. The engineer produces a model solution within the design context. The model solution is a minimal application that uses only those features of a component (or components) necessary to support or contradict the hypothesis.

5. The engineer identifies *ending* evaluation criteria, which include the starting criteria and criteria discovered as a by-product of implementing the model solution.

6. Finally, the architect evaluates the model solution against the *ending* criteria. Although the evaluation could result in rejecting or adopting the design solution, it often leads to generating new design questions that must be resolved in a similar fashion.

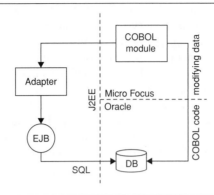

Figure 10-1   The operational system during modernization

Modernizing the Retail Supply System (RSS) consists of replacing legacy program elements with functionally equivalent EJBs. These beans are then deployed on a J2EE platform: in this case, the IBM WebSphere application server.

As modernized functionality is deployed incrementally, transactions that were processed entirely in COBOL may now be distributed across both legacy and modernized components. Figure 10-1 shows the system after incrementally deploying some modernized components. This illustration indicates that both the legacy COBOL code and the modernized EJBs may update or access the database.

Figure 10-2 shows an operation involving both legacy code and modern components. In this diagram, the legacy COBOL module updates Table 2 by means

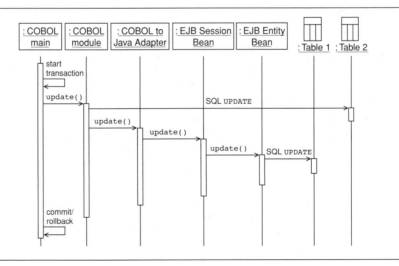

Figure 10-2   Transactional update of database records

of an SQL UPDATE. The COBOL module then invokes a method in a modernized component via an adapter that results in an SQL UPDATE to Table 1. Because the RSS modernization strategy maintains records in a single Oracle database, two-phase commit does not need to be supported in this scenario.

To perform these updates within a transaction context, it is necessary to start and commit the transaction. Some scenarios might suggest starting or committing transactions in either the legacy or the modernized components. For simplicity, we assume that transactions are always started and committed from the legacy COBOL system. The problem is how to maintain transactional integrity across the COBOL-to-EJB interface. Several possible solutions are presented in the following section.

10.3   Contingency Planning

A fundamental technique of component-based software engineering is contingency-based design. Simply put, contingency-based design pursues multiple design options in parallel. This technique is especially critical when using commercial components, because their evolution is driven by the marketplace, and their implementations are typically opaque to the architect.

Several technologies included in the SRF seemed able to maintain the transaction context between the legacy COBOL system and the modernized system. This section presents design alternatives based on these technologies, along with our initial evaluation of their feasibility.

MQSERIES

Existing RSS modernization plans call for the use of MQSeries to communicate between the legacy COBOL and modernized EJB systems. IBM's MQSeries provides asynchronous communications and uses independent queues to relay messages between communicating processes, as shown in Figure 10-3. MQSeries was discussed in some detail in Section 9.3.

MQSeries provides limited support for transactions. For example, let's assume that application A in Figure 10-3 represents the legacy system code written in Micro Focus COBOL. Application B represents a modernized component

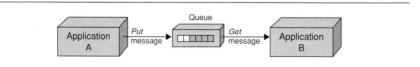

Figure 10-3   MQSeries messaging

developed as an EJB and deployed in the WebSphere application server. The queue is an input queue for the modernized component. We assume that the legacy code passes a message via MQSeries to the modernized component to perform a function. We also assume that this function must be accomplished as part of a transaction. To do this, the Micro Focus COBOL program element must start a transaction and pass a message. However, once the EJB component removes the message from the queue, the transaction context is no longer maintained. This means that any database operations performed by the EJB component takes place outside the transaction context.

Because of this limitation in transaction propagation, we did not develop MQSeries further as a solution to the model problem. However, we maintained it as a possible design contingency in case an asynchronous, message-oriented approach became a requirement.

OBJECT TRANSACTION SERVICE

Object Transaction Service (OTS) is a distributed transaction-processing service specified by the Object Management Group (OMG). This specification extends the CORBA model and defines a set of interfaces to perform transaction processing across multiple CORBA objects. CORBA uses IIOP as an interoperable protocol for communication between distributed objects.

As of the EJB v1.1 specification, RMI over IIOP has become the standard mechanism for supporting communication between a client and EJBs and between EJB containers. IIOP is well suited for this purpose because it supports the propagation of both a transaction and a security context.

To use OTS as a solution, we would need to find COBOL-language bindings to a CORBA and OTS implementation. The optimal solution would be to use ComponentBroker, IBM's OTS implementation. Because this product is an integral component of WebSphere, we could be confident that it would work in our target environment. Unfortunately, IBM ComponentBroker did not have a Micro Focus COBOL interface.

Although this approach appears to have potential, we had difficulty identifying a Micro Focus COBOL-to-CORBA binding. A possible workaround was to use a Java CORBA binding, accessed through a Micro Focus COBOL-to-Java language interface. However, we decided not to develop an OTS model problem at this time but maintained it as a potentially viable design contingency.

ORACLE PRO*COBOL

The Pro*COBOL precompiler is a programming tool that supports embedded SQL statements in high-level programming languages. It accepts the program as input, translates the embedded SQL statements into standard Oracle runtime library calls, and generates a source program that can be compiled, linked, and executed.

Although it claims to be compatible with Micro Focus Object COBOL, Pro*COBOL does not provide a solution for transaction management. Pro*COBOL is used primarily to preserve business logic in legacy COBOL programs when data is migrated to an Oracle database. Although Pro*COBOL supports transactions in embedded SQL statements, it does not solve the problem of maintaining a transaction context between legacy and modernized components. As a result, we eliminated this contingency as a possible design solution.

NET EXPRESS

Micro Focus Net Express is an integrated development environment (IDE) for developing procedural COBOL/Object COBOL-based applications. Net Express provides mixed-language programming support for procedural COBOL, Object COBOL, and Java mixed-language programming, as well as WebSphere distributed-transaction technologies.

For mixed-language programs, Net Express supports calling Java code from Micro Focus COBOL, as well as calling Micro Focus COBOL from Java code. Net Express also supports wrapping Micro Focus COBOL within an EJB. Because each approach supports mixed-language programs, we examined each.

Wrapping COBOL Code.   Wrapping COBOL code within EJBs would allow the system to be migrated quickly to a J2EE environment, although not one consisting of 100% Pure Java code. To implement this approach, each legacy program element must be wrapped as an EJB, and all the internal calls must be converted to invoke the new Java methods, requiring the COBOL code inside the Java code to call Java again. This approach has several apparent consequences.

- Turning legacy program elements into EJBs guarantees that the legacy architecture is maintained, because the decomposition of the system remains constant, and the calls between program elements remain the same. As a result, this approach is incompatible with the RSS desire to migrate to a new target architecture.

- The majority of the modernized system, especially the business logic, is still implemented in COBOL. This means that any maintenance problems that existed will remain and be further complicated by the problems associated with maintaining a multilanguage system.

- Modernizing the system in this manner is not conducive to incremental development and would require a big-bang deployment of COBOL-filled EJBs.

- The primary advantage of this approach is that it is a relatively inexpensive way to create a componentized system. However, the characteristics of this modernized system would not be very different from those of the legacy system. As a result, we eliminated this approach as a possible design contingency.

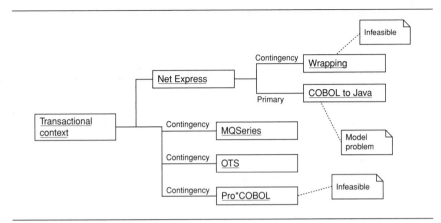

Figure 10-4   Contingency plan

Calling Java from COBOL.   The second approach using Net Express is to call Java directly from the Micro Focus COBOL program elements. This approach would invoke EJB methods directly from Micro Focus COBOL and support WebSphere distributed transactions. As this approach appears to satisfy our requirements, we decided to construct a model problem to evaluate this design contingency.

Figure 10-4 illustrates the results of the contingency-planning process. We have eliminated two contingencies: wrapping COBOL code using Net Express and using Oracle Pro*COBOL. Of the remaining three contingencies, we decided to implement a single model problem using Net Express to call Java from COBOL.

10.4   Definition of the Model Problem

To start the model problem, we created a two-part hypothesis that establishes the design question.

- **Hypothesis part 1:** The Micro Focus Net Express IDE can be used to support mixed-language programming with Java.
- **Hypothesis part 2**: The Java subroutines, invoked from Micro Focus COBOL, can interface with an EJB server and perform transactions with an Oracle 8i database.

If the first part cannot be supported, the second part is irrelevant.

After defining the design question, we identified the starting evaluation criteria that will determine whether the hypothesis can be supported.

- **Criterion 1:** Committed updates from both the COBOL process and EJBs are applied correctly to the database.

- **Criterion 2:** A rollback operation preserves the state of the database before the start of the transaction.

The final step in defining the model problem is identifying any implementation constraints on the model solution. These constraints are set by the design context and are an important part of the model-problem definition. In this case, both criteria can be trivially satisfied unless further constraints are specified.

- The transaction must be started from the Micro Focus COBOL program and use the Java Transaction Service (JTS).
- The Micro Focus COBOL program and the EJBs must write to the Oracle 8i database as part of the same transaction.
- The Micro Focus COBOL program must write to the Oracle 8i database, using JDBC and SQL.

Taken together, the design question, starting evaluation criteria, and constraints define the model problem. In the next step, the engineer must produce a model solution situated in this design context.

10.5   Solution of the Model Problem

This section describes our experience with the setup and development of the model solution.

DESIGN OF THE MODEL SOLUTION

To implement the model solution, we first must identify the sequence of steps to be followed. In particular, the model solution must

1. Start a transaction, using the JTS from a Micro Focus COBOL program
2. Write to the Oracle 8i database, using JDBC and SQL
3. Invoke an EJB method that also writes to the same Oracle 8i database as part of the same transaction
4. Return control to the COBOL program
5. Either roll back or commit the database changes made by both the COBOL and EJB programs

For purposes of evaluation, it is often convenient to start with an existing prototype. Sample programs shipped with development tools are often ideally suited for this purpose. In our case, the model solution is based on a sample banking program that manages client accounts by using EJBs. The EJB application consists of a database, a Java client, and two EJBs: an account bean and a transfer

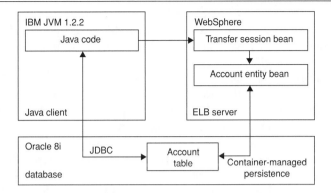

Figure 10-5   Initial architecture

bean. As Figure 10-5 illustrates, the account bean is an entity bean that persists in a relational table, and the transfer bean is a session bean that withdraws funds from one account and deposits that amount in another account in the context of a single transaction. The Java client is a simple program that accepts a request from the user and invokes the beans to perform account creations or transfers. The client uses the Java Naming Directory Interface (JNDI) to get references to various resources and the Java Transaction API (JTA) to start, commit, and roll back transactions. We used a Java client program to verify the operation of the banking application: EJBs, transaction logic, and interaction with the Oracle 8i database.

This client program was later used as a basis to construct a test adapter, as shown in Figure 10-6. The Java client was replaced with a combination of Micro Focus COBOL and Java code developed using Net Express Micro Focus COBOL.

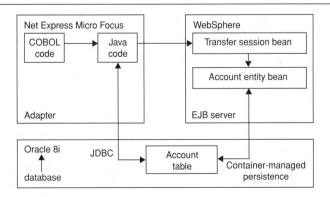

Figure 10-6   Model-solution architecture

BUILDING THE TEST ADAPTER

As stated earlier, the test adapter required mixed-language programming using COBOL and Java. Therefore, our first step was to understand how Micro Focus COBOL interfaces with Java.

We obtained an evaluation version of Micro Focus Net Express IDE v3.1 and began working with the product to determine how to invoke Java methods from a COBOL program. The Java demonstration programs provided as part of the IDE software package contained helpful information on how to call Java from COBOL and vice versa. These examples were interesting because none of them showed how to call Java from a COBOL executable or how to pass strings from COBOL to Java. Examples typically consisted of a Java program calling a COBOL procedure linked into a dynamic link library (DLL). Then, while executing the COBOL code inside the DLL, the COBOL program would invoke a Java method.

Because we could not find an example that met our needs, we developed a simple test program that passed an integer from COBOL to Java. Figure 10-7 and Figure 10-8 show the respective Java and COBOL sections of the program.

Next, we expanded our test program to include passing a string, having a return value, and catching Java exceptions in the COBOL portion of the program. Our updated COBOL and Java programs are shown in Figures 10-9 and 10-10, respectively. We tested our new mixed-language application and everything seemed to work correctly.

Once we had determined how to pass data successfully from a COBOL program to a Java program and to handle Java exceptions from within COBOL, we began building a test adapter. The test adapter was constructed from the Java client described previously. Similar to the Java client, this adapter uses the account bean, transfer bean, JNDI, and JTA but is controlled and instantiated via the COBOL portion of the program.

We determined through our test adapter that COBOL strings must be NULL terminated before being passed in a Java invocation and that Java methods receiving strings from a COBOL program must strip off any trailing spaces. Additionally, we noticed that any COBOL string used as a return value for a Java method invocation must be cleared before invoking the Java method. We did not notice this issue with our simple test program, because we were passing only one string, were not performing string comparisons, and invoked the Java method only once instead of repeatedly.

After making these modifications to the COBOL and Java portions of the program, the adapter executed correctly. At this point, it is tempting to expand the model solution further, for example, by measuring the performance of setter and getter methods in the enterprise bean to determine whether there are any start-up timing or reentrance problems. However, this effort may be wasted if performance is not a major risk or if this approach is eliminated because it fails to address another major risk. Therefore, this work should be attempted in an additional model problem intended to address a critical risk.

```
public class TestJava {
public void PassInt(int IntFromCOBOL){
   System.out.println("int from COBOL: "+IntFromCOBOL);
 }
}
```

Figure 10-7   Java integer code

```
$set ooctrl(+p-f)
program-id. COBOLCallingJava.

class-control.
 TestJava is class "$java$TestJava"
   .
working-storage section.
copy javatypes.
01 IntForJava        jint.
 01 JavaClassRef      object reference.

procedure division.
 display "Load Java Class"
 invoke TestJava "new" returning JavaClassRef
 display "Java Class Load Complete"
 set IntForJava to 123456
 invoke JavaClassRef "PassInt" using IntForJava
 invoke JavaClassRef "finalize" returning JavaClassRef
 stop run
   .
```

Figure 10-8   COBOL integer code

```
public class TestJava {
 public String PassInt(String StringFromCOBOL, int IntFromCO-
BOL) throws Exception {
   System.out.println(StringFromCOBOL+IntFromCOBOL);
   if (IntFromCOBOL==1234){
      Exception e = new Exception ("Test Exception for COBOL" );
      throw e;
    }
   return("Hello from Java");
 }
}
```

Figure 10-9   Expanded integer Java code

```cobol
$set ooctrl(+p-f)
program-id. COBOLCallingJava.

class-control.
 ExceptionManager          is class "exptnmgr"
 EntryCallback             is class "entrycll"
 JavaExceptionManager      is class "javaexpt"
 TestJava                  is class "$java$TestJava"
 .
working-storage section.
 copy javatypes.
 01 JavaClassRef     object reference.
 01 wsCallBack       object reference.
 01 wsIterator       object reference.
 01 IntForJava       jint.
 01 StringFromJava   pic x(100)
 .
linkage section.
 01 lnkErrorNumber            pic x(4) comp-5.
 01 lnkErrorObject            object reference.
 01 lnkErrorTextCollection    object reference.
 01 lnkException              object reference.
 01 anElement                 object reference.

procedure division.
 invoke EntryCallback "new" using z"JException" returning
wsCallback

 invoke ExceptionManager "register" using javaexceptionmanager
wsCallback

 *>Register a CallBack to use as an Iterator (For Errors)
 invoke EntryCallback "new" using z"DispError" returning
wsIterator

 display "Load Java Class"
 invoke TestJava "new" returning JavaClassRef
 display "Test Java Load Complete"
 display "Enter a integer to pass"
 Accept IntForJava.
 invoke JavaClassRef "PassInt" using z"Int From COBOL :"
   IntForJava
        returning StringFromJava
 display "String Returned from Java = " StringFromJava
 invoke JavaClassRef "finalize" returning JavaClassRef
 stop run
 .
```

Figure 10-10 Expanded integer COBOL code

10.6   Evaluation

After completing the model solution, the engineer and the architect must define the *ending* evaluation criteria. These criteria most often include all the starting criteria, as well as criteria that were discovered as a by-product of implementing the model solution.

In our case, the biggest surprise was the difficulty we encountered passing simple types between Micro Focus COBOL and Java. Most of these difficulties stemmed from shortcomings in the product documentation. Nevertheless, as a result of our experience, we added an *ending* evaluation criterion to test hypothesis 1: Micro Focus Net Express IDE can be used to support mixed-language programming with Java.

- **Criterion 3:** Simple data types can be exchanged between Micro Focus COBOL and Java, and Java exceptions can be handled in the Micro Focus code.

Once we completed the model problem and defined our *ending* evaluation criterion, we could evaluate the model-problem solution. Criteria 1 and 2 were easily satisfied by the solution. Criterion 3 was at least partly satisfied, in that we could communicate both integers and strings—these being the most critical data types—and provide exception handling in the COBOL code. As a result, we adopted the Net Express contingency of calling Java from Micro Focus COBOL as the primary contingency.

We also identified other areas of concern, including performance and scalability, while building the model problem. But as the model problem was not designed to evaluate these qualities, we did not add them as criteria.

10.7   Summary

Model problems are an effective component-based software engineering technique for evaluating design contingencies. In this chapter, we developed a model problem to evaluate the feasibility of maintaining transactional integrity from COBOL to EJBs, using Micro Focus COBOL, WebSphere, and Oracle 8i. We created and demonstrated a model problem that satisfied the *ending* evaluation criteria for the model problem—increasing our confidence in the viability of the design option.

As a result of this model problem, the system architect identified this design solution as the principal design contingency. Becoming the principal design contingency does not guarantee that the solution will be adopted, but typically the principal contingency will receive the most resources to further verify the viability of the approach and reduce design risk. For example, we identified some additional risks during the implementation of the model solution, including how well the COBOL types defined for interacting with Java map into the COBOL types used in the RSS. At the same time, we did little to verify the performance, robustness, and scalability of this approach. These attributes must be considered further.

Although the principal contingency is not always adopted, it is an important step nonetheless. As a result of this decision, other design solutions are potentially starved of evaluation resources. If, for example, we had selected the OTS approach, we may never have applied the resources to identify the mixed-programming language approach as a viable design option. Time is also an important factor. As time passes, the design becomes more entrenched in the principal contingency. This design solution then becomes a design constraint in other model problems and as engineering expertise is acquired in the requisite technologies. Eventually, the cost of replacing the principal design solution with a contingency becomes prohibitive.

11

Business Object Integration

Better to light a candle than to curse the darkness.
—Chinese proverb

SRF, the RSS corporatewide architecture, mandates the development of business objects that communicate asynchronously using XML messaging. The XML messages deliver OAGIS business object documents (BODs). The business objects are implemented using Enterprise JavaBeans and other J2EE technologies. The rationale for mandating this approach is to evolve from a collection of isolated systems to an environment in which collections of business objects cooperate to provide required capabilities. Each business object becomes the steward for a particular data collection, and other business objects requiring access to this data go through the appropriate steward. The objective is to eliminate not only the need for redundant, and hence inconsistent, data collection and storage but also redundant functionality.

There are, however, some practical concerns on how to apply the SRF to the RSS modernization effort. RSS is a transactional system that distributes functionality across many business objects. If all of them are implemented on the same platform, is it necessary to restrict their communication to asynchronous message passing of large-grained BODs, or can the Enterprise JavaBeans used to implement these business objects communicate with one another using method invocation? How will intersystem and intrasystem communication affect the overall performance of the system? We need to evaluate each integration approach in more detail to understand how and when each approach should be applied in the RSS modernization effort. We also need to look at the competing architectures for distribution and communication inherent in each approach.

11.1   Where Are We?

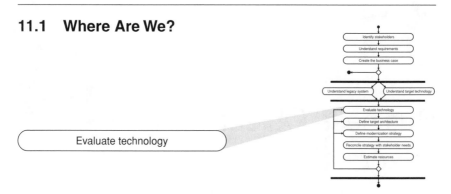

We have now developed an understanding of both the legacy system and the target technologies. We have used this knowledge to perform a series of situated technology evaluations to determine how each technology should be used in the modernization effort. We can now consider how best to use these technologies to achieve the qualities required by our target system.

11.2   A Tale of Two Architectures

Two architectures are included in the SRF: one based on the J2EE and the other based on B2B integration. Although they may be complementary, the two architectures address different needs. As a result, it is necessary to understand when we should prefer one architecture to the other.

In this chapter, we evaluate both architectures and supporting technologies against RSS requirements. Because working implementations of each approach are unlikely to be available at this point in the process, it is necessary to perform an architecture-level analysis, using an approach akin to the architectural trade-off analysis method (ATAM) [Clements 01]. Specifically, we generate *scenarios* based on RSS requirements. According to the authors of ATAM:

> A scenario is a short statement describing an interaction of one of the stakeholders with the system. A user would describe using the system to perform some task; his scenarios would very much resemble use cases in object-oriented parlance. A maintainer's scenario would describe making a change to the system, such as upgrading the operating system in a particular way or adding a specific new function. A developer's scenario might talk about using the architecture to build the system or predict its performance. A customer's scenario might describe how the architecture is to be re-used for a second product in a product line. [Kazman 01, p. 13]

Each architecture is evaluated to determine how well it supports each scenario. Order placement is an example of a scenario derived from RSS. In order placement, inventory is checked when an order is placed. If stock is available, it is placed on reserve and will not be decreased until the order is shipped. If stock is not available, the Regional Supply Center is notified and a requisition created for the item(s) out of stock. An order does not get created in the system and stock is not placed on reserve until fund availability is verified. If the order creation is successful, the warehouse system is notified.

Data from the architectural evaluation is analyzed to determine where and how each architecture should be applied in a modernization effort. Before beginning this evaluation, we provide a brief description of both architectures in the following sections.

J2EE ARCHITECTURE

J2EE applications are typically transactional systems that implement components as enterprise beans running in an EJB server. These components communicate using synchronous method calls [J2EE 02], although binding does not occur until runtime.[1] The J2EE implementation specified in the SRF is IBM WebSphere. We use this product as an example of a J2EE architecture, although our analysis of this architecture is largely product independent.

Figure 11-1 illustrates the sequence of interactions involved in implementing order placement using a J2EE-style architecture. The entire sequence takes place within a transaction context, so the entire transaction can be rolled back if any operation fails. This architecture greatly simplifies handling error conditions.

B2B ARCHITECTURE

The second method is based on the nontransactional, integration approach represented by business-to-business integration (B2B). A fairly broad range of integration approaches falls under the category of B2B. For our purposes, we consider only B2B integration that involves

- Asynchronous message passing using some form of message-oriented middleware (MOM)

- Business objects that communicate using a common, standardized business data–interchange format, such as those proposed by ebXML, OAGIS, or RosettaNet.

In particular, we use IBM MQSeries as a MOM implementation and OAGIS as a business data–interchange format because both are specified in the SRF.

Figure 11-2 illustrates the sequence of activities required to implement the order placement scenario in a B2B architecture. Although the possibility exists

---

[1] J2EE also supports asynchronous messaging between components through the Java Message Service (JMS). Here, however, we are considering only the synchronous communication mechanism provided by RMI/IIOP.

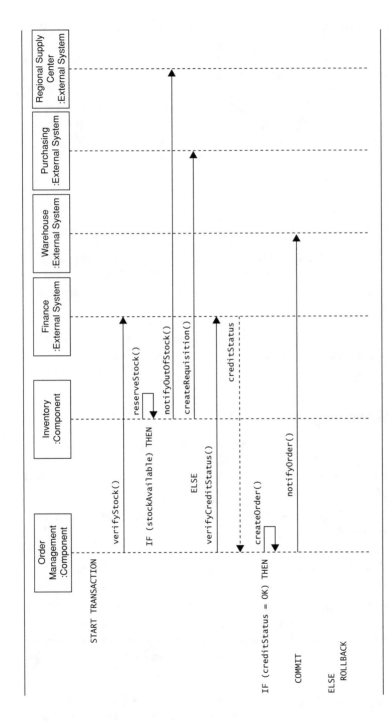

Figure 11-1 Order placement scenario in the J2EE architecture

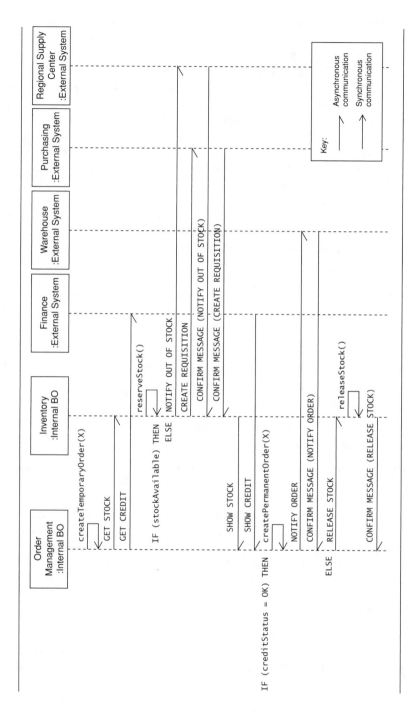

Figure 11-2 Order placement scenario in the B2B architecture

that an asynchronous message may time out and not be processed, this error condition is not depicted in the sequence diagram, for clarity. Nevertheless, the system/business object sending the BSR must include logic to react appropriately to this situation: for example, roll back a transaction, send a message to a log file, or request user intervention. CONFIRM messages occur only if confirmation is specified.[2]

The B2B sequence is significantly different from the J2EE sequence because of the lack of a transaction context. In the B2B scenario, the entire order placement use case must be implemented as a sequence of operations that can be rolled back using compensating operations. To a large extent, this requires the business object that initiates the transaction to keep track of the state of the transaction. The business object must also know how to reverse the results of any previous successful operations at each point of failure.

Significant trade-offs exist in performance, modifiability, data integrity, and other business and system qualities between the J2EE and B2B architectures. The remainder of this chapter evaluates these trade-offs.

11.3 Quality Attributes

Quality attributes are desired system qualities against which a system can be measured. There are two broad categories of quality attributes [Bass 98]:

- **Observable via execution.** Examples include performance, security, availability, and data integrity.

- **Not observable via execution.** Examples include modifiability, portability, reusability, and integrability.

In addition to the qualities that apply directly to a system, business goals, such as time to market, cost, projected system lifetime, targeted market, rollout schedule, and legacy systems use, also influence a system's architecture.

The following sections consider system qualities inherent in both the transactional approach represented by the J2EE architecture and the nontransactional approach represented by the B2B architecture. In most cases, we use the quality attribute definitions provided by Bass, Clements, and Kazman [Bass 98].

PERFORMANCE

Performance refers to the responsiveness of the system: the time required to respond to stimuli, or events, or the number of events processed in a specified interval of time. The level and type of communication between components in a

---

[2] Because each BOD in the OAGIS is named after the information contained in the BSR, we have decided to use the term BSR to indicate a message containing an OAGIS BOD.

system is important because communication latencies can often affect system performance.

Scenario. RSS requires completing most transactions in fewer than 2 seconds. Some lengthy transactions, such as those requiring reports, are exempted from this requirement but are nonetheless expected to perform quickly. RSS currently handles 2,000 transactions a minute. The modernized system must accommodate a 50 percent growth in the user base, increasing this number to 3,000 transactions a minute.

To evaluate performance in each architecture, you must consider the number of interactions required to support a particular use case. Ideally, you would know the percentages of each use case making up the anticipated 3,000 transactions per minute. If you do not have this information, you might evaluate this scenario based on an average number of interactions per use case and then based on a worst-case number of interactions per use case. You will also want to evaluate each of these situations for both success and failure conditions.

B2B.   There are several performance concerns in the B2B architecture:

- The amount of message traffic between business objects
- The time that it takes to complete an end-user transaction
- The amount of resources that must be locked at any given time

The amount of message traffic is of particular concern in a low-bandwidth network. Here, available communication bandwidth can be quickly consumed, causing contention, retries, and unpredictable response times. It might make sense to evaluate the scenarios against several possible deployments. These include having all the business objects on the same machine, all the business objects on the same 100MB network, and all the business objects distributed across the lowest-bandwidth connection envisioned in the system. Rough performance calculations could be performed on a sheet of paper. Additional precision may require prototyping and measurement or running simulations.

Given the 2-second requirement, time to complete end user transactions is an issue. Moving from a network database to a relational database, from COBOL to Java, and adding additional levels of security all lead to performance concerns in the RSS target system. Therefore, there is a concern whether any user transactions could complete in 2 seconds, even with relatively low-level loads on the system.

Another concern is the amount of resources that need to be locked in the system at any given point in time. There is likely to be a breaking point at which resource contention will lead to deadlock, causing system performance to rapidly degrade.

For example, the order placement scenario for B2B, shown in Figure 11-2, requires several OAGIS BODs to be transferred between business objects. The exact number can vary considerably. If stock and funds are available, it is 6 BSRs. If stock is not available but funds are available, it is 10. If you must reverse the order because funds are not available, it is 12 plus additional processing. Depending on the company's policy, you might also want to cancel the requisition, although not all companies do so if the items might be needed in the future. An additional BSR must also be accounted for if the order is placed from another system. In the worst case, a transaction updating n records may require $2n$ BSRs.[3]

To evaluate the effects of BSR-based communication on the network, you must determine the average size of the BODs being sent. In no case are BODs smaller than 2K, including headers and data. Ideally, the actual size of the BODs should be used in the calculations, although a rough number may suffice. The next step is to multiply the average size of the messages by the number of messages per second—or other time unit—to determine whether sufficient bandwidth exists for the anticipated message traffic without reaching contention.

Estimating the duration of an end-to-end user transaction is more difficult, as you must estimate data access performance, the number of times data will be accessed, as well as processing and communication time. As B2B technologies are designed for business-to-business integration, the parsing, construction, and communication using BSRs can add considerable overhead in an application such as RSS, for example.

- BSRs have no return value. If necessary, BSRs respond with another BSR (the GET ITEM BSR responds with a SHOW ITEM BSR), or a CONFIRM BOD BSR is returned if the confirmation option is selected in the BOD control area.
- BSRs must be assembled according to a predefined BOD.
- BSR communication requires interaction with an XML parser.

The selection of the communication infrastructure also affects the performance of message-based systems. The selection of a messaging product greatly influences both performance and QoS. Messaging products can offer different qualities of service, depending on the importance of guaranteed message delivery and processing. Messaging products can offer increased performance when acknowledgments are not required, a slower but more reliable service when an eventual acknowledgment is required, or a transactional capability that ensures complete delivery or failure of messages.[4]

J2EE.   Performance in J2EE applications is a widely discussed topic in the Java enterprise community because performance is driven by multiple factors.[5] However, these factors are a function primarily of application server configuration and application design.

---

[3] High coupling between business objects could also mean that they are not well architected.
[4] For a list of basic MOM products, see http://www.sei.cmu.edu/cbs/mls/links.html#middleware.
[5] For a list of more than 100 practices for improved J2EE performance, see http://www.sei.cmu.edu/cbs/mls/links.html#precisejava.

Given the large number of user interactions that a typical J2EE application must support, finite server-side resources must be optimally shared. Such resources may include databases, message queues, directories, and enterprise systems, each of which is accessed by an application using a connection object that acts as a resource entry point. Managing access to those shared resources is essential for meeting high-performance requirements for J2EE applications.

The most difficult part is choosing the best J2EE platform from the large number of options and configurations available. The application server is a critical resource; its implementation must be efficient and must ensure that scalability allows performance to grow in an effective manner.

Application design is also critical in J2EE performance. For EJB, the design of session beans and entity beans, as well as the mapping of entity beans to database tables, can impact performance. For example, implementing an entity bean per table in a database schema will affect performance because a large number of entity beans would be created each time data is needed from tables that have a one-to-many relationship between them.

Evaluation.   The B2B architecture and the J2EE architecture have significantly different objectives. The goal of the B2B architecture is integration between business objects. The goal of the J2EE architecture is Web-based application development based on enterprise beans. When these architectures are used for something other than their intended purposes—for example, using J2EE for B2B integration—the performance implications must be carefully examined.

Applications based on the B2B architecture do not perform well if the business objects have a high degree of interaction. Therefore, implementing components as business objects is inadvisable if the component requires a high degree of external interactions to perform a task. Also, in the B2B architecture, rollbacks are handled using a *compensating transaction* or a *saga* (see Section 8.3). As a result, performance in these systems can degrade rapidly if transactions commonly fail. This is especially true if *compensating transactions* may also fail.

As a rule, distributed-method invocation adds overhead when communication can be handled effectively asynchronously.[6] For example, you may not need to wait for a logging or audit trail method to complete, provided that the infrastructure can provide guaranteed message delivery. A more serious problem is that synchronous, distributed transactions over the Internet or other wide area network (WAN) require locking data records and other resources for the duration

[6] For asynchronous communication in J2EE, one possibility is to use CORBA, which supports deferred synchronous communication. A deferred synchronous request/response allows an application to make a request to a CORBA object. An empty result is immediately returned. The application can then perform other operations and later poll the ORB to see whether the result has been made available. Other, more sophisticated asynchronous communication can be achieved only by developing an architecture on top of the lowest levels of CORBA.

of the invocation. Unfortunately, these durations are indeterminate because of unpredictable WAN latencies.

SECURITY

Security is a measure of the system's ability to resist unauthorized attempts at usage and denial of service while still providing its services to legitimate users. Not all threats can or need to be eliminated. In many circumstances, exposure can be reduced to an acceptable level, using authentication, authorization, signing, encryption, and auditing. For an explanation of these terms and an overview of enterprise information system security, see [Kassem 00].

Scenario. The retailer in our case study has a large number of systems that users must access. Currently, each system requires its own password and implements a widely disparate set of security mechanisms. As these disparate, separate systems evolve to a set of Web-enabled business objects, it is necessary to establish an overall security solution for the enterprise. In particular, end user access must be through a single retail portal that will provide identification and authorization for the entire system of systems. The user's security context must then be associated with all interactions with business objects so that proper authorization and auditing can take place.

B2B. No security is built into OAGIS, because it is simply an XML content specification. Therefore, the MOM transporting the OAGIS BODs must provide the security infrastructure.

Policy Director for MQSeries, a security solution for MQSeries, provides access control services that restrict which users or applications can get or put messages on specific queues. It also allows MQSeries applications to send data with confidentiality and integrity, using keys associated with the sending and receiving users or applications. These services are provided transparently by MQSeries, meaning that existing applications are supported without change.

Policy Director for MQSeries provides an interceptor process that sits between an MQSeries application and MQSeries itself. This interceptor captures all calls made by the application to MQSeries for services. It determines whether the request for MQSeries services is authorized and whether the data in the transaction should be (1) encrypted and/or digitally signed before it is placed in the queue requested or (2) unencrypted and/or signature verified before it is presented to the requesting application. These interceptors receive policy information from a master policy server—management server—that is managed by an administration console. These components are identical to the ones delivered in Tivoli's Web access control product: Tivoli Policy Director.

The use of XML in B2B also introduces security concerns because information is transmitted and stored as plaintext. As more and more companies use XML to transmit structured data across the Web, the security of documents becomes increasingly important. The World Wide Web Consortium (W3C) and the Internet Engineering Task Force (IETF) are defining an XML vocabulary for digital signatures [IETF 01]. The W3C working draft of XML encryption requirements provides requirements for an XML syntax and processing for encrypting digital content, including portions of XML documents and protocol messages [W3C 01].

The two primary requirements in security for XML data are (1) encryption to keep confidential information private and (2) digital signatures to provide authenticity, integrity, and nonrepudiation. The problem with XML is that published schemas contain data about the tags used in specific XML documents, and the tags themselves can be quite long. These tags could be used to provide enough known plaintext for an attack.

J2EE.   Security services provided by Web components, such as JSPs, Java servlets, and applets, extend to the J2EE architecture. In the J2EE architecture, a container provides an authentication and authorization boundary between external callers and the components it hosts. A caller to a component inside a container has an associated credential that is compared to the access control rules for the target component. The containers implement the security mechanisms on behalf of the hosted components. J2EE security mechanisms combine the concepts of container hosting and the declarative specification of application security requirements with the availability of security mechanisms embedded in the application.

Remote method invocation in J2EE uses the RMI over IIOP. IIOP allows the security context to be communicated with the request, so that the business object receiving the request will have the security identity of the user. This information can be used for authorizing access to services and resources and for providing an audit trail.

Evaluation.   The B2B architecture allows components—business objects—to be implemented on any platform, but they must rely on the MOM infrastructure to provide secure communications, as well as additional layers inside the business objects to handle security. The J2EE architecture provides almost transparent security mechanisms, as long as all components are compliant with the J2EE architecture. But regardless of the architecture, security technologies should be used in conjunction with appropriate logging, auditing, and recovery procedures.

AVAILABILITY

Availability measures the proportion of time the system is up and running. Availability is measured by the length of time between failures, as well as by how quickly the system is able to resume operation in the event of failure.

Scenario.   Availability requirements in RSS vary, depending on the operations. For example, when a customer purchases an item at the point of sale, the business object that verifies customer funds must be available so that the transaction can be completed. This introduces a requirement for high or continuous availability, especially if stores are open 7/24. These transactions typically require 99.999 percent or higher availability.

On the other hand, transactions such as requisitions from suppliers require a different type of availability. These transactions require the business object to be *eventually* available to process the request. This allows the originating system to send the requisition and then forget about it. This type of transaction assumes an infrequent failure rate of, say, less than 2 percent. When the transaction cannot be processed, a message must be returned to the system originating the request, and the originating system must be designed to handle these notifications.

B2B. Availability in the B2B architecture depends greatly on the communication infrastructure. MQSeries, for example, provides guaranteed message delivery that supports the RSS requirement of sending certain classes of messages, such as requisitions, and then forgetting about them. Also available are tools that can be used with MQSeries or other MOM products to provide high availability through backup systems, automatic switchover, monitors, tuning, and logging systems.

J2EE. Achieving high levels of availability requires such capabilities as

- **Failover.** This capability automatically switches to a standby system if the primary system fails or is temporarily shut down for servicing.
- **Support for field-replaceable units (FRU).** This capability allows a component to be replaced in an operational system.
- **Support for on-line upgrades.** The capability allows upgrading an application and its software to a new version without disrupting the service offered by the application.
- **Logging.** This feature allows tracing a running application to diagnose the cause of abnormal behavior.

The J2EE platform does not provide API support for these functions. Hence, availability in the J2EE architecture depends on the particular application server. Many J2EE implementations support such features as transparent failover and clustering; tier duplication; real-time scalability, including load balancing, efficient connection pooling, and caching; addition of CPUs (central processing units); and reconfiguration or redeployment of the network architecture.

Evaluation. Availability requirements for different RSS transactions requiring different qualities of service differ significantly. The B2B architecture can adequately support "available sometime" availability. The J2EE architecture is better suited for continuous availability, although the exact capabilities are vendor specific.

DATA INTEGRITY

Data integrity refers to the validity of data: a measure of the trust that users have in the data that is delivered by the system. Data integrity is a major requirement for all systems that incorporate databases, particularly distributed databases. Data-integrity issues include two-phase commit, replication, and support for long transactions.

Data integrity can be compromised by human errors entering data, errors transmitting data from one computer to another, software bugs or viruses, hardware malfunctions, and natural disasters. Assuming that these problems can be managed, data integrity depends on conservation of the ACID properties (see Section 8.3) during transaction processing.

Scenario. The classic data-integrity scenario is a money transfer: Money is subtracted from one account and added to another account. If the two account balances are stored in separate database tables, a power outage occurs, and the software crashes between steps, what will happen to the account balances?

B2B. The B2B architecture commonly describes scenarios that have been designed to eliminate the need for transactions—in most cases. For example, in an order scenario, an item is *reserved* until it is determined that the funds are available for purchase, after which the item is *purchased* and removed from inventory, *assigned* to an order, or *released* because funds were unavailable. This process requires additional steps but eliminates the need for transactions in a distributed environment.

OAGIS also provides scenarios that require data redundancy. In this instance, the data required by a business object can be accessed without sending a BSR to a remote business object and waiting for a response. Guidelines for data synchronization, as well as a set of SYNC BODs to support cases of data replication, are also provided by OAGIS. The actual synchronization procedures need to be defined by the organization. In effect, the B2B architecture transfers the responsibility for maintaining data integrity from the infrastructure to the application layer.

J2EE. J2EE provides built-in transaction management. The J2EE platform supports both programmatic and declarative transaction demarcation. The component provider can use the Java Transaction API (JTA) to programmatically demarcate transactions in the component code. Declarative transaction demarcation is supported in EJBs, where transactions can be started and committed by the EJB container. In both cases, the J2EE server manages the necessary interactions between the transaction manager and the database and propagation of the transaction context.

Evaluation. For transactional systems, the J2EE architecture is a better option because it fully supports transaction management. Implementing transactions with the B2B architecture requires the application to maintain data integrity.

MODIFIABILITY

Modifiability, the ability to make modifications quickly and cost-effectively, is largely a function of the locality of the change. Modifications include extending or changing capabilities, deleting unwanted capabilities, adapting to new operating environments, and restructuring.

Scenario.   The retailer in our case study plans to replace existing systems with a set of distributed business objects. As systems are modernized, already completed business objects will need to be upgraded or replaced with newer, better implementations. Completed systems will need to be modified to use the new business objects.

B2B.   Using a messaging system for communication permits dynamic and flexible systems to be built. This allows business objects to be modified, replaced, or added without affecting the rest of the system. However, questions about the sufficiency of the standards that define the interface to the business object remain a major issue.

- How successful is the standard in the marketplace? That is, how many vendors are supporting the standard?

- Is the standard still evolving? Are competing standards in the marketplace? Is this standard likely to become the predominant one? If not, is there room in the marketplace for more than one standard?

- How well defined is the standard? Are data semantics, as well as syntax, adequately defined? Are compliance tests available? To what degree are vendors allowed to deviate from the standard? In summary, how easy will it be to replace a business object with a different implementation from a different vendor or development team?

Many of these questions are germane in evaluating OAGIS. Several standards potentially compete with OAGIS, including BizTalk, RosettaNet, and ebXML. OAG, the promoter and maintainer of OAGIS, has more than 60 members supporting the OAGIS effort. Supporters include users, software vendors, and solution providers. The ebXML standard, on the other hand, is jointly sponsored by the United Nations Center for Trade Facilitation and Electronic Business (UN/CEFACT) and the Organization for the Advancement of Structured Information Standards (OASIS). Both of these groups cite broad industry support for ebXML.

One—admittedly nonscientific—way to get a feel for a standard's pervasiveness is to perform a Web search. For example, Figure 11-3 shows sample searches using AltaVista for RosettaNet, ebXML, and OAGIS. AltaVista found 9,117 results for RosettaNet, 32,311 results for ebXML and 665 results for OAGIS, with the first of these a false positive. As a result, we must consider the viability of OAGIS carefully. A limited number of results can be reasonable if the technology has a well-defined niche.

Search: rosettanet

We found 9,117 results:
Rosetta Intro
www.rosettanet.or.kr/ • Translate

Search: ebxml

We found 32,311 results:
ebXML - Enabling A Global Electronic Market
... central integration engine by way of an ebXML-compliant system that
plugs into the ... open forum to exchange ideas on implementing ebXML.
Development of the ebXML specifications is an on-going effort ...
www.ebxml.org/ • Related pages • Translate
More pages from www.ebxml.org

Search: oagis

We found 665 results:
OAGIS Homepage
Beratung, Dienstleistungen und Produkte für Geoinformatik (GIS) und
Computerkartographie ... Mittwoch, 13. Februar 2002 Herzlich willkommen bei
OAGIS! Wenn Sie zum ersten Mal
auf unseren ...
www.oagis.com/ • Related pages • Translate
More pages from www.oagis.com

Figure 11-3 Sample search results for RosettaNet, ebXML, and OAGIS

The stability of the standard is also an issue. If the standard does what you
need, you will not want it to change. If the standard does not yet support your
requirements, your issue may be how likely it is to evolve. In general, industry
standards evolve more rapidly than standards approved by national and international standards bodies.

OAGIS, for example, has the following release history.[7]

- July 1995: OAG published a white paper describing the approach.

- Jan. 1996: Release 1 specifications for financial transactions are approved.

- June 1996: Release 2 of OAGIS Specifications are released, containing
  more APIs approved by OAG membership.

- Sep. 1996: Release 3 of OAGIS brings total to 24 APIs approved and committed to by OAG membership.

- Nov. 1996: Release 4 of OAGIS brings the number of APIs to 42 approved
  by Open Applications Group.

- June 1997: Release 5 of OAGIS completes most of the major ERP-to-ERP
  integration content required.

- Aug. 1997: The first version of the OAG Middleware API Specifications
  (OAMAS) is released for comment.

---

[7] See http://www.sei.cmu.edu/cbs/mls/links.html#openapplications-2.

- Feb. 1998: XML is adopted as a metadata language.
- June 1998: Release 6 of OAGIS adds functionality for supply chain integration.
- Oct. 2000: Release 7.0 of OAGIS includes 170 XML transactions.
- Feb. 2001: Release 7.1 of OAGIS published with 182 XML transactions.
- Apr. 2002: OAGIS Release 8.0 announced.

A cursory examination of the history suggests that, although the evolution of the standard has slowed down since 1996, the standard is still evolving rapidly. This may be a concern if stability of the standard is an issue.

Finally, how well defined is the standard? In the case of OAGIS, the syntax for data structures is well defined. However, the specific semantics of the data are left largely to the business objects to interpret. This is true for XML content standards in general. Also, the BOD set is basic. It is based on common business operations, or horizontal requirements, that can be extended by the business object developer, or vertical requirements. Any BODs defined by the developer would, of course, be outside the standard unless these BODs were eventually incorporated into the standard.

J2EE.   The J2EE architecture is similar to the B2B architecture, relying on standards to support component replacement [Seacord 02]. When standard business object interfaces are defined, replacement should be relatively simple. When standard business object interfaces are undefined, extensive code modifications would be needed to replace a business object. In our scenario, no generally accepted interface standards are available for an enterprise bean implementation of the required business objects, so modifiability is likely to be a problem.

There may be another problem in supporting the scenario. Although enterprise beans could easily be moved to other application servers on other platforms, performance could be a problem when these business objects are widely distributed across a WAN, as discussed in the section on performance.

Evaluation.   Because it promotes loose coupling, the B2B architecture is a better option when modifying or replacing business objects is a concern. An issue arises when the B2B architecture is used to integrate transactional-based applications. This is why nontransactional applications are often limited to transient data exchange and messaging across organizational boundaries.

PORTABILITY

Portability is the ability of the system to run in different computing environments.

Scenario.   RSS business objects are implemented on the Sun Solaris platform. Microsoft acquires Sun Microsystems and forces users to migrate to a Windows NT platform.

B2B. B2B does not place any restrictions on the implementation of business objects. The portability of these objects depends on their implementations. Also, B2B does not restrict where business objects are deployed, as long as they share a common understanding of exchanged BODs.

J2EE. J2EE is based on the promise of "write once, run anywhere" [J2EE 02]. J2EE works on any platform with a compliant JVM and a compliant set of platform services, such as an EJB container. J2EE platform specifications are published and reviewed publicly. In addition, numerous vendors offer compliant products and development environments. However, J2EE is a single-language platform. Interactions with objects implemented in other languages can be accomplished through CORBA or the Java Native Interface (JNI).

Portability is accomplished using Java transparency of location provided by RMI. Enterprise JavaBeans are also relatively portable to other EJB servers and hence other hardware platforms [Comella-Dorda 00].

Evaluation. The B2B architecture does not address portability. Additional architectural constraints must be placed on business objects if portability is an issue. The J2EE architecture does address portability at many different levels and is one of the principal drivers of Java-based technologies. As long as business objects are implemented as enterprise beans, portability should not be a major issue. Business objects in the B2B architecture could always be implemented as enterprise beans to address portability.

REUSABILITY

Reusability involves designing a system so that a portion of the system can be reused in other development efforts.

Scenario. Business objects developed for RSS may be used in future modernization of other legacy systems.

B2B. Reusability in the B2B architecture occurs at the business object or application level. Therefore, the B2B style of integration ideally suits this particular reuse scenario but does not provide an advantage when building a new business object.

J2EE. Business objects implemented as enterprise beans in the J2EE architecture provide finer-grained reuse than does the B2B architecture. These components may be reused in developing other business components, but because these components provide substantially less functionality than a complete business object, the overhead of reusing these components may outweigh the benefits of reuse.

Evaluation.   B2B and J2EE provide reusability at differing levels of granularity. B2B more closely supports the given reuse scenario, but reuse can be effectively applied at both levels.

INTEGRABILITY

Integrability is the ability to make separately developed components of the system work correctly together.

Scenario.   Different business objects are simultaneously developed by different development teams, at different geographic locations, in different time zones and with different cultures: for example, India and Kansas.

B2B.   Integrability in the B2B architecture is accomplished through BODs. BODs are predefined XML specification documents (DTDs or XML schema) that contain the message format for the information being exchanged between business objects. Business objects must agree on the BOD(s) being exchanged before they can be integrated.

OAGIS provides a list of BODs that cover common information exchange operations in B2B communication. The OAG is continually adding BODs to satisfy new business needs and requests from the user community. In reality, though, there is no guarantee that all the BODs needed by an organization are defined. In this case, the creation of BODs is required, especially for A2A communication within the same organization. A process that guarantees that all applications communicate using the same BODs is necessary.

J2EE.   Enterprise JavaBeans defines a common mechanism for developing and deploying components into an application server. Enterprise beans are required to provide certain interfaces, but they exist largely to support life-cycle management. The bean provider defines the functional API exported by the enterprise bean. The functionality supported by an enterprise bean is not constrained by the EJB specification and is not restricted by the EJB server.

There exists the possibility that independently developed specifications define APIs for replaceable enterprise beans, but these fall outside the EJB specification. Beyond eliminating the potential for architectural mismatch between enterprise beans and between enterprise beans and EJB servers, the EJB component model does little to support integrability of separately developed business objects.

Evaluation.   The B2B architecture goes further than the J2EE architecture in supporting systemwide integration of business objects. The B2B architecture defines messages and BODs that can be shared between business objects. J2EE makes no attempt to identify and define these functional interfaces. This is not meant to imply that integration issues do not exist in a B2B environment: They do. The development team must still be concerned that compatible versions of applicable standards—OAGIS and XML, for example—and compatible versions of middleware products are used. Data semantics, error recovery, and other integration issues also need to be managed.

11.4 Summary

The B2B and J2EE architectures each have distinct advantages. The B2B architecture is emerging as a solution for integrating business objects over the Internet or other WANs. This makes it an attractive option for integrating business objects, although the relevant standards are still evolving.

J2EE has significant momentum and a large share of the application server market. Web-based applications benefit greatly from J2EE because developers can focus on business logic and not spend time developing infrastructure that provides no direct business value.

The B2B and J2EE architectures differ mainly in their views of distribution. The B2B architecture views distribution as integrating applications running on different platforms and from different vendors in an asynchronous manner. The J2EE architecture views distribution as integrating application components and providing support for distributed transactions in a synchronous manner.

A transactional architecture, such as the one supported by the J2EE architecture, is recommended when system development is driven by the following scenarios.

- Business objects are deployed on a single machine or on a high-performance LAN.
- Business objects are tightly coupled.
- Data integrity is an important issue and transactions may span multiple business objects and legacy components.

A nontransactional architecture, exemplified by the B2B architecture, is more appropriate in the following situations.

- A business object may be replaced in the future with a third-party component or application.
- Asynchronous communication between different applications running on possibly different platforms is required.
- Communication is B2B or A2A.

B2B and J2EE are not mutually exclusive as business object integration approaches. For example, applications can be developed using the J2EE framework and communicate with other applications using the B2B framework, as shown in Figure 11-4. J2EE applications communicate synchronously with a BSR interface that creates and sends outgoing BSRs and receives and interprets

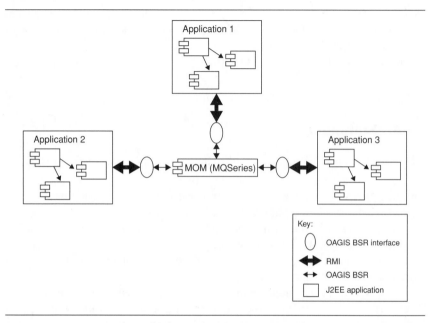

Figure 11-4   Integration of the B2B and J2EE architectures

incoming BSRs. The BSR interface communicates asynchronously with other BSR interfaces, using the MOM infrastructure—hiding all OAGIS and MOM details from the J2EE applications. The BSR interface can be shared by one or more J2EE applications. This BSR interface can be custom developed or can be provided by the framework component of existing XML messaging efforts, such as BizTalk, ebXML, or RosettaNet (see Section 9.5).

As always, you need to select the architecture that best fits your requirements, business goals, and resources. This architecture needs to work today, as well as in the future.

12

Target Architecture

The physician can bury his mistakes, but the architect can only advise his clients to plant vines.
—Frank Lloyd Wright, *Time Magazine* (Oct. 4, 1953)

In a modernization effort, the target architecture represents the as-desired system, providing the technical vision for the modernization effort. Without this vision, similar operations might be implemented completely differently, making it impossible to predict, model, gauge, or control the qualities of the system. The target architecture can also help to identify and resolve potential design risks resulting from inconsistent or contradictory requirements.

In its current configuration, the target architecture for RSS represents a best-of-breed integration of the J2EE and the B2B architectures described in the previous chapter. Both of these technologies are specified in the organization-wide SRF developed by the corporate architecture team. As discussed previously, the goal of the SRF is to promote interoperability and commonality. However, to be broadly applicable throughout the organization, the SRF must be necessarily vague in some respects. As a result, it is necessary to adapt the SRF to the requirements of a specific development effort, such as RSS, before it can be used successfully on that project.

In the case of RSS, we adapted the SRF by defining a collection of generic architectural patterns. Each of these patterns defines common operations and how they are supported by the SRF in the target RSS system.

12.1   Where Are We?

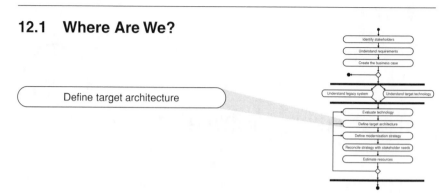

In Chapter 11, we evaluated the quality attributes of a modernized system, based on the approaches to system development proposed by the B2B and J2EE architectures included in the SRF. In this chapter, we propose a target architecture based on these technologies and on the constraints and requirements of the modernization case study.

12.2   Forces Affecting the Architecture

In general, the architecture of a system is the description of elements from which systems are built, interactions among those elements, patterns that guide their composition, and constraints on these patterns [Shaw 95]. Data, organizational, and technology requirements can all influence the architecture. The architecture must reflect the constraints imposed by these often incompatible requirements.

DATA REQUIREMENTS

Data requirements are driven by functional requirements—for example, to maintain and report inventory status—and by technical requirements—for example, to support a relational data model. Examples of RSS data requirements follow.

Reports and Queries. Reports and queries, including flexible and ad hoc queries, involve extracting, relating, and summarizing data from one or more tables. Reports evolve and new reports are often added. In the RSS, support for ad hoc query capability is required so that users can enter their queries in SQL or by using query tools.

Persistent Summaries and Roll-ups. Summaries and roll-ups are reports produced from consolidated information that involves the extraction of data from multiple tables. Roll-up and summary information is stored in the database. The process for collecting and analyzing this data may be computationally intensive, potentially requiring the creation of interim tables to store data temporarily.

Data Warehousing.   A data warehouse is a collection of data designed to support management decision making at the enterprise level. Data warehouses are described in detail in Chapter 7.

Complex Transactions.   RSS must support high volumes of transactions involving data elements in dispersed areas of the system in an efficient manner.

ORGANIZATIONAL REQUIREMENTS

Figure 12-1 illustrates the distributed nature of the retail organization in our case study. Data stored in the headquarters, in any warehouse, and in any outlet has to be accessible to authenticated users throughout the system.

Managing distributed data can be extremely challenging. Some goals of managing distributed databases, as enumerated by Ozsu [Ozsu 99], include

- Transparent management of distributed, fragmented, and replicated data
- Improved reliability/availability through distributed transactions
- Improved performance
- Easier and economical system expansion

TECHNOLOGY REQUIREMENTS

Technology requirements are often suggested or imposed by existing organizational integration frameworks or standards. These frameworks exist for a variety of reasons. By identifying standard products, an organization often hopes to share expertise among development projects and to lower licensing costs by leveraging site or multiple-license discounts. Although these frameworks can help in each of these endeavors, there must be a process for deviating from the framework when the technology choices are inappropriate for a project.

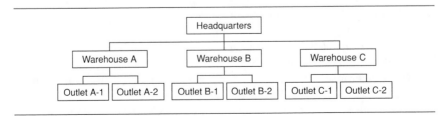

Figure 12-1   Distributed organization

The following technologies are contained within the SRF.

- The *Java programming language* is the principal language for development. Other, more specialized languages may be used, such as JavaScript for Web pages and PL/SQL for stored procedures in Oracle.

- Business logic is defined in *enterprise beans* that are run in an EJB server. The EJB server provides security, transaction, naming, and other services.

- Dynamic Web pages are described using a combination of *Java Server Pages* (JSPs), *Java servlets*, and *HTML*.

- *OAGIS* defines the *XML* business content to be exchanged between business objects.

- *MQSeries* is a message-oriented middleware package used in the SRF for exchanging BSRs between business objects.

- *Oracle* is the relational database management system (RDBMS).

12.3 Overview of the Architecture

As discussed in Chapter 11, both the J2EE and the B2B architectures have strengths and weaknesses but are not mutually exclusive. The B2B architecture supports widely distributed business objects. The J2EE architecture supports transaction systems. Common sense dictates using the B2B architecture for inter-action between business objects and decomposing each business object using the J2EE architecture. Bass, Clements, and Kazman [Bass 98] refer to this as hierarchical heterogeneous architecture styles: A component of one style, when decomposed, is structured according to the rules of a different style.

The question now becomes, "How can RSS be described within this architecture?" RSS, as we have already stated, is a very large system encompassing a wide range of functionality that will be distributed across multiple business objects in the B2B architecture. However, RSS, which has historically been a transactional system, is being modernized by a single development team and will be deployed on a single platform or collection of platforms connected by a high-speed LAN. Therefore, does it really make sense to implement this system as a collection of business objects communicating asynchronously without the support of a transaction manager?

On the one hand, building the system as a collection of business components would allow business objects to be easily shared/integrated with other systems within the enterprise. The overall system configuration would be highly configurable. Business objects could be easily relocated to a remote site running on a low-bandwidth WAN connection or replaced with a COTS product. On the other hand, system performance might suffer.

This interesting question is not easily solved without modeling the multiple-business object approach to determine whether performance will be adequate. In the end, we decided to decompose the system into multiple J2EE-based business objects and to provide a common BSR interface to each business object for ease of integration with external systems. Business objects on the same platform or LAN communicate directly using the transactional-based method invocations, whereas business objects on remote systems or systems accessible only through low-bandwidth WANs are integrated using OAGIS BSRs. The identified business objects include[1]

- **Order Management:** Processes purchase orders and back orders, services customer inputs and outputs, provides a help capability to the customer, and interfaces with the accounting and procurement systems
- **Inventory:** Maintains the status, location, stock level, and rules for issue of inventory items
- **Catalog:** Provides information for item identification, selection, pricing, and source identification
- **History/Audit:** Tracks information required for historical or audit requirements
- **PickList:** Provides the functionality to prioritize the pulling of items from inventory and provides work-flow capabilities
- **Work-in-Process (WIP) Confirmation:** Provides status, update, tracking, and suspense capabilities for requisitions, shipped items, and others
- **Requisition:** Provides capabilities for generating requisitions and funds confirmation
- **Demand Planning:** Processes usage and inventory data to determine inventory needs
- **Match Document:** Processes invoices, provides acknowledgment of the received invoice, and establishes supply-point segments for received items

Figure 12-2 shows the relationship of these business objects in RSS.

Business objects on a single platform or LAN communicate using EJB-based transactional method invocation (RMI/IIOP). These J2EE-based business objects exchange BSRs with external systems over MQSeries. Business objects communicate with the RSS operational database to perform operations on behalf of applications. The data warehouse synchronizes as required with the operational database to update data values.

Data for each business object is stored in a single operational database because we have already selected performance over modifiability as the critical attribute driver for the architecture. It is our decision to allow a high degree of coupling between business objects running on the same platform.

In essence, the RSS architecture is a three-tier layered architecture. The application components represent the presentation tier, the business objects represent the business logic tier, and the database represents the data tier.

---

[1] As might be expected, the exact list and the makeup of business objects evolved continuously during the planning effort.

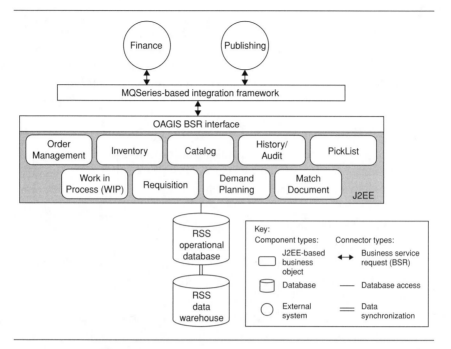

Figure 12-2   RSS high-level architecture

A simplified view of an application is shown in Figure 12-3. RMI is used to communicate between application components and business objects. SQL is used as an interface between business objects and the database. A more detailed view of the architecture is shown in Figure 12-4 and is discussed in the following sections.

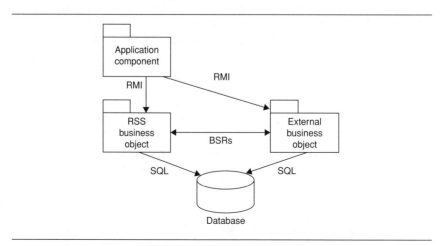

Figure 12-3   Simplified view of an RSS application

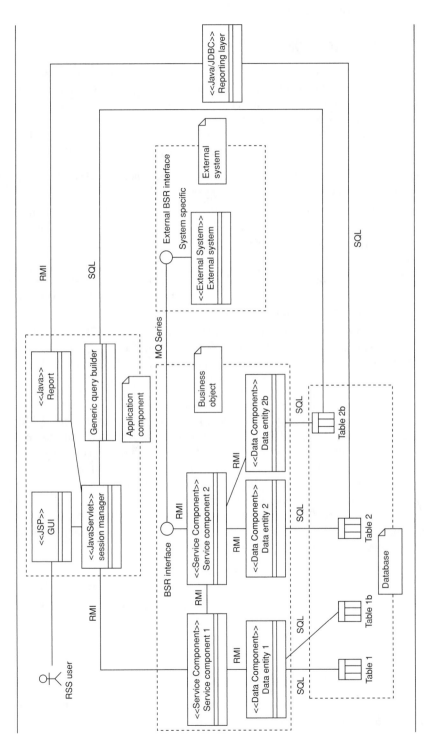

Figure 12-4 Detailed view of the RSS architecture

197

APPLICATION COMPONENTS

Application components are responsible for providing information from the user to the computer system and for presenting information from the computer system to the user. Application components include user interfaces, reports, query building, and application-specific work flows.

The structure of an application component is shown in Figure 12-5. The application component contains the following elements:

- **Graphical user interface (GUI).** The GUI is implemented as HTML pages, with dynamic content provided by JSPs or Java servlets.

- **Reports.** Preset reports are implemented in Java and use the services of the reporting layer. The reporting layer provides a level of abstraction, using the JDBC layer to access the database. This makes the reports independent of the database implementation.

- **Generic query builder.** The generic query builder allows the user to construct ad hoc queries to the database. It can be an applet, a JSP, a servlet, an SQL prompt, or any commercial query-building tool.

- **Session manager.** The session manager is a Java servlet or JSP that implements work flow and session management. The session manager accepts the user's input, invokes the service components located in the business objects, and then issues a response to the client.

Application components can communicate with business objects by using BSRs, nonstandard component APIs, or a combination of both. Using BSRs maintains a greater degree of independence between applications and business objects. In particular, using nonstandard interfaces to business objects can create a dependency on a particular implementation of a business object for the application component. However, the granularity and performance of BSR-based communication may be inadequate to support user interactions. As a result, it is acceptable to use non-BSR communication with business objects in this situation. The architecture uses RMI to communicate between application components and business objects.

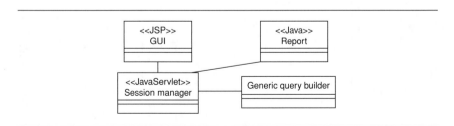

Figure 12-5 Application component structure

Application components access data through the business objects, except for reports and ad hoc queries. Database access for reports is done through a reporting layer, whereas ad hoc queries access the database directly.

BUSINESS OBJECTS

Business objects encapsulate the business logic and data of a business entity. Business objects communicate internally using RMI, externally using BSRs, and with the database layer using SQL. Each business object defines one or more *service components*, one or more *data components,* and *wrapper components* as required. A service component provides the functionality of a business object. A data component encapsulates data elements maintained in the RDBMS. A wrapper component is used for communication with legacy systems that do not have a BSR interface.

SERVICE COMPONENTS

Service components provide the business logic for a business object. Service components communicate with one or more data components to obtain required information, to respond to a call from another service component or application, to respond to a BSR, or to generate a BSR.

Service components must use the BSR interface to communicate with external business objects and systems. Service components also provide interfaces for use by application components, other service components within the business object, and other local business objects.

Service components do not access the database directly; they access it through data components. Service components perform bulk operations on data components on behalf of Java servlets in application components.

The Session Entity Façade pattern [J2EE 01a] provides functionality similar to that provided by a service component. The service component acts as a façade—a unified, simple interface to all the service's clients. Those clients use the service component as one-stop shopping for functionality and data access.

Service components are implemented as EJB session beans. Session beans act as agents for clients and are typically instantiated for each client session. Order placement is a good example of functionality that would be implemented as a session bean.

Accessing data components through service components also simplifies transaction management. For example, if the session bean implementing the service component specifies transactions as required, all entity beans invoked by the session bean will run in the same transaction context as the session bean.

EJB defines stateless and stateful session beans. *Stateless session beans* are components that model business processes performed in a single method call. These beans hold no conversational state on behalf of clients, meaning that they are free of a client-specific state after each method call. For a stateless session bean to be useful, the client must pass all client data that the bean needs as parameters to business logic methods. Because they can support multiple clients, stateless session beans can offer better scalability for applications with a large number of clients. Typically, an application requires fewer stateless session beans than stateful session beans to support the same number of clients.

Stateful session beans hold conversations with clients that span multiple method invocations. Stateful session beans store a conversational state within the bean. This state must be available for that same client's next method request.

The RSS architecture uses stateless session beans to provide generic services to multiple clients. For example, a service that manipulates multiple rows in a database and represents a shared view of the data can be modeled as a stateless session bean. One example of such service is a catalog listing products and associated prices. Because all users are interested in this information, the stateless session bean can be easily shared. Stateless session beans are the best choice for implementing behavior to visit multiple rows in a database and presenting a read-only view of data.

Session beans encapsulate a business task. As a result, there is typically a strong correlation between service components and system use cases. In RSS, examples include order placement, requisition, and delivery.

Often, use cases contain steps that are common to other use cases, such as obtaining a list of items. These steps are usually extracted from the use case and modeled as use cases themselves. They are associated to the original use case with the *include* relationship. These steps may be modeled as session beans or simply as reusable Java classes.

DATA COMPONENTS

Data components provide encapsulation. They communicate with the database to obtain or update information. In this architecture, data components are implemented as entity beans. Data components represent data in a database and add behavior to that data. Instead of writing database logic in an application, the application accesses data through the remote interface to the entity bean.

Data components can use either bean-managed or container-managed persistence. With bean-managed persistence (BMP), database calls are implemented within the bean, using, for example, JDBC. With container-managed persistence (CMP), there is no persistence logic inside the bean; rather, the EJB container manages data persistence based on information provided in the deployment descriptor.

Even though container-managed persistence allows beans to be smaller and eliminates the need to develop data-access logic, bean-managed persistence proves to be better in large and complex systems, for three reasons

1. There is usually a need to develop logic, especially for finder methods.

2. Complex data fields may not be directly mappable to underlying storage.

3. There may be relationships between entity beans that must be specified.

Data components should represent coarse-grained objects, such as those that provide complex behavior beyond simply getting and setting field values. These coarse-grained objects typically have dependent objects with real domain meaning only when they are associated with their coarse-grained parents. These finer-grained, dependent-data subcomponents can be implemented as Java classes.

Data components apply the Aggregate Entity pattern. This pattern uses an aggregate entity bean to model, represent, and manage a set of interrelated persistent objects rather than representing them as individual fine-grained entity beans [Larman 00]. An aggregate entity bean consists of a tree of objects.

For example, an invoice can be represented as a coarse-grained entity bean. The lines in the invoice are dependent objects. This representation avoids the problems that emerge when the entity bean schema matches the relational schema. To use the same invoice example, this would mean defining a separate entity bean for each invoice header and for each line in the invoice. Examples of problems that could emerge include

- Excessive communication overhead between the coarse-grained entity bean and the dependent entity beans
- Significant overhead resulting from the presence of a large number of entity beans
- Overhead resulting from fine-grained management for fine-grained components, especially in bean creation
- Overhead resulting from numerous, dynamically established connections between entity beans
- Added development complexity resulting from distributed debugging

Figure 12-6 shows the Aggregate Entity pattern, in which entity beans represent independent objects with associated sets of dependent objects, or subcomponents, thus providing a coarse-grained, entity bean schema. The Aggregate Entity pattern states:

> In general, an entity bean should represent an independent business object that has an independent identity and life cycle, and is referenced by multiple enterprise beans and/or clients. A dependent object should not be implemented as an entity bean. Instead, a dependent object is better implemented as a Java class (or several classes) and included as part of the entity bean on which it depends [Harpner 99, p. 99].

This form of aggregation requires access to subcomponents always to be performed through the entity bean. One way to reduce the overhead of having to go through the entity bean is to have *group operations*. In Figure 12-6, for example, Entity Bean 1 could have a method `SetSubentity1( … )` that sets all the attributes in Subentity 1 without having to call an individual set method for every attribute.

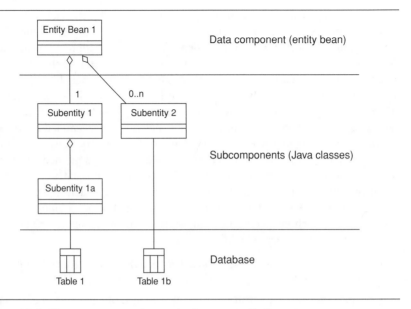

Figure 12-6 Data component internals: Aggregate Entity pattern

Elements identified as data components have common qualities. In particular, they

- Are referenced by more than one component or client
- Have an independent life cycle that is not bound or managed by the life cycle of another element
- Require a unique identity
- Provide complex behavior beyond simply getting and setting field values
- Usually have dependent objects—ones that have no real domain meaning when standing alone

WRAPPER COMPONENTS

A wrapper component is an adapter that allows a service component to communicate with an external system that does not have a BSR interface. Figure 12-7 illustrates how to use BSR-to-API and API-to-API wrappers. Use a BSR-to-API wrapper to communicate with an external legacy system that may eventually become a business object of its own. Use an API-to-Native-API wrapper when a component communicates with an external legacy system that is accessed only by components in the same business object or that will eventually become a part of the same business object when modernized.

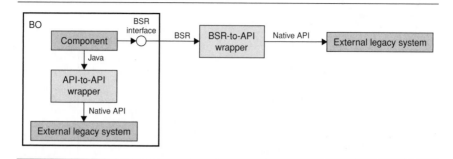

Figure 12-7   Types of wrapper components

BSR INTERFACE

The BSR interface provides service for communication between business objects. This interface can be constructed using a layered architecture:

- An *interface* layer, which receives information in an OAGIS XML BOD from the messaging system.

- An *interpreter* layer, which interprets the message content. This layer includes an XML parser. Business objects interface with the interpreter to send and receive information.

- An *application* layer, which provides the core application functionality: the business objects.

The BSR interface package must receive BSRs, parse the BODs contained in the BSRs, and translate the BODs into calls to service components. The BSR interface package also must generate BODs and send BSRs when requested from a service component or as a confirmation/reply to a BSR.

Figure 12-8 shows the parts of a BSR interface:

- **BSR interpreter.** The BSR interpreter receives XML messages, parses them, and generates the appropriate calls to the service components inside the business object.

- **BSR constructor.** The BSR constructor receives requests from service components to construct BSRs to send to external systems. The BSR constructor is also called from the BSR interpreter if the incoming BSR requires another BSR to be generated as a confirmation or reply.

- **XML parser.** XML parsers are available from several sources, as discussed in Section 7.5.

- **Data type definition (DTD) or XML schema repository.** The DTD/ schema repository contains the DTDs or schemas for all the BODs defined by the OAGIS, as well as user-defined BODs. This repository can reside in the database or on any file system.

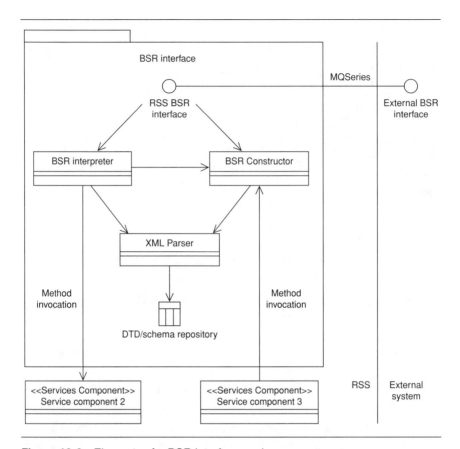

Figure 12-8 Elements of a BSR interface package

Figure 12-9 illustrates the operations that take place when the BSR interface receives a BSR.

1. The external BSR interface sends a BSR over MQSeries to the RSS BSR interface.

2. The RSS BSR interface invokes the BSR interpreter that knows how to handle the incoming BSR.

3. The BSR interpreter invokes the XML parser to extract the information from the BOD associated with the incoming BSR.

4. The XML parser obtains the DTD/schema from the DTD/schema repository.

5. The BSR interpreter invokes the service component that knows how to process the incoming BSR and passes it the information that was extracted from the BOD.

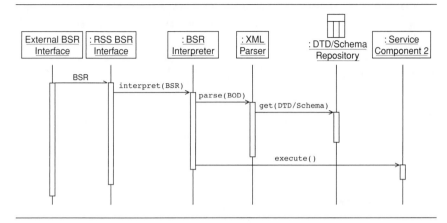

Figure 12-9   Processing an incoming BSR

Figure 12-10 shows the operations that take place when a service component invokes the service of a BSR interface.

1. An RSS service component that needs to communicate with an external system sends a request for BSR construction to the BSR constructor.

2. The BSR constructor invokes the XML parser to construct the BOD to be sent in the BSR.

3. The XML parser obtains the DTD/schema from the DTD/schema repository.

4. The BSR constructor requests the RSS BSR interface to send the BSR to the external system.

5. The RSS BSR interface sends the BSR to the external BSR interface.

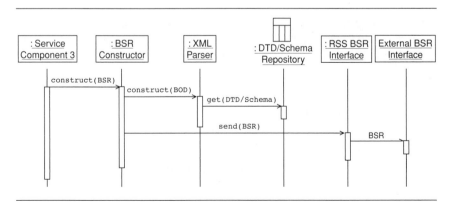

Figure 12-10   Processing an outgoing BSR

If a BSR is required as a reply to an incoming BSR, the BSR interpreter requests the services of the BSR constructor, and the operations in steps 2 through 5 take place.

The BSR interface receives incoming messages from MQSeries and sends the BSRs to the interpreter. The BSR interface also accepts outgoing BSRs and sends them to the MQSeries queue of the intended recipient system.

Alternatively, the BSR constructor can communicate with the external BSR directly. The problem with this approach is that two components must now interact directly with MQSeries instead of isolating this interface to a single component.

12.4 Architectural Patterns

Architectural patterns are templates that represent generic functions required by the system. Patterns can be used as a guide by component developers. This section describes some patterns that can be applied in developing an enterprise information system: data access within the system, business object, data access involving an external system, report, ad hoc query, batch roll-up, continuously updated roll-up, transaction, and data warehouses.

Each architectural pattern describes the motivation for using the pattern, as well as a UML sequence diagram accompanied by a step-by-step explanation of the component interactions defined by the pattern.

DATA ACCESS WITHIN THE SYSTEM

Motivation. This pattern is used when an operation accesses data that is fully contained within the system. This pattern should not be used if the operation communicates with an external system using BSRs.

Interaction Sequence. Figure 12-11 shows the sequence of operations for accessing data from a single data component. An operation requiring access to multiple tables would include calls to other data components that have access to the tables.

The sequence of operations for data access within the system is as follows.

1. The GUI confirms the operation to the session manager.

2. The session manager invokes the service component that performs the operation.

3. The service component communicates with the data component that has access to the data.

4. The data component executes the SQL command to select the data.

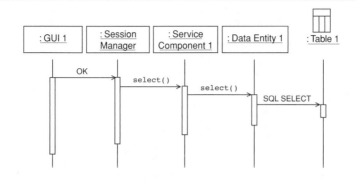

Figure 12-11   Data access within the system

DATA ACCESS INVOLVING AN EXTERNAL SYSTEM

Motivation.   This pattern is used when an operation accesses data that is not fully contained within the system. In this case, access to an external system is needed to complete the operation. This pattern assumes that the BSR that returns the data requested by the system exists. If not, a BSR for this purpose must be defined.

Interaction Sequence.   Figure 12-12 shows the sequence of operations for a simple example that communicates with an external system. An operation requiring access to multiple tables would include calls to other data components that have access to the tables.

The sequence of interactions for an access operation involving an external system is as follows:

1. The GUI confirms the operation to the session manager.

2. The session manager invokes the service component that performs the operation.

3. The service component communicates with the data component that has access to the data.

4. The data component executes the SQL command to obtain the data.

5. Because it has to obtain data from another system, the service component sends a request to the BSR interface.

6. The BSR interface constructs a BSR and sends it to the BSR interface of the external system.

7. The BSR interface of the external system invokes the component that performs the operation.

8. The external components obtain the necessary data.

9. The external BSR interface constructs a BSR with the obtained data and sends it to the RSS BSR interface.

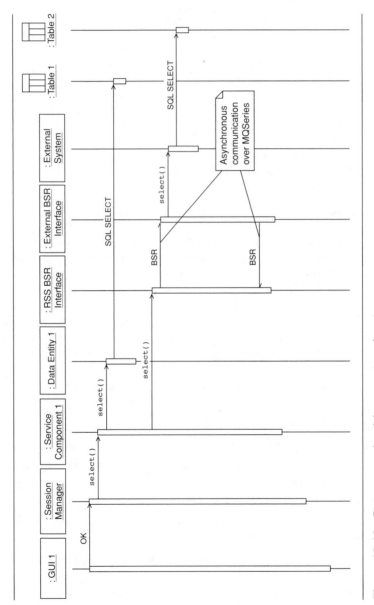

Figure 12-12 Data access involving an external system

208

REPORT

Motivation.   A report is a formatted and organized presentation of data. The report pattern is used when a report must be produced in the system. The output for a report can be printed on paper, written to a file, or sent to an external system. It can be generated from the application component or as part of an operation in a service component.

The report is an exception to the rule of always going through business objects to access data, because SQL is recognized as the best way to handle reports. An example of this is the J2EE Fast-Lane Reader pattern, which states:

> The Fast-Lane Reader pattern can accelerate the retrieval of large lists of items from a resource. Instead of going through an enterprise bean, an application accesses data more directly by going through a data access object. This way, the application avoids the overhead associated with using enterprise beans (remote method invocation, transaction management, data serialization, etc.). [J2EE 01b]

Reports use the JDBC-based reporting layer to access data used only for display, because, in this case, transactional support is unnecessary. (When the application needs to update the database transactionally, it uses enterprise beans.)

Another option for reports is stored procedures in the database. These procedures can be written in SQL as either PL/SQL-stored procedures or Java-stored procedures.[2] However, this option makes the reports database dependent. If the database changes, all the procedures stored in the database must be ported to the new database. Additionally, even though most databases support standard SQL, some have enhancements or additional features that, for example, work only for that particular database and can be used only inside PL/SQL. If this is the case, the procedures will not work when ported to the new database. Another potential problem is that the new database may not support Java-stored procedures.

Interaction Sequence from an Application Component.   The sequence of operations for a report executed from an application component is shown in Figure 12-13. The report output is not represented in the sequence diagram but should be defined in the report.

The sequence of interactions for a report executed from an application component is as follows.

1. The GUI confirms the operation to the session manager.

2. The session manager invokes the report script.

3. The report script invokes the Java program, which uses JDBC to access the database, for the report in the reporting layer.

4. The reporting layer obtains the information from the tables in the database.

---

[2] These are the options for writing stored procedures in Oracle. Other databases may have other options.

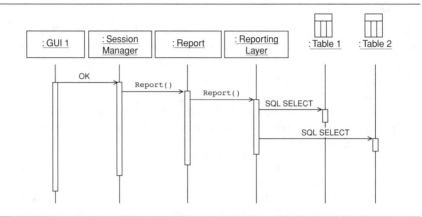

Figure 12-13 Sequence diagram for a report executed from an application component

Interaction Sequence from a Service Component. The sequence of operations for a report executed from a service component is shown in Figure 12-14. The report output is not represented in the sequence diagram but should be defined in the report.

The sequence of interactions for a report executed from a service component is as follows.

1. The GUI confirms the operation to the session manager.

2. The session manager invokes the service component that performs the operation.

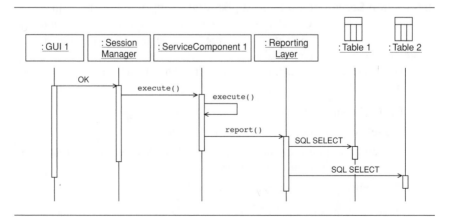

Figure 12-14 Sequence diagram for a report executed from a service component

3. The service component executes the operation.

4. The service component invokes the Java program, which uses JDBC to access the database, for the report in the reporting layer.

5. The reporting layer obtains the information from the tables in the database.

AD HOC QUERY

Motivation.   This pattern is used to obtain information from the database when no predefined report or operation returns the data in the desired form. Ad hoc queries are also an exception to the constraint of going through business objects to access data.

Interaction Sequence.   Figure 12-15 shows the sequence of operations for an ad hoc query using a generic query-builder tool. Another option for entering ad hoc queries is to use SQL directly.

The sequence of interactions for an ad hoc query is as follows.

1. The GUI confirms the query to the session manager.

2. The session manager invokes the generic query builder.

3. The generic query builder sends the user query to the SQL engine.

4. The SQL engine retrieves the results from the tables in the database.

ROLL-UPS

Roll-ups are persistent reports (summaries) that require consolidating data from one or more tables, potentially located on different machines or different locations.

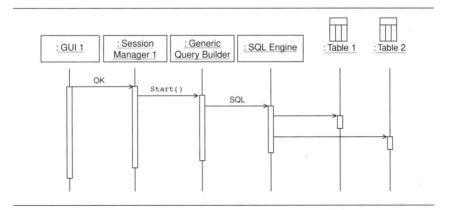

Figure 12-15   Sequence diagram for an ad hoc query

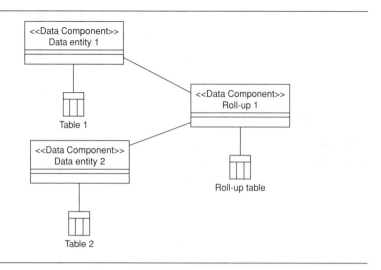

Figure 12-16   Roll-up data component

There are two types of roll-ups. *On-the-fly* roll-ups are generated as needed from the operational data and can be treated as reports. *Persistent* roll-ups are incrementally updated so that the information can be quickly provided when required. Persistent roll-ups use tables to synchronize roll-up data with operational data. Roll-up tables have an associated data component, shown in Figure 12-16, located inside a business object. The roll-up tables are either batch updated or continuously updated, but the actual roll-up generation is a report and is treated as such.

BATCH ROLL-UP

Motivation.   The batch roll-up pattern is used when an operation requires data to be extracted from different sources and consolidated in a persistent table that does not need to be immediately synchronized with the tables from which it obtains its data. A procedure is executed on demand to synchronize the roll-up table with its related tables.

Interaction Sequence.   Figure 12-17 shows a sequence diagram for a roll-up table that needs to synchronize with one other table. If the number of related tables is greater, a SELECT operation has to be performed against each of the tables to obtain the necessary data.

The sequence of interactions during on-line transaction processing—day-to-day operations—is as follows.

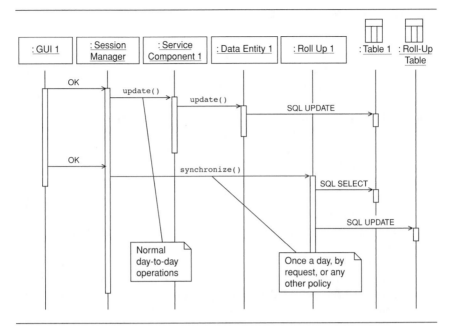

Figure 12-17   Sequence diagram for a batch roll-up

1. The GUI confirms the operation to the session manager.

2. The session manager invokes the service component for the operation.

3. The service component communicates with the data component that has access to the data.

4. The data entity executes the necessary SQL command to update the data.

   The sequence of operations during synchronization once a day, by request, or any other policy is as follows.

1. The GUI confirms the operation to the session manager.

2. The session manager sends a synchronization request to the roll-up data component.[3]

3. The roll-up data component obtains the necessary data from the table associated with the roll-up table.

4. The roll-up data component updates the roll-up table.

---

[3] This is an exception to the rule of going through a service component to access a data component. It is not necessary to create a service component, because this is a simple batch synchronization operation on the data.

CONTINUOUSLY UPDATED ROLL-UP

Motivation. This pattern is used when an operation requires data to be extracted from different sources and consolidated in a persistent table that must be immediately synchronized with the tables from which it obtains its data. In a continuously updated roll-up, the roll-up table must be updated every time any of its associated tables is updated. This operation is based on the Subject-Observer pattern [Gamma 95]. In this case, the roll-up table acts as the *observer* by registering an interest in knowing when its associated tables have been updated. The associated tables are the *subject*. After this, every time an update occurs, the roll-up table is notified.

Interaction Sequence. Figure 12-18 shows a sequence diagram for a roll-up table that synchronizes with one table. If the number of related tables is greater, a select operation has to be performed against each of the tables to obtain the necessary data.

Only once, the roll-up data component registers an interest in changes made to Table 1 by sending a registration message to the data component associated with the table. During normal day-to-day operations, the sequence of operations is as follows.

1. The GUI confirms the operation to the session manager.

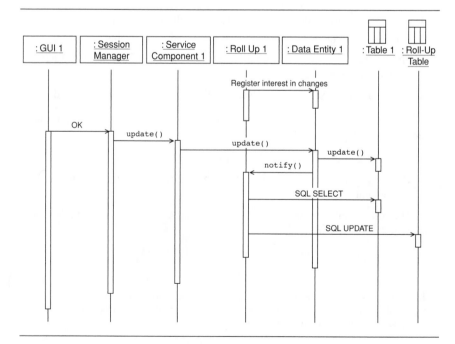

Figure 12-18 Continuously updated roll-up

2. The session manager invokes the service component for the operation.

3. The service component communicates with the data component that has access to the data.

4. The data component executes the necessary SQL command to update the data.

5. The data component notifies the roll-up data component that there has been an update.

6. The roll-up data component obtains the necessary data from the table associated with the roll-up table.

7. The roll-up data component updates the roll-up table.

The operations that take place after the notification can be considered part of the transaction or can be executed outside of the transaction if the response time is inadequate.

TRANSACTIONS

Motivation. This pattern is used when an operation updates data that is entirely contained within the system. Transactions that span to external systems are not covered in this pattern, because transaction context cannot be maintained when component interactions rely on MQSeries.[4] Also, because of the asynchronous nature of message-based communication, the time required to perform the transaction across components can vary.

A transaction is an *atomic* operation that follows the ACID properties for transaction-processing systems (see Section 8.3). A transaction involves two or more operations on the database, where either all or none of the operations are done. An operation to commit to keep changes (or a rollback operation to remove changes) ends a transaction.

Interaction Sequence. Figure 12-19 shows a sequence diagram for a transaction that updates multiple tables as part of the same transaction. The number of tables updated as part of the transaction is irrelevant, as the EJB framework manages all updates within the same transaction context.

The sequence of interactions for a transaction is as follows.

1. The GUI confirms the operation to the session manager.

2. The session manager invokes the service component that performs the operation.

3. The EJB framework creates a transaction context.

[4] This rule does not apply when the business objects are running on the same platform or LAN and are coupled using J2EE transactional method invocation instead of asynchronous message passing.

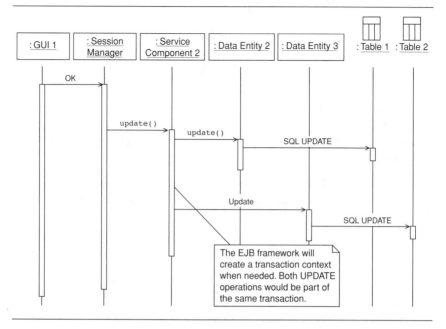

Figure 12-19   Transaction

4. The service component communicates with the first data component partici-pating in the transaction.

5. The first data component executes the necessary SQL command to update the data.

6. The service component communicates with the second data component par-ticipating in the transaction.

7. The second data component executes the necessary SQL command to update the data.

8. The EJB framework commits or rolls back the transaction.

DATA WAREHOUSES

This pattern is used to interface to data warehouses and data marts. Because data marts are usually subsets of data warehouses, the data warehouses communicate with the operational database, and then the data marts populate themselves from data in the data warehouse. This pattern depends on the specific tool that is used for data warehouse population.

Data warehouses can be populated using either a pull or a push mechanism. With a *pull mechanism*, the data warehouse–population application pulls the data from the operational database either by request or through automated update procedures. In this case, an interface to the operational database has to be implemented. With a *push mechanism*, the operational database pushes data to the data warehouse either by request or through automated update procedures. In this case, an interface to the data warehouse–population application has to be implemented.

Motivation.   If a pull mechanism is implemented, the functionality for data warehouse population resides in a third-party data warehouse–population tool. This tool can be treated as a business object, with population operations using BSRs if the tool has a BSR-based communication interface. The tool can also be treated as an application-specific component, with population operations using the reporting layer.

Interaction Sequence using BSRs.   The pull option for data warehouse population using BSRs is shown in Figure 12-20. The population interactions that take place inside the business objects are omitted in the pull option for data warehouse population using BSRs. The sequence of steps in this option is as follows.

1. The data warehouse–population application communicates with its BSR interface to request a population operation.

2. The BSR interface constructs a BSR and sends it to the RSS BSR interface.

3. Components inside the RSS obtain the information and use the RSS BSR interface to construct a BSR that sends the requested information to the data warehouse–population application.

4. The data warehouse–population application populates the data warehouse with the obtained data.

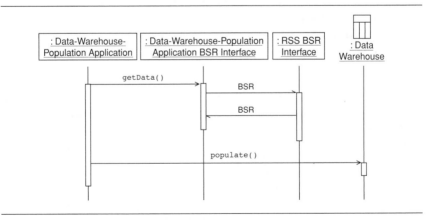

Figure 12-20   Pull option for data warehouse population using BSRs

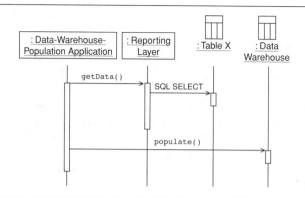

Figure 12-21 Pull option for data warehouse population using the reporting layer

Interaction Sequence Using the Reporting Layer. The pull option for data warehouse population using the reporting layer is shown in Figure 12-21. The sequence of steps in the pull option for data warehouse population using the reporting layer is as follows.

1. The data warehouse–population application communicates with the reporting layer to obtain the data.

2. The reporting layer performs the necessary SQL SELECT operations to obtain the data.

3. The data warehouse–population application populates the data warehouse with the obtained data.

Motivation. If a push mechanism is implemented, the functionality for data warehouse population resides within the system. As in the previous option, if the tool has a BSR-based communication interface, communication can take place through BSRs. If this is not a possibility, an adapter for communication with the tool should be implemented as a wrapper component.

Interaction Sequence Using the BSRs. Figure 12-22 shows the push option for data warehouse population using BSRs. The operations that take place inside the business objects are omitted in the push option for data warehouse population using BSRs. The sequence of steps in this option is as follows.

1. RSS uses its BSR interface to construct a BSR that sends information to the data warehouse–population application.

2. The data warehouse–population application BSR interface sends the data warehouse–population application the incoming data.

3. The data warehouse–population application populates the data warehouse with the incoming data.

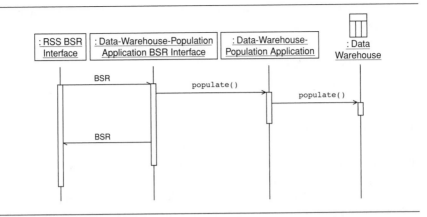

Figure 12-22   Push option for data warehouse population using BSRs

4. (Optional) The data warehouse–population application BSR interface constructs a confirmation BSR and sends it back to the RSS BSR interface.

Interaction Sequence Using a Wrapper Component.   Figure 12-23 shows
the push option for data warehouse population using a wrapper component. The
operations that obtain the data from the data components in the push option for
data warehouse population using a wrapper component are omitted. The
sequence of steps in this option is as follows.

1. A service component sends a request to a wrapper component to populate
   the data warehouse. Data obtained from the operational database is attached
   to this request.

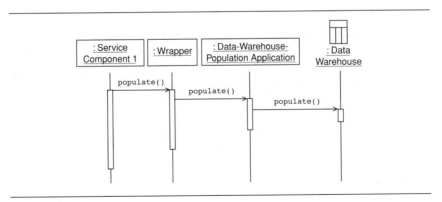

Figure 12-23   Push option for data warehouse population using a wrapper
component

2. The wrapper component sends the request and data to the data warehouse–population application.

3. The data warehouse–population application populates the data warehouse with the incoming data.

12.5 Summary

The target architecture in this phase of the modernization planning process is a high-level design that cannot always anticipate and accommodate all implementation details. Some details may impose demands that conflict with the architecture. In these cases, it may be necessary to either reevaluate the architecture or determine what can be done to accommodate the additional demands.

The architectural patterns included in this chapter provide templates to create an architecture for a system based on the J2EE platform for business objects and XML Messaging, based on OAGIS, for communication between systems. The information in this chapter can also be used to identify and resolve potential design risks resulting from inconsistent or contradictory requirements.

Applying these architectural patterns should result in a system with the following characteristics:

- Fulfillment of the data requirements
- Capability of communication with other systems through a BSR interface
- Compliance with the given technical requirements
- Decoupling of data components from data representation
- Conservation of ACID properties for transactions provided by the EJB framework
- Use of J2EE design patterns representing best practices

As always, sound engineering judgment should be used in applying the architectural patterns included in this chapter, because it is difficult, if not impossible, to predict all possible scenarios. This architecture should be maintained and updated to reflect lessons learned during early iterations of the development process.

13

Architecture Transformation

> *By three methods we may learn wisdom: First by reflection, which is the noblest; second by imitation, which is the easiest; and third, by experience, which is the bitterest.*
> —Confucius, *Analects*, 16.9

Now that we understand both the legacy and target architectures, we can develop an architectural transformation strategy: How do we get there from here? In our case study, we refer to this architectural transformation as "componentization"; we are moving from a largely unstructured legacy system to a modern, component-based architecture. Architectural transformation is a principal goal of the RSS modernization effort. The existing architecture—or lack thereof—is considered to be a major cause of the lack of maintainability in the existing system. Therefore, the ability of each transformation strategy to achieve the as-desired architecture is a critical consideration.

Of course, the architectural transformation strategy in our case study is further complicated in that it must take place within the context of an incremental development and deployment strategy. Carving up the legacy system into "chunks" that can be incrementally developed and deployed makes it challenging to achieve the as-desired architecture. This initial "chunking" of the system is, in effect, the initial architectural decomposition of the system. This means that the as-desired architecture is influenced, or constrained, by the legacy architecture and that our ability to transform the architecture is localized to the boundaries of each chunk. As the use of adapters can play a major role in addressing this issue, we begin this chapter by examining the development and use of data and logic adapters in legacy system modernization before discussing the overall transformation strategies.

13.1 Where Are We?

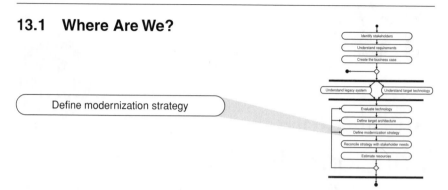

In the preceding chapters, we defined a target modernization architecture. The next step is to create a modernization strategy, using available technologies, that gets us from where we are today to the modern architecture.

13.2 Data Adapters

Data adapters are required when the data and code are migrated simultaneously. These adapters synchronize data between the modernized and legacy databases during incremental data migration. Data adapters provide the mapping between a legacy database schema and a modernized database schema, as shown in Figure 13-1.

DATA REPLICATION

Data replication is the process of copying and maintaining database tables in multiple databases. Replication provides users with fast, local access to shared data and greater availability to applications because alternative options exist for data access. Even if one site becomes unavailable, users can continue to query, or even update, data at other locations. Changes applied at one site are captured and

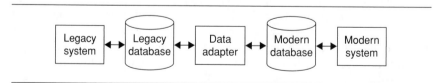

Figure 13-1 Generic data adapter

stored locally before being forwarded and applied to the master repository at another site.[1]

Data replication can also enable decentralized access to legacy data stored in mainframes. Local instances are replicated from portions of the centralized legacy database and are stored in a modern database. The local copy of the data wraps and buffers the original data source. Applications using the data obtain the benefits of local access to a modern database instead of remote access to an obsolete data repository.

Data replication, however, can have problems with data coupling—especially if local data sets overlap. Data elements may need to be updated by both legacy and modernized systems, for example, when the code accessing a particular data element cannot be migrated in a single increment. The following sections describe mechanisms for supporting data replication.

Scripts. Scripts provide a simple mechanism for synchronizing replicated data. Scripts transform data from one system to another according to a predefined mapping between data elements. Scripts are usually run in batch mode, periodically, or on demand. Scripts do not typically require significant changes to the application.

Scripts also have disadvantages. For example, it can be difficult to determine the most recent changes to the data when synchronizing databases updated by both systems. One solution is to timestamp the data so that the most recent update can be used. This solution may not work when data is updated using values that have already been replaced in the other system. Ozsu and Valduriez provide additional information on problems related to data replication [Ozsu 99].

Extraction, Transformation, and Loading (ETL). ETL tools extract data from a source database; transform the data into a suitable format, using rules or lookup tables or by creating combinations with other data; and then load the data into a target database that may or may not have previously existed. ETL tools may be stand-alone tools or act as middleware residing between a client and a database. Even though ETL tools are used mostly for data warehousing and data marts, they can also support data replication between legacy and modernized systems.

ETL has broad tool support and can be used in batch or on-the-fly mode. Some ETL tools also support bidirectional transfer, or data that moves from the legacy system to the modernized system and vice versa. ETL, however, can lead to inefficiencies because it is an additional component running on the system. In addition, ETL tools may not be available for all legacy platforms and may take considerable effort to master.

---

[1] We realize that data replication may exist without one repository acting as the master, or primary, copy. The challenge with styles of replication that do not use a master copy is often determining which repository contains the latest updates.

Database Triggers.   Database triggers are fragments of logic that execute within a database when specified conditions are established or events occur. Database triggers can be used to synchronize data between a legacy database and a modernized database. When used for synchronization, they are programmed as POST-UPDATE or POST-INSERT triggers associated with each replicated table. The logic inside the trigger propagates changes, synchronously or asynchronously, to the corresponding set of tables in the other system. These triggers can be programmed on the legacy database, on the modernized database, or on both databases.

An advantage of using database triggers for data synchronization is that data changes can be propagated on-the-fly, depending on the communication mechanism and infrastructure. Additionally, if it is programmed on the modernized database to update the legacy database, a database trigger can simply be disabled once the legacy database is migrated.

The disadvantage of database triggers is that they increase the workload of the DBMS. Also, mapping between the two databases might be complicated, especially if they have different structures—for example, if the legacy database is network and the modern database is relational.

The use of database triggers as data adapters is most effective when the legacy and modernized databases rely on the same database management system. In this case, the mapping rules are maintained in the database and not in an additional tool or layer, thereby improving efficiency. If the databases do not rely on the same DBMS, the triggers can be programmed to invoke either scripts or an ETL tool.

DATA-ACCESS LAYER

A data-access layer maps between data elements so that they appear in a prescribed format to the client application. For example, a data-access layer may make a network database appear as a relational database to a client program.

An advantage of a data-access layer is that the data remaining on the legacy system does not need to be replicated; all data-access operations are performed through the relational view of the legacy database. Although most data-access-layer tools provide read-only access, some can write to the legacy database.

A disadvantage is that a data-access layer provides two points of access to a single data element. As a result, it is necessary to serialize data access to guarantee data integrity.

A data-access layer should be used only as an interim solution during incremental modernization. Mapping from a hierarchical database to a relational database produces a design that is nonoptimal because of the underlying differences between the two database types (see Section 7.3).

DATABASE GATEWAY

A database gateway is a specific type of software gateway that translates between two or more data-access protocols [Altman 99]. Many vendor-specific protocols

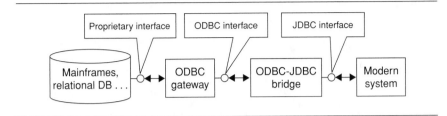

Figure 13-2   Gateways and bridges

are used to access databases. The de facto industry standards include ODBC, JDBC and ODMG; see Chapter 7 for additional information on these standards. A database gateway typically translates a vendor-specific access protocol into one of these de facto standards. Using a database gateway to access legacy data improves connectivity, enables remote access, and supports integrating legacy data with modern systems.

Given that there are multiple standards, the protocols supported by the legacy system database gateway and the protocols supported by the modernized system may not match. Figure 13-2, for example, shows a legacy system that uses an ODBC gateway, whereas the modern system requires a JDBC interface. One solution is a special gateway, called a bridge, that translates one standard protocol into another—in this case, a JDBC-ODBC bridge, also called a Type 1 JDBC driver; refer to Section 7.4 for a description of the various JDBC driver types.

HYBRIDS

Hybrid data adapters combine two or more of the data adaptation techniques described in this chapter to solve a data synchronization problem. One example of a hybrid solution is a data-access layer for read access and scripts for batch data synchronization. Another example is using database triggers to call an ETL tool to perform on-the-fly data synchronization.

COMPARISON

Table 13-1 summarizes the strengths and weaknesses of the data adaptation techniques presented in this section.

Table 13-1   Comparison of Data Adaptation Techniques

Technique	Result	Strengths	Weaknesses
Script	Provides data synchronization for replicated data	Simple to implement; doesn't require extensive changes	Difficult to maintain data cohesion in nontrivial cases

Table 13-1   Comparison of Data Adaptation Techniques *continued*

Technique	Result	Strengths	Weaknesses
ETL	Provides data synchro-nization for replicated data	Tool support	May lead to inefficien-cies; availability of tools; difficult to master
Database trigger	Provides data synchro-nization for replicated data	Not an additional com-ponent in the system; eases legacy system turn-off	Loads the DBMS with additional work; difficult to implement
Data-access layer	Makes a legacy data source appear in a prescribed format	Data does not need to be replicated	Inefficient; dual-access points
Database gateway	Translates a propri-etary access protocol to a standard access protocol	Low cost/tool support	Limited impact on maintainability

13.3   Logic Adapters

Logic, or functional, adapters encapsulate not only legacy data but also the business logic in the legacy system. Wrappers are a form of logic adapter that can be used to encapsulate legacy logic within a modern interface. The logic-wrapping techniques described in this section can access legacy data, if required, in addition to legacy logic.

OBJECT-ORIENTED WRAPPING

The conceptual model of object-oriented wrapping is deceptively simple: Individual applications, common services, and business data are all represented as objects. In reality, object-oriented wrapping goes beyond simply requiring analysis, decomposition, and OO abstraction. The encapsulation, reengineering, and coexistence of object with legacy (ERCOLE) project describes an exemplifying process to wrap legacy applications with OO systems [De Lucia 97]. Of the multiple difficulties involved in wrapping a legacy system, two are of special relevance: the definition of appropriate object-level interfaces and the need for integrated infrastructure services.

Translating the monolithic and plain semantics of the legacy system to an object-oriented system can be a difficult task. A good knowledge of the domain can greatly help. For example, Stets describes an experience in which the Win32 API is translated into objects, using specific knowledge of the structure of the operating system [Stets 99]. Unfortunately, developers wrapping a system rarely have such deep domain knowledge. Some techniques have been developed to streamline the legacy-to-OO mapping. In one such method, every coarse-grained persistent item is mapped to an object, and services are assigned to objects with an algorithm that minimizes coupling [Cimitile 97]. Although these and other techniques are useful in extracting objects from legacy systems, the mapping problem is far from being solved.

COMPONENT WRAPPING

Component wrapping is similar to OO wrapping, but components, unlike objects, must conform to a component model. Although there are several commercially viable component models, we focus here on developing logic wrappers using EJB, because this is the prevalent component model used in our case study (see Section 9.2 for more information on EJB).

The first step in wrapping a legacy system using EJB is to separate the legacy system into logical units—shown in Figure 13-3 as function 1 and function 2. The difficulty of dividing the legacy system into discrete functions depends on how the separation was defined in the legacy system interfaces and whether new interfaces must be built. Although a black-box approach is preferable, it still may be necessary to peer into the black box to truly understand the legacy system [Plakosh 99].

The next step in wrapping the legacy business logic is building a *single point of contact* to the legacy system. It is a good idea to centralize all the communication knowledge in a single software artifact. The communication method used will depend on the particular situation. Options include RMI-IIOP, sockets, or even MOM. This has the advantage of uncoupling the EJB server from the legacy system and allowing asynchronous communication. This single point of contact can be implemented internally as a bean—the adapter in Figure 13-3—or externally as a *service broker*—a software component outside the EJB server. The differences depend mainly on the communication method and security restrictions. For example, to create a new thread or to listen to a socket, the single point of contact must be outside the application server because the EJB specification prevents EJBs from being multithreaded or listening to sockets.

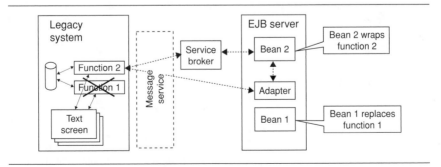

Figure 13-3 Wrapping legacy business logic using EJBs

The final step in wrapping the legacy business logic is implementing a wrapper bean for each module in the legacy system. In Figure 13-3, this wrapper is shown as Bean 2. These enterprise beans forward requests to the legacy system, using the single contact point, in a manner similar to object wrapping.

This component approach has several advantages. First, the benefits of component-based systems can be supported with relatively limited effort. We can, for example, build new EJBs that use the wrapper beans in unanticipated ways, greatly improving system flexibility. Second, wrapper beans are bona fide enterprise beans and therefore can be fully integrated with all the management facilities and services included with the application server. Finally, wrapping legacy business logic provides a road map to substitute the old system incrementally. After wrapping the functionality of the legacy system, we can reimplement wrapper beans one at a time—Bean 1 in Figure 13-3. The system and the clients will not notice any disruption, because the reimplemented bean will maintain the same interfaces provided by the wrapper bean. In time, it is possible to replace the old system completely.

Wrapping legacy business logic with EJBs is not without risk. The EJB specification is porous, and portability problems can arise among vendors' application servers [Comella-Dorda 00]. In addition, the Java programming language may be unsuitable for performance-critical or real-time applications.[2]

Another issue involves providing services for deployed components. A wrapper bean represents business logic in an external legacy system. A mechanism is needed to manage services across the legacy system and the EJB server. This mechanism, called a *connector,* represents a Java solution to the problem of providing connectivity between the many application servers and EISs already in existence [Sharma 02]. Many application servers, including BEA's WebLogic and IBM's WebSphere, support the J2EE Connector Architecture (JCA) adapters for enterprise connectivity. Using JCA to access an enterprise information system is akin to using JDBC to access a database.

Connectors, shown in Figure 13-4, manage transactions, security, and resource pooling between the server and the legacy resource. This architecture allows the development of a standard connector to access a legacy data source or system. The connector can be plugged into any application server that supports the connector mechanism. It is, of course, still necessary to implement application-level communication.

COMPARISON

Table 13-2 contrasts the two logic adaptation techniques described in this section.

---

[2] The Real-Time Specification for Java (RTSJ) is maturing, to the point that it can be applied to certain types of real-time applications [Corsaro 02].

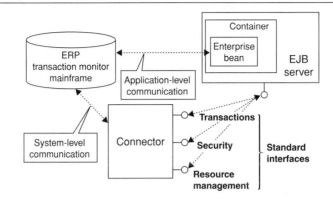

Figure 13-4   Integrating legacy business logic using connectors

Table 13-2   Comparison of Logic Adaptation Techniques

Technique	Result	Strengths	Weaknesses
OO wrapping	OO model	Flexibility	Difficult to implement
Component wrapping	Component model	Flexibility; integrated services	Labor intensive

13.4   Architecture Transformation Strategy

Now that we have examined both logic and data adapters, we can consider an architectural transformation strategy. One method for creating this strategy is to form it around a set of answers to key issues in the modernization project. Here, we develop a strategy based on the answers to the following questions.

- How will the code be migrated?
- When will the data be migrated relative to the code migration?
- Do we need to support parallel operations?

Table 13-3 lists potential answers to each of these questions. Selecting an answer to each question forms the basis for a componentization strategy. Of course, the answers to these questions must be considered collectively because certain groups of answers have more cohesion than others. The following sections describe these questions in more detail and examine the characteristics of each potential answer. We discuss the combined effects in Section 13.5.

Table 13-3   Incremental Deployment Options

Issues	Options
Code migration	A1 Based on user transactions
	A2 Based on related functionality
Data migration	B1 Before code migration
	B2 During code migration
	B3 After code migration
Deployment	C1 Deploy each increment in parallel with the legacy system
	C2 Deploy each increment as the operational system

CODE MIGRATION

Code can be split and migrated in many ways. One approach is to extract a functional thread from a program element or elements. This can be difficult to implement in practice because it requires a white-box approach. Program elements must be "opened up" and significantly modified. If the existing system is being modernized because it is fragile and difficult to maintain, as is the case with RSS, this approach may not be viable.

The remaining possibility is to migrate sets of "whole" program elements, using a black-box approach. Successfully migrating legacy code based on program element sets requires linking remaining legacy program elements to modernized logic functionality without compromising the overall functionality of the system. In the RSS example, program elements can be split across business objects, and business objects can be deployed while still incomplete—as long as the overall functionality of the system remains intact. This approach supports architectural transformation but may require some rework of business objects as the system evolves.

Figure 13-5 illustrates code migration by program element sets. A legacy component (121) is scheduled for modernization. On the right, functionality performed by 121 is reimplemented as part of the modernized architecture. However, the 121 component is still invoked by the 345 program element and invokes the 129 component element, neither of which has been modernized. In this case, it is necessary to develop a shell and an adapter for the 121 program. The shell maintains the external interfaces of the 121 program element. The adapter accepts requests from the 121 shell and invokes methods in the modernized components to implement this functionality. Results can then be returned to the 121 shell, which will use this data to satisfy its external requirements before calling program element 129.

In the remainder of this section, we consider two approaches for selecting program elements for migration in a given increment. The first approach is to select program elements based on user transactions; the second is to select program elements implementing related functionality.

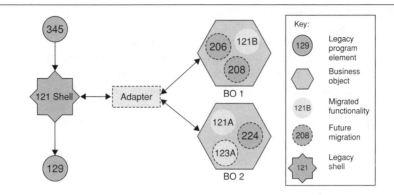

Figure 13-5   Code migration by program element sets

User Transactions.   User transactions—user or external system requests that result in the execution of a series of program elements—can be used to identify functionality to be migrated to the modern system. As each user transaction is modernized, it is turned off in the legacy system and redirected to the modern system. A top-level GUI/routing program determines whether user transactions should be invoked in the modern system or the legacy system.

User transactions can also be used as input in both static and dynamic analysis techniques. Trace programs can identify program elements invoked during the execution of a given user transaction. However, tracing program execution does not guarantee that all the program elements that *may* be invoked during execution of the user transaction have been identified, particularly with respect to exception handling. Not only do these programs need to be identified, but also any reachable program elements must be migrated. Reachable program elements are program elements that can be called, either directly or indirectly, by a program element in the user transaction.

Migrating program elements based on user transaction sets has the advantage that complete use cases can be migrated and executed on the modern platform. The disadvantage is that it can force the migration of large amounts of functionality in one increment. If suitably sized increments cannot be found, it will be impossible to build the system within the incremental development and deployment paradigm. Also, migrating large amounts of functionality in a single increment, particularly an early increment, reduces the opportunity to refine the target architecture based on lessons learned.

To successfully migrate the code based on user transactions, most of the transactions must be fully executable within a small set of program elements. If the majority of transactions require a large number of program elements, it will be impossible to find suitably sized increments.

Related Functionality. Program elements that implement related functionality can also be selected for migration in the same increment. In theory, these program elements demonstrate greater cohesion than those that execute as part of user transactions. Groups of functionally related program elements should correspond more directly with business objects in the target architecture, making it easier to complete business objects in each increment. Also, working in a related functional area makes it easier for developers to understand the requirements for that area and to develop appropriate designs. The major problem with this approach is identifying program elements that implement related functionality. Some methods for accomplishing this are described in Chapter 15.

DATA MIGRATION

The second question to consider when selecting a componentization strategy is when to modernize the database and migrate the data. Like other aspects of the legacy system, the database schema has evolved over time and not necessarily in an optimal fashion. One of the goals of the componentization effort is to improve the representation of data in the database. This, in turn, will eliminate redundancy, improve performance, reduce storage requirements, and reduce the potential for database anomalies.

In general, there are no guarantees about the mapping between the legacy and modernized databases. Some existing database tables may be split up; others may be grouped. New database tables will be created and existing tables eliminated. This may result in a complex relationship between database fields in the legacy and modernized systems.

There are three options for data migration: *before*, *during*, and *after* the code migration. Regardless of which strategy is adopted, when migrating from a network, or hierarchical, to a relational model, the database will most likely pass through a series of states, as shown in Figure 13-6. In RSS, for example, the data is initially stored in a network database (DMS). The first step is to migrate this data to an equivalent relational form. This translation requires modifying the structure of the data to compensate for the differences between relational and network database models. The next step is to replace the database schema that reflects the

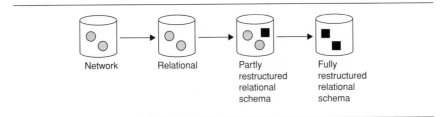

Network   Relational   Partly   Fully
                        restructured restructured
                        relational   relational
                        schema   schema

Figure 13-6   Database migration

structure of the legacy tables with a modernized database schema. Eventually, the entire database will be migrated to the modernized structure, as shown at the right in Figure 13-6.

Data Migration before Code Migration.   Migrating the data before the code has several advantages. It certainly simplifies the code migration. Modernized code can be developed to the target data architecture and does not need to be mapped to legacy data elements. Migrating the data first is also a focused effort with a single goal, so it is easier to accomplish. Finally, migrating the data first reduces the risk of retaining the legacy architecture, because the code migration will be based on the new database schema.

Unfortunately, this approach also has disadvantages. Migrating the data requires restructuring the legacy system to accommodate the modified tables or providing a reverse data adapter from the legacy to the modern database tables. This is a major concern if the legacy system is being modernized because of its lack of maintainability. In this case, restructuring the legacy code to support the new database schema can be extremely risky.

Another disadvantage is that migrating the data and restructuring the legacy code will consume considerable time and resources. As a result, it should be attempted only if the target database schema is well understood and architecturally sound. This is extremely difficult when dealing with a large, complex system that is being incrementally developed and deployed. The impossibility of designing an optimal database schema without understanding the associated business logic being modeled is accepted as a truism by most developers involved in these efforts.

Because a large up-front investment must be made to migrate the data, there is not much latitude for further refinement of the database schema. This often means that the project must choose between living with the initial assessment or overrunning budgets and schedules. Changing the database schema downstream requires changing the legacy system again and restructuring the modernized code. In general, this high-risk approach depends largely on "getting it right the first time." If you do not have a high degree of confidence in your understanding of the data requirements for the modernized system, this may not be the best approach.

Data Migration during Code Migration.   Perhaps the most direct and obvious approach is to migrate the data and code at the same time. Theoretically, this is the least expensive approach because it requires minimal rework. Unfortunately, migrating both the code and the data simultaneously expands the focus of each increment and increases the complexity of the effort. It is particularly difficult when data elements or logic cannot be easily untangled from the legacy system. This approach can quickly degrade into a big-bang deployment.

There are several techniques for combining data migration and code migration. One technique is to identify several database tables to be migrated. By starting with a small number of isolated tables, it may be possible to identify and migrate the program elements accessing these tables in a single increment while minimizing the amount of code that must be migrated. However, it is likely that these program elements will continue to reference the remaining legacy database tables, requiring the development of data adapters.

A second technique is to create new database tables in the modernized system and to use data adapters to maintain the data in a consistent state. To fully synchronize these databases, data adapters must be maintained in both directions. These data adapters are often difficult to develop and maintain. In addition to simply maintaining data consistency, the order in which data elements are updated may be critical to the proper operation of the system. It may also require significant knowledge of the business logic simply to get the data adapters to function properly.

Although both of these techniques are feasible, both introduce significant complexity, making this a high-risk approach. The major problem with data migration during code migration is data replication and synchronization, because transactional integrity and recovery is an issue. If both databases are updated in a distributed transaction, there may be a requirement to ensure that they stay strictly in step. Synchronization may require that two-phase commit be achieved through compensating transactions or be supported by other means, as explained in Chapter 8. In any case, it is a problem to be addressed, especially if the modernized and legacy systems are connected using MQSeries because two-phase commit cannot be used.

Data Migration after Code Migration.   Migrating the data after the code has some interesting advantages. For example, it provides additional time to refine the database schema. This approach requires constructing modernized components using the legacy database schema. This is possible using a persistence layer to map component state data to the persistent store. The modernized logic uses only component/object interfaces to access data elements, which is good software engineering practice, anyway. Implementing reports that directly access the database structure using the report pattern, described in Section 12.4, is a special case. Reports can be migrated after the database or go through a mapping layer as well.

Isolating dependencies on the legacy database to the persistence layer can simplify migrating the data after the code. However, code in the persistence layer will still require modification. This effort will involve replacing fairly complex code that maps state data to fields in one or more legacy database tables with calls that map component state data directly to modern database tables. The mapping between component state data and the database schema can be straightforward because the database schema can be designed to mirror the state data.

The persistence code that maps to the legacy database structure may be slow because it must emulate the modern data structure using the legacy system data structure. The good news is that performance will improve when the data migration is completed and the mapping layer removed.

DEPLOYMENT STRATEGY

Every time new functionality is deployed to the field, there is an operational risk that the system, including both modernized and legacy components, will not function properly. Deploying each increment in parallel with the modified operational legacy system can mitigate these risks. Alternatively, these risks may be acceptable when weighed against the additional costs and development risks of parallel operations and deploying each release directly to the field as an operational system. These options are analyzed in the following sections.

Parallel Operations.   Operational risk can be reduced by running the previous version of the system in parallel with the current release, as shown in Figure 13-7. In this approach, the modernized system is put into operation, but the legacy system is maintained as a "hot" backup. If the new system fails to function properly, control can be switched over to the legacy system. This solution provides a fallback capability that allows on-line verification and testing of the new increment.

Parallel operations provide additional benefits. Users of the system are able to perform a side-by-side comparison of the user interfaces of both the modern and legacy systems. This may help the user learn the new interface and identify places where it is deficient. Parallel operations can also aid in system verification by allowing users to enter similar or identical operations in both the modern and legacy systems to make sure that the results are the same or, in a defensible way, different.

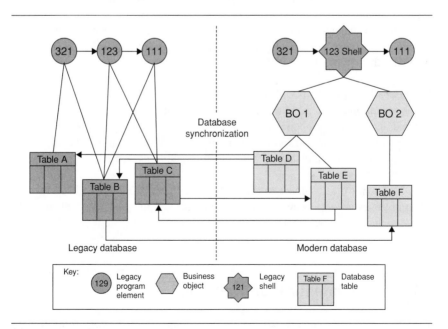

Figure 13-7   Parallel operations

For this to be feasible, the legacy system must have access to the latest data. Providing this access can be problematic because the format and structure of the database tables may have changed between incremental deployments, depending on the data migration strategy. This situation requires synchronization of the database, using one of the data replication techniques described earlier in this chapter.

Deploying in parallel can reduce operational risks, but care must be taken not to corrupt the legacy system while wiring the two systems together. Introducing complex trigger mechanisms, for example, could easily corrupt the legacy system. In general, changes to the legacy system should be minimal and nonpervasive. Another concern is that invoking procedures to synchronize multiple database tables after each update can affect performance. After the modernized system has been deployed, used, and validated, the legacy system and modernized system can be decoupled and the modernized system can run independently.

Although parallel operation can reduce operational risk, it can also increase development risk, degrade performance, and significantly increase maintenance costs. Difficulties may arise in data synchronization and locking between the modern and legacy systems. This can further increase development costs and affect the schedule.

When deploying in parallel, each incremental system release is deployed alongside the legacy system. Once the final release has been verified, the backup system can be stood down. This has several implications for the overall life cycle of the system. First, it will be necessary to maintain two separate databases from the first incremental deployment until the backup system is stood down. This will increase maintenance and support costs over the life of the project. Also, code and database changes will need to be removed from the completed system. Parallel operations make sense when system availability is critical and the risks associated with this approach are negligible or easily mitigated.

Non-Parallel Operation.   Another strategy is to deploy each increment as part of the operational system. In this approach, the deployed system consists of modernized and legacy components. Nonparallel deployments typically reduce cost and development time and force users to use the new system immediately, potentially increasing acceptance, without injecting additional technical and software development risks.

The major disadvantage to this strategy is that there is no fallback mechanism in the event of a system failure. Therefore, you must have complete confidence in the system before deploying it as the operational system.

13.5   Componentization Trail Maps

Each unique set of answers to the three architectural transformation strategy questions forms a *trail map*. A trail map describes a time-phased approach, consisting of up to three phases. Table 13-4 shows several sample trail maps. The

Table 13-4 Sample Trail Maps

Trail Map	Phase 1	Phase 2
A1-B3-C1	Componentization by user transactions (A1) Parallel operations (C1)	Data migration (B3) Parallel operations (C1)
A2-B2-C2	Componentization by related functionality (A2) Data migration (B2) Operational (C2)	
A2-B3-C2	Componentization by related functionality (A2) Operational (C2)	Data migration (B2) Operational (C2)

first trail map shows componentization by user transactions (A1) in the first phase, followed by the data migration in the second phase (B3). All increments are deployed in parallel with the operational system (C1). The second trail map is a big-bang approach whereby everything gets developed and deployed in one phase. Twelve trail maps are possible given the three independent variables.

Each trail map can be evaluated by cost, schedule, risk, and complexity. In any modernization effort, however, different stakeholders will have different opinions on the best way to proceed. It is important to develop consensus before moving forward.

To obtain that consensus in our case study, we held a componentization workshop to discuss the risks and benefits of each approach. After considering the ramifications of each trail map, the stakeholders agreed on the A2-B3-C2 trail map, in which the modernized components are developed based on related functionality, followed by the data migration. Parallel operations will not be used.

Once the architectural transformation strategy has been selected, it must be further developed. The code migration strategy must be refined by identifying the program elements to migrate in each increment, determining the number and types of adapters that must be developed, and revising the cost estimation accordingly. The data migration strategy must be refined by determining the number and type of data adapters, if necessary, and data migration procedures. This process is described in Chapter 15.

The fact that the RSS team selected this trail map does not mean that it is the only appropriate architectural transformation strategy. Each trail map, like each modernization effort, has its own unique characteristics.

13.6   Use of Adapters in RSS

At the beginning of this chapter, we discussed both data and logic adapters. The architectural transformation strategy selected for RSS requires the development of logic adapters to redirect calls to legacy program elements to the replacement logic implemented as EJBs in the modernized system. Figure 13-8 illustrates the

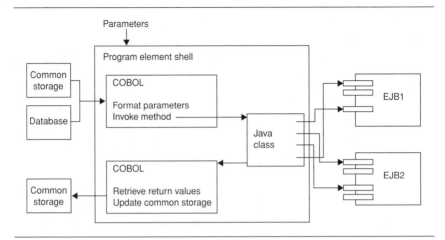

Figure 13-8 Legacy system adapters

composition of an adapter that replaces a COBOL program element with modernized logic. In broad terms, the adapter satisfies the external requirements of the program element and provides a mapping between legacy and modernized functionality.

The adapter satisfies the external requirements of the legacy program element in the *shell*. The shell is written in the same programming language as the legacy system, and also supports the same calls and accepts the same parameters. The shell also extracts and formats required information so that it may be passed as parameters to a Java class, which invokes the necessary sequence of methods in the EJBs to execute the functionality. Using the adapter, functionality in the modernized system can be decomposed differently than in the legacy system. The complexity of the adapter may vary, depending on how different the modernized architecture is from the legacy architecture. The adapter must absorb these differences for the modernized system to avoid legacy constraints.

Once the Java class has invoked the necessary EJB methods, control is returned to the COBOL shell, which must now modify common storage according to the changes that *would have been made* by the replaced legacy program elements. Fortunately, it is not necessary for the legacy component to update the Oracle database. These modifications are made directly from the EJBs through their persistence layer.

In addition to replacing the legacy program element, the adapter also replaces all its dependent program elements. In other words, before the adapter relinquishes control to the calling program, all changes to state data controlled and to external data components—side effects—normally accomplished by the program element must be performed as a consequence of the call to the adapter. To some degree, the functionality and database modifications should be implemented through a logical decomposition of activity in the modernized system.

However, as the EJBs have no knowledge of, or access to, common storage, the COBOL shell must make these updates on return from the Java class.

Developing the shell and adapter code is not trivial and can significantly increase the cost of modernizing. Conversely, reducing scaffolding code should reduce overall development costs. As a result, reducing the number of adapters is a driver in determining the order in which to migrate program elements.

13.7 Summary

In this chapter, we evaluated strategies for transforming the architecture of the legacy RSS to a modern, component-based architecture. The strategy we followed in this chapter can be applied in other architectural transformations and other decisions for which the consequences are not immediately apparent. The strategy is simple: When selecting among several unknown paths, walk down each path a hundred yards before deciding on the most appropriate route.

Once the transformation strategy is understood, we can consider an optional, preparatory step. The purpose of this step is to prepare the system for architectural transformation, or componentization, in the case study. The preparatory step may involve code reduction, retargeting, refactoring, or another form of reengineering. Whatever steps are taken, the development team must be confident that these steps will reduce the overall cost, and possibly complexity, of the architectural transformation. Precomponentization options for RSS are considered in the next chapter.

14

System Preparation

The men of experiment are like the ant; they only collect and use. The reasoners resemble spiders, who make cobwebs out of their own substance. But the bee takes a middle course: it gathers its material from the flowers of the garden and of the field, but transforms and digests it by a power of its own.
—Francis Bacon, *Novum Organum*

System preparation is an optional, potentially beneficial, but often risky step that occurs before architectural transformation. In system preparation, we try to evolve the legacy system to a point where it will be much easier to perform the desired architectural transformation. The benefit is a reduction in overall modernization costs. The risk is that the system preparation does not go as planned and that the development team gets mired in the legacy code.

Before deciding on system preparation possibilities, it is critical to perform an analysis of the available alternatives and to consider the strengths and weaknesses of each. The analysis of alternatives is primarily a brainstorming exercise. The architect may ask three or four of the design engineers to develop and present alternative system preparation approaches. At this point, the feasibility of these approaches is unlikely to have been demonstrated unless a member of the design team has recently completed a similar, successful modernization project. Even so, it is unlikely that the same plan will survive intact, as technologies will have evolved since the previous project was conceived. Feasibility, then, is something that must be established in more detail later. The analysis of alternatives establishes some potential approaches and provides a starting point for evaluating trade-offs and for understanding system requirements.

In this chapter, we analyze several alternatives for system preparation work in RSS. Only then can we agree on a plan.

14.1 Where Are We?

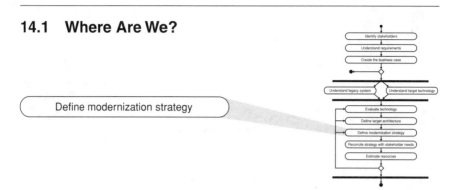

Implementing the modernization trail map selected in the previous chapter requires dealing with several problems. In essence, we have components running on different hardware platforms, written in different languages, and storing data in different databases. A logical process step at this point is system preparation planning, in which we attempt to identify steps that can reduce the complexity of the componentization effort and, in turn, overall costs for the modernization effort.

14.2 Analysis of Alternatives

The most important consideration in developing an incremental modernization approach is how to support the gradual evolution of the system. We can safely assume that at any given point after the initial incremental deployment, some functionality and data will remain in the legacy system and some will be migrated to the modernized system. However, this can be achieved in many ways. For RSS, code is migrated first and then data is migrated, according to the selected trail map. Having functionality and data exist in both the legacy and modernized systems means that distributed transactions will be executed across the two systems, that is, partly in the HVTIP environment and partly in the EJB environment.

The approach selected for evolving the system will affect the technologies that can be applied during modernization. Again, depending on the modernization approach selected, it may be necessary for modern logic to access legacy logic or data or for legacy logic to access modern logic or data. But we cannot select the technology until we understand the modernization approach, and we cannot select a modernization approach until we have established technical feasibility. To resolve this catch-22 situation, we initially focus on the desirability of the approach and then evaluate the technical feasibility of the most desirable approach, because establishing technical feasibility can be a time-consuming, expensive process.

In addition to simply identifying a modernization approach that supports the incremental development and deployment of the system, it is necessary to ensure that the system can meet the interim quality objectives, as recorded in Section 4.4. These objectives include performance, availability, and security. Some common questions that must be answered follow.

- Performance: What volume of data is extracted? How frequently is data extracted? How many transactions need to be supported per second? What is the size of these transactions? What response time is required?

- Availability: What are the requirements for system availability? Does the system need to be constantly available, or can it be taken down for periodic maintenance? How long can these outages last?

- Security: What levels of security are required? Does the system need to support multiple classes of users, each with a different level of access?

In the following sections, we analyze and contrast several plans. Although they are potentially viable, we have not validated all of them in practice and do not recommend that they be applied without further consideration. These plans fall on a continuum from least to most aggressive. All the alternatives take into account the prior work on Web enablement and the reports database on Oracle (see Section 2.2 for more details). Selecting a final plan requires a risk-benefit analysis.

PLAN 1: DMS ON OS 2200

Plan 1, illustrated in Figure 14-1, is the least aggressive system preparation step. The legacy system is retained largely intact, with various middleware components used to integrate modern and legacy elements. After code migration, data will be migrated from DMS to Oracle. Adapters can have logic on either platform, both platforms, or even be a middleware solution. Logic adapters transfer control from the OS 2200 environment to the Solaris environment (COBOL to Java), and inverse-logic adapters transfer control from the Solaris environment to the OS 2200 environment (Java to COBOL). EJBs use a data adapter to access the legacy DMS database. The Oracle database used for report generation and data mining is populated daily from data residing in the DMS database. Applications are accessed from a Web browser.

After the construction of several model problems, it was agreed that transactions would always start from the OS 2200 environment and then execute functionality in the Solaris environment before returning to the OS 2200 environment to complete the transaction. Once a use case is completely migrated, transactions execute entirely on the Solaris environment.

Data Access.   Plan 1 requires that enterprise beans, running on the Solaris platform, access data stored in the DMS. This can be accomplished in many ways.

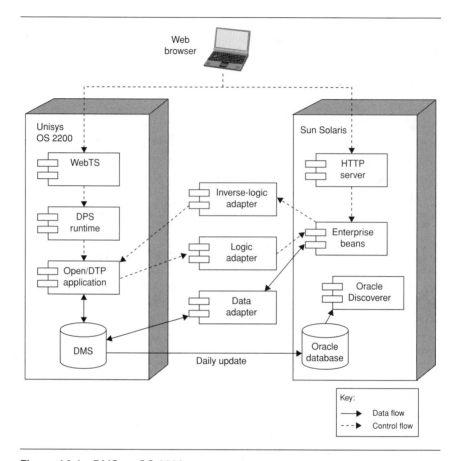

Figure 14-1   DMS on OS 2200

The first option is to allow the enterprise beans to access the database directly, bypassing any existing application programs. In this case, an enterprise bean directly formats a database access request, using JDBC. This request is then sent to the OS 2200 Data Access via a JDBC-to-ODBC bridge. OS 2200 Data Access provides the relational view of the nonrelational DMS data structures.

A second option is for the enterprise beans to invoke a data adapter program that runs on the same system as the database. In this case, the database is not accessed directly by the remote requestor: The database adapter provides functionality that can read or update the DMS as necessary. This option has only one point of contact to the database instead of embedded DMS data-access code in all beans.

One way to implement this second option is to use RMI to invoke a Java method running on the Java Virtual Machine (JVM) on OS 2200. The Java method, running locally on OS 2200, can access the DMS, using JDBC.[1] To be successful, the version of RMI running on the Solaris JDK must be compatible with the version of RMI running on the OS 2200 JVM. This can best be determined through a small model problem or prototype.

A third implementation approach is to send messages to data adapters, using MQSeries invoked with JMS from an enterprise bean. The data-access routines, in this case, would likely be written in COBOL, because MQSeries on Unisys provides bindings for this language.

Control Integration.   Legacy program elements are written primarily in COBOL. As a result, MQSeries is a reasonable mechanism for control integration because it is available for both the Solaris and Unisys platforms, and because both Java (JMS) and USC COBOL bindings are available.

Another possibility is to use the JNI to interface between Java *shells* running in the OS 2200 JVM and COBOL programs on the legacy system. EJBs running on the Solaris platform can simply invoke methods in these Java shells, using the RMI.

Transactions.   Because transactions will include logic and database access from the legacy program elements and modern system components, a transaction context must be maintained across both systems. To support transactions across both systems, COBOL programs must be modified to use Open/DTP. This change will allow any X/Open-compliant transaction monitor to maintain transactions, using, for example, the Java Transaction Service (JTS) interface. This approach might be used in conjunction with Java RMI methods to perform database access on the DMS.

A second approach is to use MQSeries on OS 2200 to support queued transactions, as described in Section 8.4. Given that transactions start on the OS 2200 side and continue in the EJB environment before returning to OS 2200 to complete, MQSeries is the only available option. As of December 2001, the Unisys Transaction Integrator did not support OS 2200 applications invoking enterprise beans, although Transaction Integrator now supports this. If the transactions originate on the EJB side, the Transaction Integrator currently supports connections to the OS 2200 system, using Open/DTP. MQSeries supports this scenario as well.

Evaluation.   Plan 1 is the easiest plan to implement. However, its success depends on the level of integration necessary between the legacy and modern systems.

Plan 1 requires migrating the legacy system from HVTIP to Open/DTP. This migration is usually relatively easy but depends to some degree on the HVTIP feature set used. The Open/DTP code is temporary scaffolding that will eventually be replaced.

---

[1] Performance problems may occur when JDBC is used from within the JVM on the OS 2200 system. Performance may be improved by using a native OS 2200 program to extract the data from the DMS.

Plan 1 adds initial complexity because of the need for enterprise beans to use JMS and MQSeries to access data in the DMS. There is also a performance risk in using an asynchronous messaging system to distribute data access across two platforms. Ideally, collocating the two platforms and establishing a high-bandwidth LAN connection between them can minimize performance issues. Interaction between the legacy system and the modernized system is greatest when functionality is equally split between the two systems.

Another, somewhat political, issue is the selection of an EJB server. In the RSS modernization effort, there are organizational pressures to use IBM Web-Sphere as an EJB server. However, Unisys has qualified the BEA WebLogic to work with Transaction Integrator and Open/DTP [Bye 01]. This pressure to use IBM WebSphere creates uncertainty and risk. If the IBM WebSphere EJB server were used, there is uncertainty as to how well it would integrate with Unisys software. Although in theory this software should work well, our experience has taught us that untested component ensembles seldom integrate seamlessly. Ensuring that IBM WebSphere could be integrated with the Unisys software requires the development of one or more model problems.

There is one other possibility: We could use BEA WebLogic for the modernization effort. This possibility shifts the uncertainty to compatibility between BEA WebLogic and IBM WebSphere, which may be used for other modernization efforts within the organization. Again, ensuring that BEA WebLogic can interact with IBM WebSphere requires the development of one or more model problems. In the case of RSS, it may also require organizational approval to select an EJB server other than the preapproved one.

The greatest disadvantage of Plan 1 is the business expense of maintaining the Unisys system during the entire modernization process.

PLAN 2: RDMS ON OS 2200

Plan 2, shown in Figure 14-2, involves migrating the data from the DMS to the RDMS for the OS 2200. The data remains on OS 2200 but is converted into relational form. The RDMS schema should be closer, if not similar, to the eventual Oracle schema because differences between the network and relational database models, discussed in Section 7.4, must be resolved.

Data Access.   Enterprise beans running on the Solaris platform can access data in the RDMS either directly or indirectly through data adapters on the legacy platform. Instead of using Unisys Data Access to access the DMS, data in the RDMS can be accessed via JDBC, using the UniAccess ODBC Server. (Uni-Access ODBC, an Applied Information Sciences product that provides SQL access to the RDMS, is described in Chapter 7.) Using UniAccess to access the RDMS has an advantage in that there is no need to define a relational-to-network mapping layer; therefore, the UniAccess solution can be more efficient.

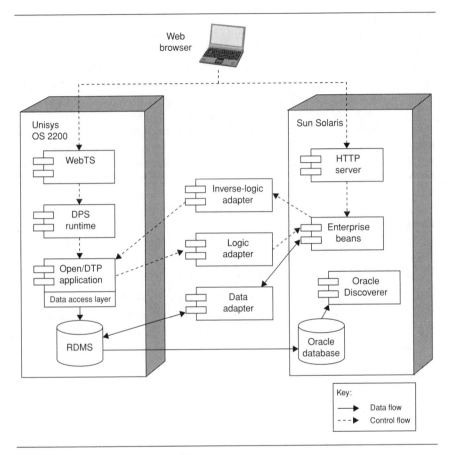

Figure 14-2   RDMS on OS 2200

Programs on the legacy side need to be modified to access the RDMS. Ideally, a data-access layer can provide the mapping between the old and new schemas and provide a single point of contact to the database instead of rewriting all the data-access code in the legacy programs.

The implementation options for accessing data through data adapters are unchanged from Plan 1.

Control Integration.   The options for control integration are unchanged from Plan 1.

Transactions.   This approach is similar to Plan 1 in that COBOL programs are modified to use Open/DTP, allowing transactions to be maintained across both systems, using any X/Open-compliant transaction monitor.

Evaluation.   Plan 2 is similar to Plan 1 except that the data is migrated from the network database (DMS) to a relational database (RDMS) on the Unisys platform. This requires changing the schema to accommodate the differences between network and relational databases. In turn, this requires changing COBOL program elements on the legacy platform, in addition to the changes required to support Open/DTP.

Changes to the legacy system are always troublesome; this is one of the reasons it is being replaced. Although the migration from the network to the relational database structure requires modifying the schema, these modifications are minimized for this intermediate step. Enterprise beans on the modernized platform will need to provide a mapping between the modernized data structures and the legacy structure of the RDMS database. This mapping layer and modifications to the legacy code and to the database will all contribute to the overhead of Plan 2.

PLAN 3: ORACLE ON THE SOLARIS PLATFORM

Plan 3 calls for porting the database from the DMS on OS 2200 to Oracle on Sun Solaris. This approach also requires Open/DTP to allow distributed transactions to be maintained across both systems. An architectural view of this approach is illustrated in Figure 14-3.

Data Access.   Moving the database from the DMS to Oracle requires modifying the legacy COBOL code to access data in Oracle or creating data adapters. Figure 14-4 illustrates one way in which this can be accomplished. This approach requires that both control and data pass through multiple components.

Moving the database from the DMS to Oracle also requires restructuring the database schema to support a relational model. Beyond this, any modernization of the schema is optional but not without consequence. Migrating this schema toward the target schema requires adapting the legacy code to work with the modified data structures. Maintaining the legacy database schema requires a mapping between the objects in the modern system and the legacy data structures, possibly in the persistence layer of the enterprise beans. Both cases require developing scaffolding code that will later be discarded, and both have performance implications because data being accessed will now also need to be transformed.

Control Integration.   The options for control integration are unchanged from the first two plans.

Transactions.   With all the data in Oracle on the Solaris platform, it is no longer necessary to support distributed transactions or two-phase commits. This simplifies transaction management, particularly if BEA Tuxedo can be used as the transaction manager for both the OS 2200 applications and the EJBs.

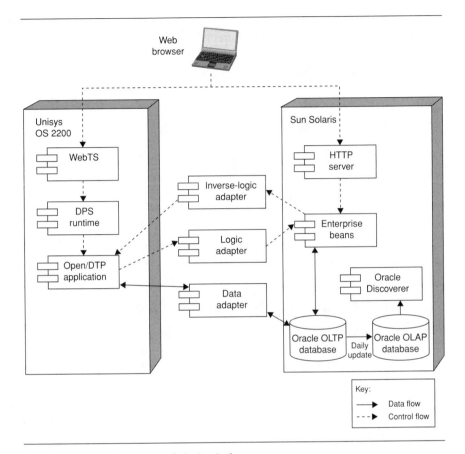

Figure 14-3 Oracle on the Solaris platform

Evaluation. Plan 3 has many of the same complications and difficulties as Plan 2. Both plans require migrating the data to a relational database. Plan 3 has some potential advantages over Plan 2 in that Plan 3 may simplify transaction management. Our assumption that two-phase commits can be eliminated in this scenario must be verified by using model problems or other techniques. BEA Tuxedo may function as a transaction manager for both the legacy application and EJBs running in the BEA WebLogic EJB server, which is tightly integrated with BEA Tuxedo. The same may not be true of the IBM WebSphere EJB server, which incorporates the Encina transaction manager.

Overall, Plan 3 may require relatively expensive modification of the legacy code to work with Oracle. Further, the overall effort falls short of eliminating the dependency on the legacy hardware.

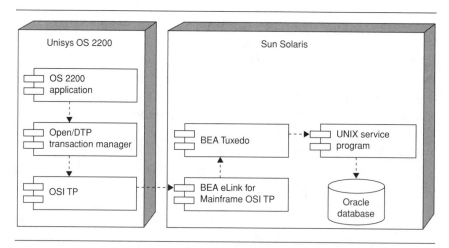

Figure 14-4 Accessing the Oracle database from an OS 2200 application

PLAN 4: EVERYTHING ON THE SOLARIS PLATFORM

Plan 4 is to migrate everything to the Solaris platform but to do so as quickly and inexpensively as possible. This eliminates the dependency on the legacy hardware and gets everything into a Solaris environment, where it will be, theoretically, simpler to integrate with the modernized components.

Retargeting the code from OS 2200 to Solaris requires the following changes.

- The code must be ported to Solaris.
- The DMS must be replaced with Oracle.
- HVTIP must be replaced with an open-systems transaction manager.
- Dependencies on the DPS must be eliminated.
- All remaining dependencies on OS 2200 must be eliminated.

To minimize changes because of language differences, the code must be compiled for the Solaris platform, using a COBOL compiler, such as Micro Focus COBOL. This will eliminate the need to transform the code into another language, such as Java or C++. Unfortunately, differences between Micro Focus and Unisys COBOL could make this translation challenging.

Once the legacy system is ported to Solaris, development of the modern components can begin. Although both legacy and modern components can now operate on the same platform, it is still necessary to integrate legacy and modern components. Ideally, integration issues can be solved to allow flexibility in deployment—for example, having both the legacy and modern systems run on the same server or on different servers.

Data Access. Data is stored entirely in Oracle, greatly simplifying data access.

Control Integration. Control integration can be handled using a variety of mechanisms. Previous options for control integration, such as MQSeries and RMI, are still viable, but other mechanisms may now be possible as well. One such potential solution is to use CORBA and IIOP. The Java ORB is unsuitable for this application because it lacks a Micro Focus COBOL-language binding. However, suitable language bindings may be available from another ORB vendor. Another control integration option is to use JNI to invoke Java methods directly from COBOL and/or COBOL methods directly from Java. Unless combined with a distribution mechanism, using the JNI would require both the legacy and modernized systems to run in the same process space.

Transactions. Maintaining transactions in the context of Plan 4 is the subject of Chapter 10. In Chapter 10, we considered several alternative solutions and established the somewhat qualified feasibility of one approach.

Evaluation. Plan 4 completely eliminates the need for the legacy Unisys system. This saves dollars that would otherwise be spent on legacy system maintenance. Moving both the code and the data to Solaris brings us closer than previous plans to our eventual goal of replacing the legacy system architecture. In addition to sharing many of the complications of earlier plans, porting the legacy system to Solaris requires that all dependencies on OS 2200 be eliminated.

Anecdotal evidence suggests that moving from a Unisys platform to a Solaris system by using an Oracle database improves the performance, although simply assuming that this is the case is ill-advised. All performance and response-time issues rely, however, on how well the entire system is set up and tuned. This means that the operating system, the database, and the applications programs must all be properly optimized during the testing phase to ensure good performance in production.

PLAN 5: EVERYTHING ON SOLARIS+

Plan 5 is a slightly more aggressive variant of Plan 4. Code and data are still ported from the legacy platform to Solaris. However, instead of using Micro Focus as a target language, we convert to the Java programming language and J2EE environment to further narrow the gap with the target environment. This conversion is a direct mapping, with no architectural transformation.

This approach has several advantages. In narrowing the gap between the modern and legacy systems, we simplify control integration and data access, as well as support for transactions that span legacy and modernized system components. This approach reduces the entire problem to a Java development effort rather than requiring the development staff to be proficient in two significantly different languages and development environments.

EVALUATION OF ALTERNATIVES

Migrating the existing system off the Unisys hardware turned out to be the overriding issue in selecting a plan, because of the high cost associated with maintaining the system on the legacy hardware. In the case of RSS, computing services were being provided by an independent third party. The yearly bill for operating the Unisys platform at full capacity is $15.5 million a year, whereas the cost of operating the Solaris platform at full capacity is $6.9 million. Any modernization plan that incrementally migrates functionality from the legacy system to the modernized platform would require that both systems be operational at the same time. In some cases, this meant yearly operational costs exceeding $23 million. Money spent on maintaining the existing system came out of the overall budget, with the result that high operational costs resulted in fewer funds remaining for modernization.

All the plans considered in this section may be valid under different circumstances. The RSS team selected Plan 4 as the least-aggressive system preparation plan that accomplished the goal of migrating the existing code base off the Unisys hardware platform and onto a Solaris platform before starting componentization.

14.3   Summary

Many forms of reengineering can be applied to the modernization effort before beginning the architectural transformation effort. Many of these techniques may be perceived as beneficial to the overall process. However, the benefit of these changes must be carefully weighed against the cost and schedule implications. This is especially true when multiple reengineering efforts are being considered, because this often causes diminishing returns. In the final analysis, you must remember that the legacy system will eventually be replaced, and any improvements made to it will become irrelevant. The focus must remain on reducing the cost and schedule associated with accomplishing the end goal of the modernization.

15

Code and Data Migration

with Santiago Comella-Dorda

> *Give me where to stand, and I will move the earth.*
> —Archimedes, *Mathematical Collection*,
> book VIII, proposition 10, section 11,
> Pappus of Alexandria (date unknown)
> translated into Latin (1588)

As noted at the end of Chapter 13, RSS stakeholders selected an architectural transformation strategy that dictated that code be migrated in the first phase, followed by the database in a second phase. Parallel operations would not be used. In Chapter 14, we selected a system preparation strategy that migrates data from DMS to Oracle without major changes to the schema and retargets the legacy COBOL code to the Solaris platform. The next step is to develop plans for *code migration* and *data migration*.

The code migration plan is a refinement of the first phase of the architectural transformation strategy and identifies which program elements are modernized in each increment. Unless objective criteria are devised, the code migration plan will be driven by external forces or by chance. The criteria for assigning program elements to increments are derived from the overall modernization goals. We established the following criteria for the RSS modernization effort.

- **Minimize the number of adapters.** Reducing the need for adapters should reduce overall development costs for the system.

- **Migrate program elements with related functionality at the same time.** Reducing the number of adapters as the only criterion may not result in an optimal migration plan because program elements with widely varying functionality will be migrated together. This lack of focus makes it difficult to comprehend and implement system requirements.

Santiago Comella-Dorda is a business analyst with McKinsey & Company.

- **Map increment size to the funding profile.** Effort must be mapped to available funding. Project funding may be constant, ramp up steadily and then ramp down, or vary, based on spending projections.

Although it is not performed until after the code migration, data migration must be planned so that the cost of the overall modernization strategy can be estimated.

15.1   Where Are We?

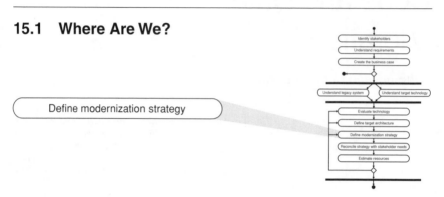

Define modernization strategy

In Chapter 13, the stakeholders agreed on an architectural transformation strategy. In Chapter 14, a system preparation strategy was selected. Before the costs of the modernization strategy can be estimated, a more detailed, tactical plan for the code migration and data migration efforts must be developed.

15.2   Structural Analysis

The structure and dependencies of the legacy system must be analyzed to determine a reasonable, if not optimal, program element migration plan. The call graph in Figure 15-1 illustrates how this might be accomplished.

Figure 15-1 contains four kinds of program elements:

1. *Root program elements*—for example, program element 418—call other program elements but are not called by any. Root program elements are invoked directly by the user or an external process. By themselves, these program elements may not be good candidates for modernization because they call other program elements. This means that the modernized Java components would have to call back to the COBOL system.

2. *Node program elements*—for example, program element 123—both call and are called by other program elements. Node program elements share the difficulty of root program elements but also require creating adapters in the legacy code so that the remainder of the legacy system can continue to function without modification.

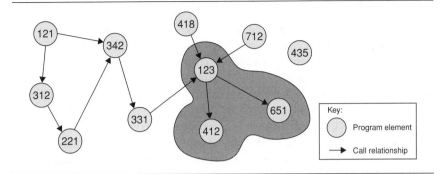

Figure 15-1 Call graph

3. *Leaf program elements*—for example, program element 412—are called by program elements but do not call any. Leaf program elements are the best candidates for migration: They do not call back to the COBOL code, and it is possible to minimize the number of adapters required by migrating entire subtrees in a single increment. The shaded area in Figure 15-1 shows where three program elements can be migrated, requiring only a single adapter.

4. *Isolated program elements*—for example, program element 435—neither call nor are called by other program elements. Many of these isolated programs are reports. Independent of other issues, isolated program elements can be migrated easily. These elements could be used as filler in any given increment because they neither increase nor decrease the number of adapters needed.

Initially, we assumed that we could use a COTS COBOL analysis tool to generate a call graph for the legacy system. The RSS team had already acquired a well-known analysis tool. Unfortunately, this tool was not able to identify the majority of call dependencies in the legacy system. These calls were made by moving the name of the program to call into a variable and then calling the value of the variable:

```
MOVE 'NGV129' PROGRAM-TO-CALL
CALL PROGRAM-TO-CALL
```

This is a relatively simple example of this problem. In other cases, the name of the program to call was established at runtime by concatenating the value of a variable to the end of a static string. In the end, we used a combination of static analysis, dynamic analysis, and manual code inspection to develop a complete call graph.

INITIAL PLAN

To generate call graphs from the available input, we developed a tool that used the Rational Rose Extensibility Interface (REI) to create UML diagrams. The System Analysis and Migration tool (SAM) converts program elements to classes and converts calls to associations. Each association is labeled with its call type, that is, Perform, Call, Copy. There are a total of 900 distinct program element names and 10,629 calls. Figure 15-2 shows the resulting UML diagram.

The initial Rational Rose model was obviously too complex to be useful. (It also exemplifies how some tools work well on simple problems but are unable to scale to real systems.) To simplify the model, we created a separate diagram for each *root element*. We also eliminated self-referential elements and reduced utility functions, which typically fetch, delete, or update a database record, to comments in caller program elements.

The result was more comprehensible. A series of charts was generated and then analyzed. Our two primary findings from this analysis involved isolated program elements and root program elements.

RSS has a total of 96 root element diagrams. Their complexity varies from 2 to more than 100 elements; however, most range from 2 to 20 elements. Figure 15-3 shows an example of a relatively complex root element diagram.

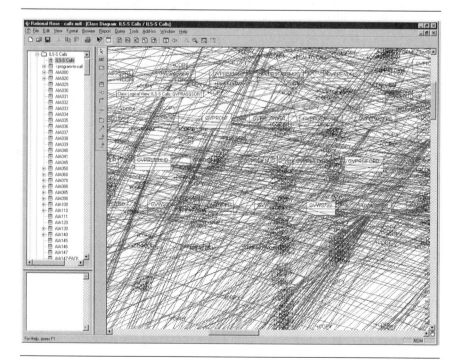

Figure 15-2 Initial Rational Rose model

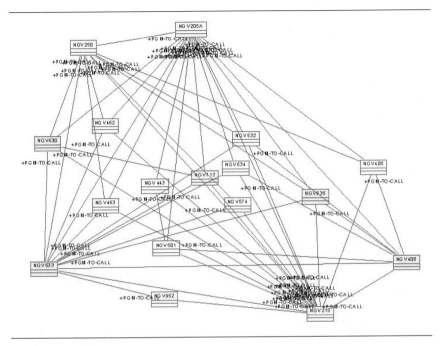

Figure 15-3   Root element diagram

The algorithm that we developed to generate the root element diagrams has some interesting features. Subtrees, for nodes within the diagram, are expanded only once in the model. This missing complexity is captured in two ways: It is recorded in the documentation for the program element class and is displayed using a shade of blue in the diagram. Darkening shades of blue indicate increasing numbers of *reachable* elements. Reachable elements are program elements that can be called, either directly or indirectly, by the program element, even if all those elements are not explicitly represented.

The documentation for each program element class contains the number of diagrams in which the class is included—root elements are included in only one diagram—the number of times that the program element is called, and the number of program elements that are called. The number of program elements in the tree is the same as the number of reachable elements. As stated earlier, calls to utility functions are reduced to comments and also included in the documentation for each program element class. Figure 15-4 shows a sample of the documentation that is provided for each program element class.

Of the 900 overall program elements in RSS, 248 are isolated program elements, which can be ported easily with little impact; that is, they do not require adapters. However, many of these program elements are reports. Reports are a special case because they do not use component interfaces and depend on the

```
NUMBER OF DIAGRAMS: 1
TIMES CALLED: 0
TIMES CALLER: 4
NUMBER OF PROGRAM ELEMENTS IN TREE: 14
NOTES:
accesses: GVPRGETPCT
…
accesses: GVPRCALLER
accesses: GVPRCNF
added to diagram: NGV227
expanded in diagram: NGV227
```

Figure 15-4   Program element class

database structure. As a result, it may make sense to identify program elements that are reports and to defer implementing them to the final data migration phase. Because these reports operate against the legacy database, they can remain unchanged until that time.

Although analyzing root program elements teaches us something about the structure of the legacy system, it is not clear that root elements form the best candidates for componentization. In RSS, root elements map directly to user-level transactions. Business objects, on the other hand, are often built as augmented encapsulations of data entities. Consequently, components in the modernized system are more likely to correspond to the legacy data entities than to transactions. If we followed the root element approach, every diagram represented in the UML models would map to several business objects in the modernized system. This would create an unwanted complexity because multiple business objects in the modernized system would be in development at the same time.

REVISED PLAN

As we had concerns with building a code migration plan around root program elements, we conceived a new approach: building the plan around database records. This approach consisted of the following steps.

1. Arrange data records into as many sets as there are increments—five in the case study. Group logically related records together to modernize related functionality.

2. For each data record set, group program elements that reference or depend on the database records.

3. For each data record set, identify program elements outside the group that invoke programs inside the group; these program elements potentially require adapters.

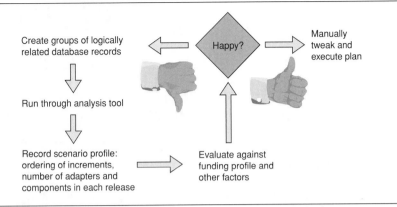

Figure 15-5   Process overview

4. For the system, determine the modernization order for the groups created in steps 2 and 3 to minimize the number of adapters that must be built and balance the size of increments.

We further reduced system complexity and improved the quality of the migration plan by eliminating database records and program elements that were likely to be eliminated in the modernized system. For example, we eliminated database records that were used to maintain global constants or information about the system—for example, the number of user terminals—because this information would be managed differently in the modernized system.

Once the database records were grouped, we ran them through the tool and analyzed the results. If these results were acceptable, we could tweak and execute the plan. If the results were not acceptable, we could reorganize the records and run the tool again. Figure 15-5 illustrates this revised process.

15.3   Code Migration Plan

We captured the results of the analysis described in the previous section in a collection of Rational Rose UML models. A separate model is generated for each increment, which in turn contains a class diagram for each database record in the set.[1]

Figure 15-6 shows a diagram for the DB53 record. The record is displayed using the table stereotype defined in Rose. Program elements shown in white must be migrated as part of this increment. Program elements in light gray have already been migrated. Program elements shown in dark gray are scheduled to be

---

[1] Database records without associated program elements are not included.

260

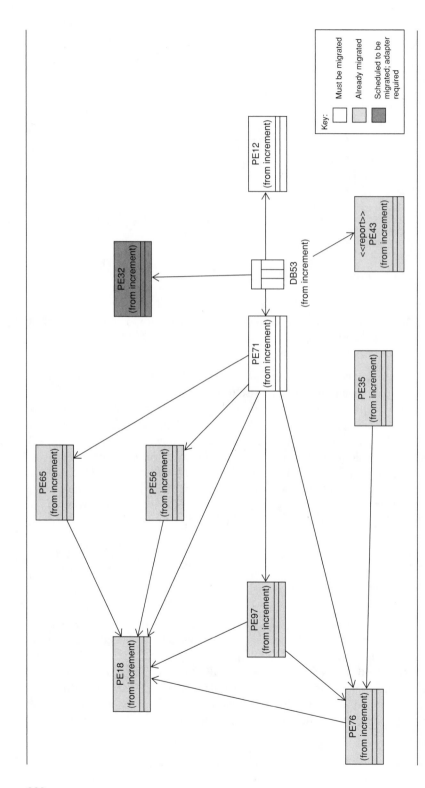

Figure 15-6 Database element set

migrated and require the use of an adapter. Adapters are required where program elements not already ported need to invoke a program element that is being migrated in the current increment.

Figure 15-7 shows sample information for each increment in the documentation for the increment package created in Rational Rose. This data includes the number of program elements ported in the increment; the number of adapters required; the number of lines of code ported in this increment, both as an absolute value and as a percentage of the overall system; and the number of lines of executable code ported in this increment, both as an absolute value and as a percentage of the overall system. Following this header information is a description of the percentage of each business object completed at the end of the increment. There is one line for each business object. The number of lines of ported code associated with each business object is given, again as an absolute and as a percentage of the total lines of code in that business object.

We used the information from SAM to generate a series of alternative code migration plans. Each plan is contained in several UML models: one for each increment and a final increment containing the flexible allocation, or isolated program elements. From these UML models for each plan, profiles can be developed that include the lines of code (LOC) allocated to each increment, the number of required adapters, and the completion rate for business objects. Management can then select the profile that best fits the available resources, or request additional profiles, if necessary. As an example, this section contains an initial profile. (Profiles obtained from running the tool against various stakeholder preferences are presented in Chapter 16.)

Figure 15-8 shows the LOC allocation for each increment. In this profile, increment 1 is intentionally small because the main concern is exploring the technical risks associated with the project. The advantage of a small initial increment is that you should be able to routinely apply lessons learned in the first increment to later increments. There is, of course, some management risk in this approach

```
NUMBER OF PROGRAM ELEMENTS PORTED: 37 NUMBER OF
ADAPTERS REQUIRED: 8
LOCs PORTED: 92308 (total=1209996 percentage=7)
EXECUTABLE LOCs PORTED: 77941 total=1016515
     percentage=7)
BO COMPLETION (this increment)
Orders LOCs: 7897 (total=110611 percentage=7)
Inventory LOCs: 3435 (total=165278 percentage=2)
WIP_Confirm LOCs: 1146 (total=53331 percentage=2)
Requisition LOCs: 1193 (total=80729 percentage=1)
:
Other LOCs: 0 (total=1309 percentage=0)
```

Figure 15-7   Sample increment output

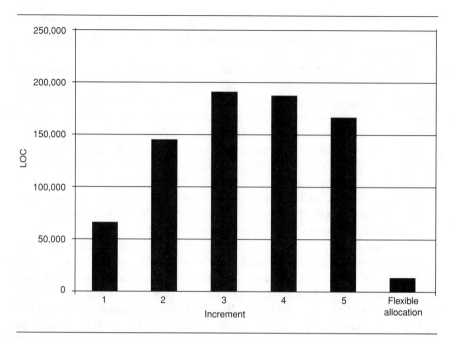

Figure 15-8 Size of increments

because the cost per line of code developed will be disproportionately high in the first increment. This is a condition that will have to be supported by management fortitude.

Isolated program elements become part of the flexible allocation and can be assigned to any increment. This is convenient because these isolated program elements can increase the size of increments to map the funding profile. Ideally, the fixed allocation will fall below the projected effort for each increment. Program elements from the flexible allocation can then be added to each increment to bring them up to the projected effort for each increment.

Figure 15-9 shows the number of adapters—calls from the legacy code to the modernized code—inverse adapters—calls from the modernized code to the legacy code—and program elements being ported and developed in each increment according to this initial profile. The height of each bar shows the combined number of adapters and program elements. Of course, no adapters are included in the flexible allocation.

Figure 15-10 shows the percentage of each business object completed after each increment. In this profile, every increment completes at least one business object. Completing business objects quickly is important to demonstrate early benefits and to finalize parts of the modernized system.

Figure 15-11 shows the initial allocation of source lines of code (SLOC) to the business objects. This chart was not part of a specific profile but helped detect

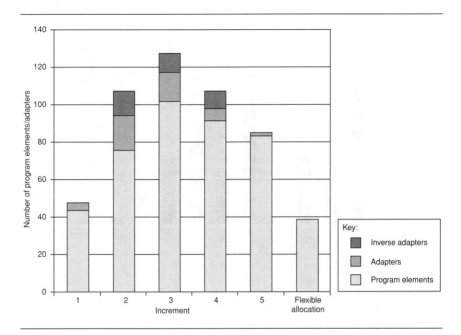

Figure 15-9   Adapters versus program elements

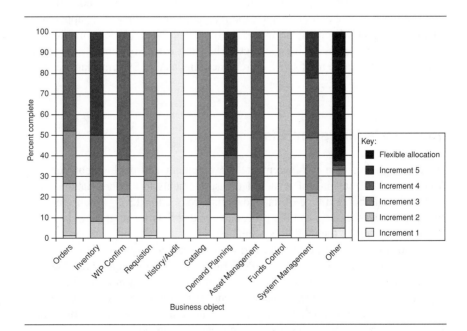

Figure 15-10   Business object completion

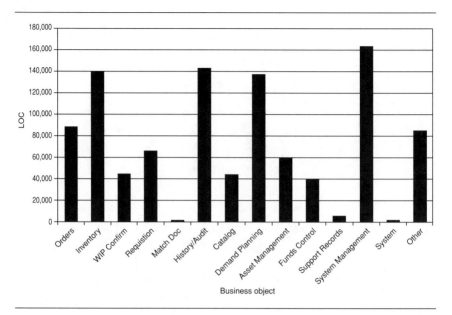

Figure 15-11   Size of business objects

business objects that had too much functionality and should be decomposed or that did not have enough and should be merged. For example, it is apparent in Figure 15-11 that Match Doc, Support Records, and System lacked functionality and were eliminated as business objects. The chart can also identify other problems, such as the large number of source lines allocated to System Management.

15.4   Data Migration Plan

A data migration plan for incremental development and deployment needs to account for the mapping of legacy database elements to modern database elements, the number and type of data adapters (see Section 13.2), synchronization procedures, if necessary, and the procedures and scripts for migrating data from the legacy system to the modern system.

The RSS architectural transformation strategy requires that code be migrated first, followed by the data. Performing the data migration after the code migration eliminates the need for data replication and synchronization between a legacy database and a modern database, reduces the complexity of the incremental development, and allows for optimization and refinement of the modern database schema based on lessons learned from each increment.

During system preparation, data is ported from DMS to Oracle. The schema in the Oracle OLTP database is an *interim* relational schema that is modified from the DMS network schema only to accommodate the differences between the database types. Data-related calls inside the legacy code are mapped to a data-access layer for interaction with the Oracle OLTP database instead of the DMS database. Figure 15-12 shows the system before code migration.[2]

Functionality inside business objects is implemented by session beans that communicate with entity beans to access and update data. In this case, the entity beans also serve as a data persistence layer. During code migration, the entity beans need to map to the interim database schema. Figure 15-13 shows the system during code migration.

The COBOL program elements and logic adapters are no longer needed once the code migration is finished, as shown in Figure 15-14. Data can now be migrated from the *interim* database schema to the *final* database schema. Because the data is already in Oracle, this is a straightforward task that can be easily accomplished using scripts, provided that the mapping is clearly understood. The interim entity beans are replaced with entity beans that map to the final database schema. The advantage of using entity beans as a data persistence layer is that the session beans that contain the business logic need not be changed to switch schemas, as long as the interfaces remain constant. Figure 15-15 shows the final system after data migration. The tasks of creating the new database schema, developing the final entity beans, and the data migration itself need to be accounted for in the cost estimate for the overall modernization strategy.

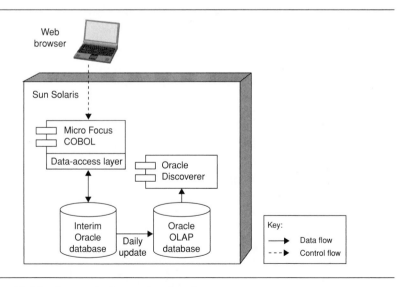

Figure 15-12   System before code migration

---

[2] Client application, communication, and transaction-management details are omitted.

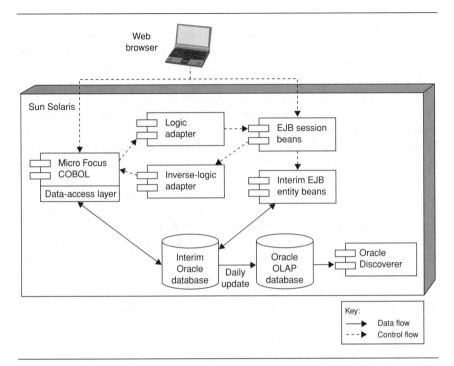

Figure 15-13 System during code migration

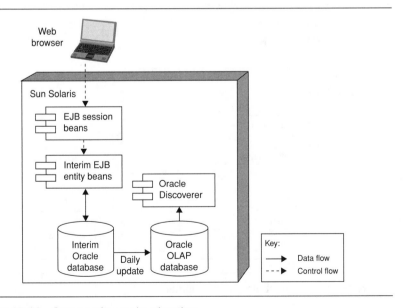

Figure 15-14 System after code migration

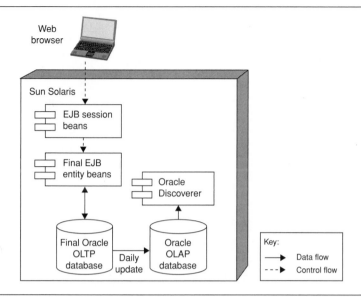

Figure 15-15   System after data migration

15.5   Summary

The technique presented in this chapter for incremental refinement of the code migration strategy provides a systematic and fact-based method that avoids the arbitrary, intuitive decision making often found in software projects. The systematization of the technique has enabled us to partly automate the process through the creation of a tool that analyzes the legacy system and generates a code migration plan.

However, the strengths of this technique are also its weaknesses, as the analysis tool necessarily lacks the insight and expertise found only in humans. The code migration plan created by the tool is generated automatically from a rigid set of predefined parameters, and the results should be treated accordingly. The plan must be tweaked by developers to accommodate particular concerns during the migration process. Nevertheless, the valuable information about the migration process that the plan provides can improve the fidelity of the cost estimation for the modernization strategy.

16

Integrated Plan

with Vivian Martin

> *I have always thought that one man of tolerable abilities may work great changes, and accomplish great affairs among mankind, if he first forms a good plan, and, cutting off all amusements or other employments that would divert his attention, make the execution of that same plan his sole study and business.*
> —Benjamin Franklin,
> *Autobiography*, Chapter 7
> written 1771–1790

> *The best plan is* only *a plan, that is, good intentions,* *unless it* degenerates into work.
> — Peter Drucker
> *Management: Tasks, Responsibilities, Practices.*
> New York: Harper & Row. 1974, p. 128.

In the previous chapters, we developed a modernization strategy for RSS. However, this modernization plan represents an idealized process based on technical considerations. The plan is aimed at minimizing development costs—number of adapters, scope of understanding required—and mapping size, based on lines of COBOL, to a schedule. However, other business drivers must be reconciled with the technical plans. These drivers may require reprioritizing business objects to field them earlier. In this chapter, we reconcile cost with stakeholder needs.

Vivian Martin is a Senior Information Systems Engineer at Tec-Masters, Inc.

16.1   Where Are We?

In this step of risk-managed modernization (RMM), we reconcile the modernization strategy with stakeholder needs. This is an essential step in building consensus for the development plan and schedule among the stakeholders. Once a plan has been agreed on, the implementation costs can be estimated.

16.2   Reconciliation Objectives

The reconciliation effort decides the order of componentization. Stakeholders evaluate the qualities of the various code migration strategies and make trade-offs. The qualities evaluated include risk, costs, measurable progress, and others derived from stakeholder priorities. This process results in a high-level schedule supported by the stakeholders.

Given the inflexibility of the legacy RSS, limited resources, and high visibility, compromise is a necessity. This was apparent as soon as stakeholders reviewed the initial migration plan. Stakeholders observed that the only business object fully completed before the end of the project in the initial code migration plan was the small and poorly understood Match Doc. The testable, measurable progress goals they sought were subjugated by the quest to minimize adapters. Migrating a percentage of program elements had no appeal as a progress measure. The lack of interim products did not fit with their expectations of an incremental approach.

The high-level schedule resulting from the reconciliation process accomplished several goals: It provided a consensus plan for which a cost estimate could be developed, established a notional schedule, and determined the order for business object completion. Order is important because extracting a program element from its environment creates loose ends that require adaptation. Adapters add complexity, can be difficult to build, and must ultimately be thrown away—all of which increase the cost of the modernization effort.

16.3   Reconciliation Plan

The reconciliation effort enables stakeholders to compare trade-offs on a conceptual level. Having a focused objective prevents the process from degenerating into confusion or emotional appeals. In the RSS case study, we used the profiles generated by SAM, discussed in Chapter 15, to contrast migration strategies at a conceptual level.

The reconciliation plan includes the following steps.

1. **Assemble the stakeholders as a group and explain the process.** This step includes briefing the stakeholders about the approach, reviewing the architecture-transformation choices, and enumerating the uses and limitations of SAM. Stakeholders are assigned the task of defining the order of business object completion.

2. **Conduct separate meetings to construct each group's "ideal" project profile.** Participants assemble a plan that satisfies their requirements. SAM is used to create *profiles* for each plan.

3. **Synthesize the profiles into combined views to demonstrate the impact of compromise.** The ideal profiles are combined to demonstrate trade-offs and their impact to the plan.

4. **Reassemble the entire group.** The entire group evaluates the results and provides input for the final consensus profile.

5. **Brief the consensus to management.** The final consensus profile is provided to the engineers developing the life-cycle cost estimates, as described in Chapter 17.

16.4   Stakeholder Priorities

Each group of stakeholders evaluates the componentization plan from its particular perspective. In the RSS case study, stakeholder views varied from, "I need to see risk mitigated early on; you can't squeeze it all out to the end" to "That sure looks like it will cause a lot of hard work on the legacy side." For the list of stakeholders in the RSS case study and their perspectives, see Section 4.2. The desires of each group, as captured during the individual meetings to construct the ideal profiles, follows.

USER REPRESENTATIVES

User representatives have the functional expertise required to carry out retail activities. These activities include, for example, ordering and shelving items, storing and picking, and resolving bottlenecks. Certain functions are so basic to the tasks the users perform on a daily basis that they have no trouble expressing their priorities.

To some degree, the user representatives' priorities are neutralized by the choice of delivering a complete, operational system with each increment. This is best explained with the question: "If I get all functionality in some form or other every time, why do I care what order that you do it in?" However, considering that desired system improvements had been collecting in a backlog of legacy change requests for some time, the users keenly felt a need to put their core, critical activities first so that the promise of maintainable components could be quickly exploited.

Their activities, listed in priority order, are as follows.

1. **Stock must be available on the shelf.** The ability to fill basic orders for items directly from the shelf is essential. Therefore, the basic management of inventory is a top priority, including computing required on-hand quantities and requisitioning new items from wholesale sources.

2. **Stock must move from the shelf to the customer.** Customers must be able to place their orders using a catalog and knowing the availability of substitutes. The retail clerk must be able to release the items to the customer and know that the inventory balance will reflect the transaction.

3. **Inventory must be controlled.** Support for receiving property into the warehouse or retail location must be automated. On-hand balances must be continually updated so that inventory position is available on demand.

4. **Allocation of assets among retail locations must be tracked.** Stockpiling of assets in one location to the detriment of another location must be avoided. Methods to monitor and rectify stock levels by lateral moves of property must be supported.

ARCHITECTURE TEAM

Work on the enterprise architecture began at the organizational level before the start of the RSS modernization effort. The architecture team had already adopted the OAG model and its integration specification, OAGIS, as described in Section 9.5 and in Chapter 11. The architecture team used the concept of a business object to coalesce and encapsulate associated business logic. Therefore, the business object was viewed as the ideal measure of progress.

The architecture team's perspective was enterprise-wide, as demonstrated in its priorities.

1. **Do things first that may be used by others.** Throughout the organization, pockets of software had developed over the years. This resulted in considerable amounts of redundant code supporting basic capabilities. Any basic capability, such as inventory, had a good chance of being reused by other groups because many departments had varying needs to keep goods on their shelves.

2. **Look at other modernization efforts in the organization.** Across the organization, other, decentralized, development groups were planning modernization efforts. In the cases where these other groups were developing similar components, it made sense to develop common components that could serve both groups' requirements.

3. **Seek early interoperability with external suppliers and systems.** The architecture team promoted the adoption of industry standards. Standardization was expected to promote interoperability within the organization. However, OAGIS was also expected to better automate activities with suppliers and to provide opportunities to use off-the-shelf software products compliant with OAGIS.

4. **Start with the Audit/History business object.** The architecture team had performed considerable analysis to support selecting the Audit/History business object for the first increment. The main points of the argument were its relatively small size and low complexity. Functionally, it was expected to be the last action taken for all transactions. This meant that legacy-side adapters would not contend with returning values from a component but would be one-way: legacy to modern business object. Another attractive feature was that auditing requirements were stable. There was little likelihood of requirements churn or disagreement among the parties as to what was expected. The architecture team conceded that Audit/History was sensitive to a myriad of transactions, lessening its direct, unchanged usability across the organization. But the team countered with the attractiveness of Audit/History as pilot work. The qualities of this business object made it a low-risk effort suitable for a newly assembled team using unfamiliar technology.

LEGACY SYSTEM MAINTAINERS

The legacy maintainers advocated tackling the modernization effort based on transactions in the legacy system. In this view, dynamic analysis would identify a particular execution path for a given transaction and set of parameters. The legacy maintainers argued that extracting a complete transaction would have little impact on the legacy system. Given the maintainers' reasonable desire to minimize impact to the legacy system, the transaction approach made sense.

Using logic similar to that used in the development of SAM, the maintainers saw the value of keeping program elements in logically related groups. As a result, the maintainers proposed logical groupings based on the transaction types that correspond to the following business events:[1]

- Receipt of goods
- Nondirected shipments

---

[1] It is interesting to note that this list is *not* ordered by the most frequently occurring transactions or by program elements that have become especially difficult and expensive to maintain.

- Changes to descriptions of goods
- Reversal of transactions
- Freezing of inventory items
- Basic inquiry
- All remaining transactions

A concern in following this approach was that these transactions might easily exercise large portions of the legacy system, resulting in one or two enormous increments that would countermand the incremental development and deployment approach.

MANAGEMENT

Management's primary concern is managing risk. Risk was considered more important than achieving the corporate architecture, avoiding costs, or avoiding rework. Management was adamant that componentization was the view around which the project would be managed. In effect, the new architecture should take its place as the system's vision.

Management had two other notable perspectives. The managers thought it important to begin with the retail supply core processes. The example given was the Inventory business object. The supply organization's ownership of inventory processes was not debatable. The managers' other perspective anticipated the scrutiny of midlevel management and of independent testers for additional operational testing. It was clear that each iteration's products must be testable as logical units.

The management view of the first-iteration priorities was as follows:

1. It should represent the overall program and mitigate as many risks as possible as early as possible.

2. It should be large enough to produce a fieldable product. This was reasoned to be about 10 percent of the entire effort, or about 6 months of work.

3. It should touch on complexity, integration framework services, and data management. Complexity would include samples of business objects, business object documents, adapters, and legacy COBOL working together. The integration framework services, such as security and portal presentation layer, should be exercised. Data management included its availability to operational data stores and data warehouse projects.

OBSERVATIONS

None of the groups provided the order in which business objects should be completed. At this point, business object order was a dependent variable in SAM.

Concerns among the groups often overlapped. Some of this stemmed from participants' previous experiences and some because a few participants contributed to more than one group. The exercise seemed to bring out the "manager" in all the participants. Recurring themes included the constraint that different priorities would impact the difficulty of the modernization effort and the view that the initial increment should serve as a pilot effort to reduce risk.

16.5 Stakeholder Ideal Profiles

To create the stakeholder profiles, we translated stakeholder priorities into inputs for SAM. As described in Chapter 15, SAM bases its analysis on logically related groups of data. The translation required mapping program elements to database records, program elements to business objects, and transactions to program elements. Subjective decisions arose in defining the boundaries of logical data groupings. Because of the tangled relationships between call structure and data access, consultation between the SAM operator and a requirements analyst was often required to resolve boundary disputes. There was also a temptation to bias data groups to better distribute size across the iterations. Unfortunately, this could bias the results so that less viable profiles appeared less costly than they were.

Figure 16-1 illustrates the relative size of the business objects and remains constant for each profile. Each profile consisted of three graphs:

1. **Size dispersed over increments.** Size for business objects was estimated using a lines-of-code (LOC) count of the corresponding legacy program elements.

2. **Ratio of program elements to adapters.** This bar graph shows the number of program elements migrated in an increment and the corresponding number of adapters produced during the increment. Adapters from the legacy system to the modern component—adapters—are distinguished from adapters from modern component to the legacy system—inverse adapters.

3. **Business object completion.** These graphs illustrate the degree to which a business object is completed at the end of an increment. As already mentioned, business object completion was a primary progress indicator.

The remainder of this section presents each stakeholder group's ideal project profile, highlights areas for potential compromise, and provides some observations.

USER REPRESENTATIVES

Figures 16-2, 16-3, and 16-4 illustrate the user representative profile. As shown in Figure 16-3, this profile resulted in two large initial increments, conflicting with the desires of both the architecture team and management for a small initial increment.

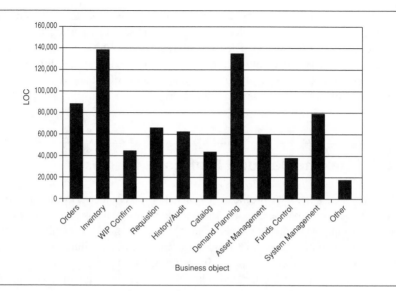

Figure 16-1 Size of business objects

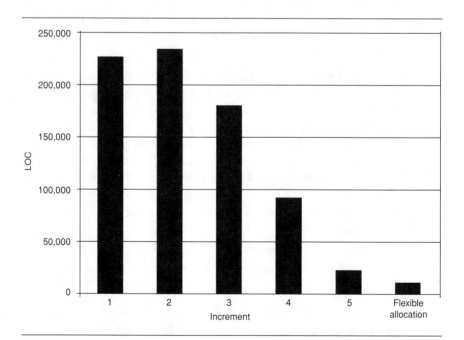

Figure 16-2 User representative profile: size of increments

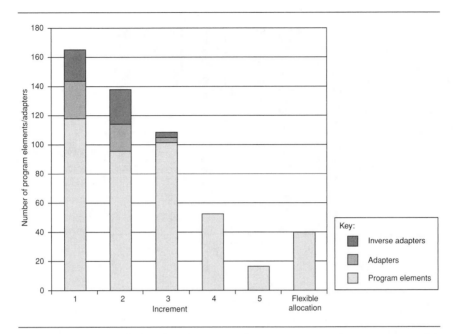

Figure 16-3   User representative profile: program elements versus adapters

Figure 16-3 illustrates the user representatives' priorities resulting in the highest number of program elements affected during the first increment (118), as well as a significant number of adapters of both types (subtotal of 48). This indicates that the first increment would be challenging and conflict with management's perception of risk. This profile also required a total of 95 adapters, a number sure to get the legacy maintainers' attention.

The user representative profile shown in Figure 16-4 results in the following order of business object completion:

- Increment 1—Requisition
- Increment 2—Demand Planning
- Increment 3—Orders, Inventory, and Work in Process
- Increment 4—Audit History, Asset Management, and Funds Control
- Increment 5—Catalog and System Management

The user representatives' low value of Audit History and Catalog—because of their limited contribution to this group's daily tasks—was another area of potential conflict. Conversely, these two business objects were attractive to management because of their relatively small size and perceived low complexity. The fragmentation of business object work over the increments appeared to be within the architecture team's tolerances.

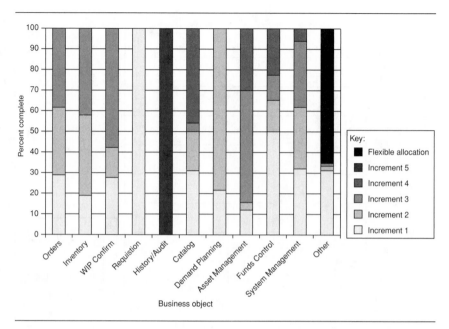

Figure 16-4   User representative profile: business object completion

ARCHITECTURE TEAM

Figures 16-5, 16-6, and 16-7 define the architecture team's profile. The architecture team's first increment represented 8 percent of the total system size, which was consistent with management requirements. The shape of the curve is appealing with its smooth ramp-up, but drops off in increment 5.

The architecture team's priorities required 77 adapters—18 fewer than in the user representative profile. The first increment does not include inverse adapters, so it fails to address management's concern that the initial increment touch all elements of the modernization effort. The third increment of the architecture team's profile includes the most program elements (99), still slightly fewer than the user representative's 118 in the first increment.

As requested by the architecture team, History/Audit finished in the first increment. To keep the increment small, the interfaces for the other business objects provided the inputs required by History/Audit, but little else was targeted. Fragmentation of business object work was surprisingly high, as several required four increments to complete, and one required work in all five. The order of completion was as follows:

- Increment 1—History/Audit
- Increment 2—Funds Control
- Increment 3—Requisition and Catalog

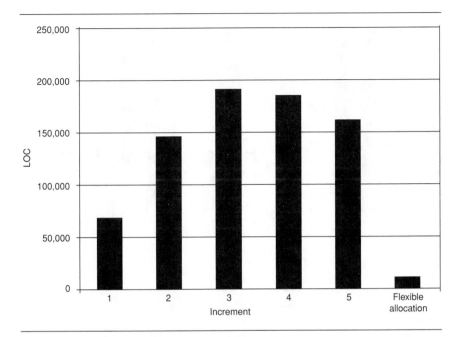

Figure 16-5   Architecture team profile: size of increments

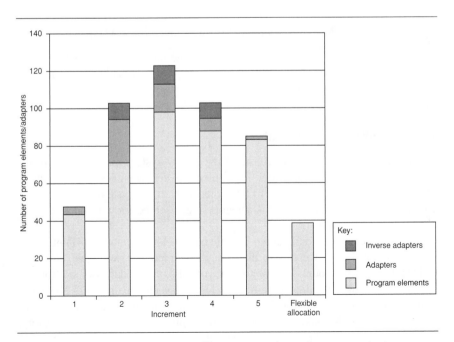

Figure 16-6   Architecture team profile: program elements versus adapters

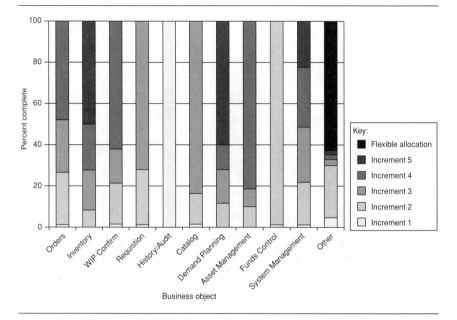

Figure 16-7 Architecture team profile: business object completion

- Increment 4—Orders, Work in Process, and Asset Management
- Increment 5—Inventory, Demand Planning, and System Management

The fact that Inventory is not completed until the last increment conflicts with those stakeholders who believe inventory to be a core, irrefutable supply function that should be addressed early.

LEGACY SYSTEM MAINTAINERS

Figures 16-8, 16-9, and 16-10 illustrate the legacy system maintainers' profile. The legacy maintainers' approach decoupled the dependencies between increments. Some 481K lines of code, or 62 percent of the total system size, were allocated to the flexible category. This category was reserved for work that could be allocated to any increment.

The legacy system maintainers' profile had the lowest number (41) of adapters. These 41 adapters were all of the legacy-to-component variety, which would reduce the overall amount of complexity involved in the modernization effort.

Business object completion for the legacy system maintainers showed a considerable degree of flexibility. The program elements in the category of flexible allocation could make a number of orders practical. For example, History/Audit could be first, followed by anyone's choice.

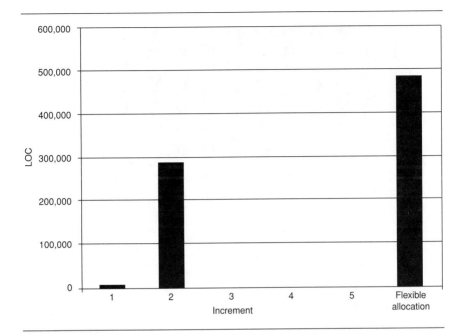

Figure 16-8   Legacy maintainer profile: size of increments

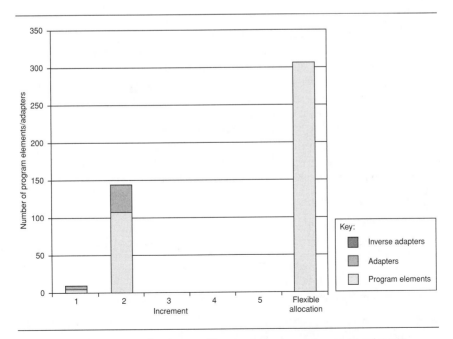

Figure 16-9   Legacy maintainer profile: program elements versus adapters

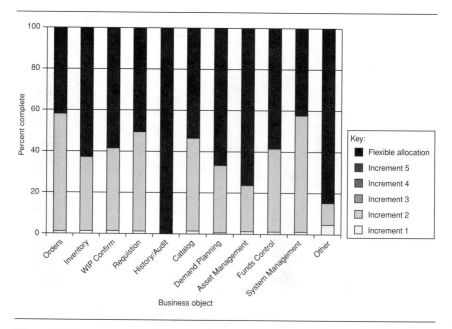

Figure 16-10   Legacy maintainer profile: business object completion

MANAGEMENT

Figures 16-11, 16-12, and 16-13 illustrate the management profile. The managers' effort did not fully align with their own desires and reflects compromise. The second increment was large, at 437K lines of code, or 56 percent of total system size.

A positive side effect of this profile was that most adapter work was concentrated in the big second increment. This could also be viewed as a risk. However, the total number of adapters for this profile was 63, not as low as for the maintainers' profile (41) but still 32 fewer than in the user representatives' profile.

Fragmentation of business object work was low, with five business objects requiring three increments. The bulk of work was slated for the second and third increments. The management profile completed business objects in the following order:

- Increment 1—History/Audit
- Increment 2—Inventory
- Increment 3—Orders, Work in Process, Catalog, Asset Management, and Funds Control
- Increment 4—Requisition
- Increment 5—Demand Planning and System Management

Completing Inventory in the second increment was a good omen for consensus building, but Demand Planning was a priority for user representatives, and they were unlikely to wait until the last increment.

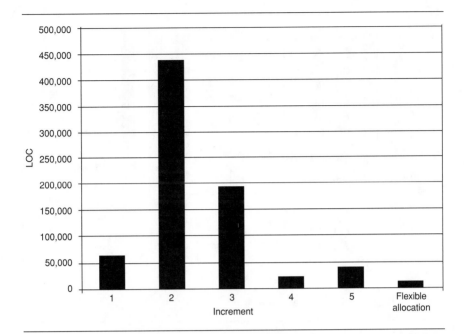

Figure 16-11   Management profile: size of increments

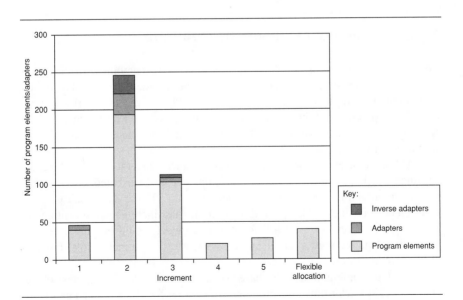

Figure 16-12   Management profile: program elements versus adapters

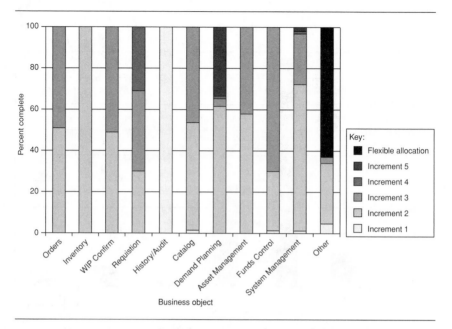

Figure 16-13 Management profile: business object completion

16.6 Stakeholder Consensus Meetings

Before the consensus meetings, several profiles were combined to encourage compromise. We looked for priorities common to two or more stakeholder groups, such as implementing Inventory in an early increment and risk mitigation. We also addressed the demonstration of progress in each increment, based on business object completion. Finally, we generated four viable compromises to start negotiations.

Although the early completion of business objects emerged as a goal, necessity dictated that a business object's development be distributed across increments, although this was not to the architecture team's liking. The result was that work on each business object would begin in the first increment and continue in each ensuing increment. At least one business object would be completed per increment. This required a modification to SAM to fix the increments in which business objects were completed.

The four combinations were based on a specified order for business object completion. We determined the groupings of data for SAM's input and generated the profile output products. The completion orders are shown in Table 16-1.

The use of PowerPoint slides was deemed too limiting for the consensus meeting. The profiles could be compared adequately only by viewing them side-by-side.

Table 16-1   Completion Orders

	Compromise 1	Compromise 2	Compromise 3	Compromise 4
Increment 1	Audit/History and Requisition	Audit/History and Requisition	Audit/History and Catalog	Audit/History and Catalog
Increment 2	Demand Planning and Catalog	Inventory and Catalog	Demand Planning and Requisition	Inventory
Increment 3	Inventory	Demand Planning	Inventory	Demand Planning and Requisition
Increment 4	Orders and Work in Process	Orders and Work in Process	Orders and Work in Process	Orders and Work in Process
Increment 5	All remaining	All remaining	All remaining	All remaining

We prepared color prints and spread them across the conference room table. The decision makers walked around the table, shuffled the charts this way and that, and made occasional pronouncements. Then they chose an order and voted unanimously for it, although the user representatives grumbled over the fact that Audit/History was given top billing in the first increment. These recommendations were applied to form the *consensus profile*.

16.7   Code-Migration Prioritization Results

Figures 16-14, 16-15, and 16-16 illustrate the consensus profile. The stakeholders liked the fact that, although the distribution of size across the increments was a little jagged, it was within projected tolerances. It ramped up to peak in the second increment, then ramped down, as shown in Figure 16-14.

The ratio of program elements to adapters was less appealing (72 adapters). However, at least it fell below the maximum number of adapters required by other profiles. The initial increment included both types of adapters—an advantage for risk mitigation.

Figure 16-16 shows the most attractive feature of the consensus profile—business object completion. Combining Audit/History and Catalog in the first increment created a good-sized piece of work that touched on many risk areas. These included internal and external interfaces using industry-standard approaches, applying adapter technology, using considerable portions of the database, and fielding of previous work on the Catalog business object. Addressing Inventory in the second increment was acceptable to the user community and prevented the business object from being the "guinea pig" in the initial, pilot increment. Both the Funds Control and Asset Management business objects were belatedly removed because these functions were being reallocated to other systems. Fragmentation

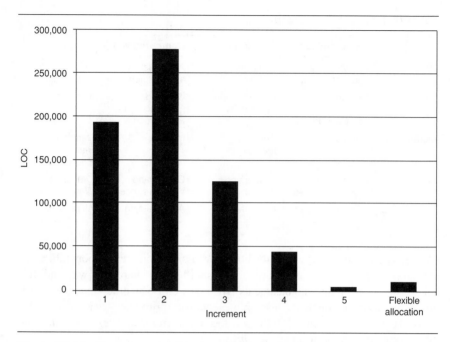

Figure 16-14   Consensus profile: size of increments

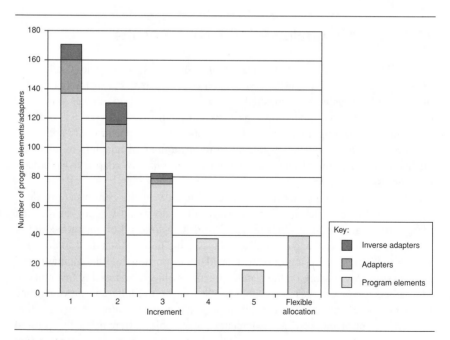

Figure 16-15   Consensus profile: program elements versus adapters

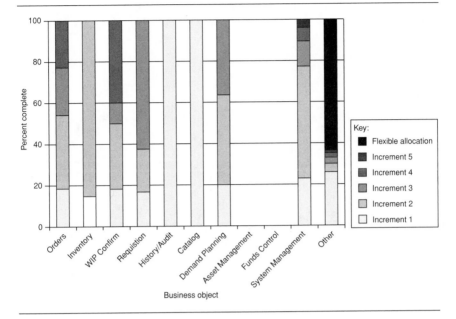

Figure 16-16   Consensus profile: business object completion

was not optimal, but with two business objects complete in one increment, one complete in two increments, two complete in three increments, and two complete in four increments, size was evenly dispersed.

16.8 Summary

Although not an ideal solution for any stakeholder group, the consensus profile was satisfactory to all. In the next chapter, we estimate the costs for the consensus code-migration strategy and determine whether the consensus plan selected is feasible.

17

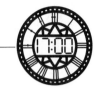

Resource Estimation

with Brad Clark, Wolf Goethert, and David Zubrow

> *For which of you, intending to build a tower, does not first sit down and*
> *estimate the cost, to see whether he has enough to complete it?*
> —Luke 14:28

In the previous chapter, the RSS stakeholders agreed on a consensus code migration plan. In this *first-fit* approach, we estimate the cost of this consensus plan to determine whether it is feasible within project constraints. Management makes the final decision about feasibility. Alternatively, in a *best-fit* approach, we cost several approaches and use cost and schedule data as evaluation criteria in selecting among them.

The RMM approach terminates when a *feasible* modernization plan has been approved. A feasible plan is one that accounts for the constraints imposed by the legacy system, target technologies, and business requirements.

If the modernization strategy is determined to be infeasible, it is necessary to identify the cause. For example, the target architecture may be too ambitious, and something more practical must be attempted. Or, the plan may simply not be implementable as defined and may need to be adjusted to account for staff and schedule constraints.

Although it is implicit in the approach that a modernization effort may be terminated at any time if it is determined to be infeasible, an explicit determination of feasibility takes place at the completion of the cost estimate. At this point, it should be apparent whether the defined approach is feasible, infeasible, or salvageable—feasible once adjusted. After this planning activity is completed, the modernization will be fully staffed with software designers, programmers, quality engineers, and other professionals. Terminating the project at this point has a broader impact on cost, schedule, and the morale of those involved.

Brad Clark is a visiting scientist at the Software Engineering Institute at Carnegie Mellon University and a technical consultant with Software Metrics, Inc. Wolf Goethert is a Senior Member of the Technical Staff at the Software Engineering Institute at Carnegie Mellon University. David Zubrow is a Senior Member of the Technical Staff at the Software Engineering Institute at Carnegie Mellon University.

At the completion of this final step in the approach, you should have an understanding and appreciation of both the legacy system and the target technologies, a defined target architecture, a defined modernization strategy, a risk mitigation plan, and a detailed cost estimate and schedule. These elements, along with more traditional software development plans for configuration management, staffing, and so forth, should be sufficient to successfully manage your modernization effort.

17.1   Where Are We?

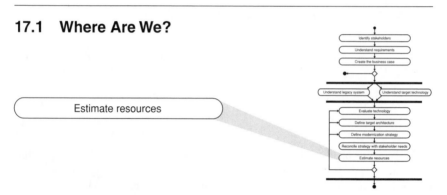

Now that we have created detailed code and migration plans, we can estimate the cost of executing the modernization strategy. Once we have estimated the costs, we can determine whether the strategy is feasible or use this plan as a measuring rod by which to assess other modernization strategies.

17.2   Cost Estimation Overview

Cost estimation is based on the simple premise that the more work to be done, the more it will cost. Figure 17-1 shows how project cost is estimated, based on the amount of work associated with developing functionality and the cost of other development tasks.

FUNCTION-BASED ESTIMATION

The top path in Figure 17-1 shows that overall cost is proportional to the functionality to be developed. This functionality could be new, reused, or replaced. In RSS, almost all the functionality required for the modernized system exists in the legacy system. The work effort to be estimated includes analysis and coding to migrate the functionality from the legacy system to the new system. Replacement, unlike refactoring, also includes redesign and reimplementation.

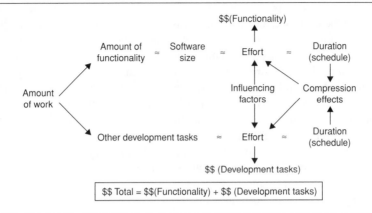

Figure 17-1   Converting work into cost and duration

Functionality can be quantified in various ways. Useful measures of functionality include the number of requirements, function points,[1] use cases, and scenarios. Functionality can be used to estimate the size of the software system in lines of code. For example, an organization may determine that one function point is equivalent to 89 source lines of code based on either published sources of conversion ratios or its own historical data.

Many cost estimation models use source lines of code (SLOC) as the software size measure. Design measures, such as design and user interface components, can also be used to estimate source lines of code. The estimated SLOC for business rules and data manipulation algorithms must be estimated from the functionality. In RSS, the size estimate must also account for the cost of developing scaffolding and other intermediate products that are a consequence of the modernization approach.

Function-based cost estimation is possible because software size strongly correlates to the effort expended to produce it. Based on this observed relationship, size estimates can be used to estimate effort. This relationship is expressed as a productivity ratio: staff months per thousands of source lines of code (KSLOC). The accuracy of the effort estimate depends on the accuracy of the size estimate and the productivity ratio. For RSS, no such productivity ratio was available. Hence, data needed to be collected to establish a productivity ratio.

Effort expresses how much labor is required over a period of time to produce required functionality. Effort is a derived measure that factors the number of people working and the time period over which they worked. Effort is expressed as staff hours, staff weeks, or staff months.

---

[1] The function-point metric is a means of measuring software size and productivity and uses functional, logical entities, such as inputs, outputs, and inquiries, that tend to relate more closely to the functions performed by the software as compared to other measures, such as lines of code.

Estimated effort is converted to cost by multiplying the number of staff months by the cost of a staff month, that is, the cost of one person working full time for one month. The cost is an average of the cost of each labor category used on the project for one month. Additional fidelity can be added by categorizing effort estimates into labor categories and applying a monthly cost for each category.

Effort can generally be converted into a staffing profile, given the available duration, or converted into the duration needed, given the available staffing. Imagine two projects require the same effort to develop a software product but finish at different times. The reason may be that one project had a large number of staff and took less time to finish. The other project had fewer staff and took longer to finish. Effort, expressed as staff months, represents a staff/time quantity. Reduce one and you need more of the other.

Many projects want to reduce the project *duration*, or the time it takes to complete the project. This is called schedule compression and generally requires adding staff. The relationship between duration and staffing is not linear. Generally, the schedule can be reduced by 25 percent—generally the maximum compression possible—if the staff is doubled. For example, a project requiring 30 person months of effort can be reduced in duration from 10 months to 7.5 months if the staffing is increased from 3 to 6 people, an increase in effort from 30 staff months to 45 staff months.

Factors other than size can influence the effort required to develop software. These factors include the ability of the people working on the project, the development environment, characteristics of the software product, and the host platform. These factors increase or decrease the effort required to produce the software and are used to adjust the productivity ratio.

TASK-BASED ESTIMATION

Another way to estimate effort is to identify development tasks and estimate the effort required for each, as indicated by the bottom path in Figure 17-1. In many cases, such as project management and QA, the support tasks are included as part of the productivity ratio rather than separately estimated tasks. Task-based estimation is used when the tasks do not produce any software—for example, the migration of data in RSS—and are not already accounted for as overhead in the productivity ratio. The cost of developing functionality is combined with the cost of these additional development tasks to form the RSS project cost estimate.

17.3 Costing an Increment

Estimating the cost of one increment is considered in the context of the cost for multiple increments. Each increment's cost is allocated a portion of the estimated final system size, which essentially establishes a "size budget" for each increment because size is strongly related to effort, which contributes to cost. Size allocations for each RSS increment were determined as part of the consensus profile and are shown in Figure 16-14.

When using an incremental development strategy to build a system, it is important to start follow-on increments at an appropriate time. For example, if the ensuing increment is started prematurely, late changes from the completing increment may have an adverse effect on cost and schedule. Ideally, each increment should start after the previous increment's software development has completed. Figure 17-2 illustrates the RSS incremental development strategy. While an increment's software is undergoing integration and testing, the next increment's software is undergoing an architectural review and detailed design. This minimizes unnecessary rework resulting from unplanned changes from a previous increment. If the overlap is increased, the cost for an increment will increase.

The size of the software to be developed depends on the functionality to be implemented (shown in Figure 17-1) and on a growth factor that takes into account the growth of the system because of requirements evolution. The two sources of functionality in RSS are the functionality embedded in the legacy code and the adapters required by the modernization strategy. Even though the adapters are not in the final system, they represent work that is a source of cost.

LEGACY SYSTEM SIZE

The existing system is assumed to be representative of the majority of RSS functionality. One approach to estimating the size for the new system in this situation is to use the legacy system's size as a basis of estimation. The estimate of size for the new system depends on a conversion ratio based on the differences in implementation languages between the legacy and modern systems.

In our case study, the legacy language is COBOL and the target language is Java. A conversion ratio of 1 COBOL SLOC to 0.58 Java SLOC can be used to

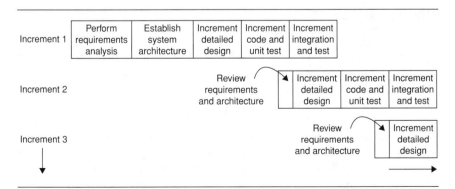

Figure 17-2 Incremental life cycle

estimate the new system size. This is based on ratios for converting COBOL and Java into unadjusted function points (UFPs). One UFP is equal to 91 COBOL SLOC or 53 Java SLOC [Boehm 00b]. Dividing the Java ratio by the COBOL ratio gives a ratio of 1 COBOL SLOC to 0.58 Java SLOC.

Increment size depends on the budget available and the amount of functionality to be converted from the legacy system to the new system. A rough estimate of the final size of the system is based on the size of the legacy system, which is about 1,230,300 executable COBOL SLOC. The estimated equivalent new-system size would be about 713,600 Java SLOC. Be mindful that this conversion ratio is based on the conversion ratios of COBOL and Java to UFP. All conversion ratios are averages and have some amount of error when applied in practice. As each increment is completed, data should be collected to update the ratios used to convert size from the legacy system to the new system.

ADAPTERS

Increment size is further increased as a result of the construction of adapters, as described in Section 13.6. Each incremental release of the system creates new adapters and discards existing adapters that are no longer needed. The sum of the sizes for all new adapters to be developed in a given increment must be estimated. Also, if regression testing is required for functionality where adapters have been discarded, a sizing factor may be assigned to this code as well.

One approach for estimating the size of adapters is to build a prototype of representative adapters and measure their sizes. In RSS, we prototyped both a regular adapter and an inverse adapter. These prototypes also provide an opportunity to collect data to estimate a productivity ratio for adapter development.

The size of these prototypes can be used for initial planning until actual data can be collected. It is important to collect size data on each adapter at the end of each increment for each class of adapter used. This data is used to improve the estimate for the next increment.

MAINTENANCE COSTS

In each ensuing increment, the portion of the legacy system that has not yet been replaced, as well as code already modernized, needs to be maintained. Unlike development costs, which occur only once, maintenance costs are recurring. Maintenance costs can also be expected to vary in proportion to the number of lines of code being maintained.

Because they are usually well known, legacy system maintenance costs can be used to estimate the cost of maintaining the recently modernized code. The cost of maintaining the legacy code is determined by dividing legacy system maintenance costs by the legacy code size, producing a cost per KLOC value. This value can then be used to estimate the cost of maintaining the modernized code by multiplying it against the estimated total lines of code to be completed at the end of each increment, including code from the previous increment. This rough estimate needs to be recalibrated using actual maintenance costs. Periodic maintenance costs should be collected and used to refine the model.

GROWTH FACTOR

A final consideration for estimating the size for one increment is a growth factor. A growth factor takes into account the system growth resulting from requirements evolution. There may be some enhancement of business processes as the system is modernized. A growth factor of 25 percent of the new increment's code size is not unreasonable.

17.4   Estimation of Cost and Duration

There are two approaches to estimating the effort, or cost, and duration for an increment: *productivity ratios* and *cost estimation models*. We discuss productivity ratios first, followed by cost estimation models.

PRODUCTIVITY RATIO APPROACH

The productivity ratio approach uses KSLOC per staff month to convert estimated size into effort, as shown in Figure 17-3. If a productivity ratio of 300 SLOC per staff month is used, the estimated effort for one fifth of the estimated RSS system size, 143 KSLOC, is 477 staff months, obtained by dividing the estimated increment size by the productivity ratio.

The productivity ratio of 300 SLOC per staff month may seem low. A useful productivity ratio is based on total estimated size for an increment and all the effort used in the increment to get the work done. This means that the productivity ratio should include the life-cycle phases that are common to all increments shown; the labor categories that support the development, such as project management, configuration management, and quality assurance; and designing, programming, and testing labor categories.

$$\text{Estimated effort (staff months)} = \text{Estimated SLOC} \div \frac{\text{SLOC}}{\text{Staff month}}$$

$$\text{Estimated duration (months)} = 3 * (\text{Estimated effort})^{1/3}$$

$$\text{Average staff} = \text{Staff months} \div \text{months}$$

Figure 17-3   Size/effort/duration relationships

The RSS duration can be estimated from the estimated effort by using the relationship between effort and duration shown in Figure 17-3. If an increment is estimated to need 477 staff months of effort, the duration is about 22.5 months, or about 21 staff members.

If an increment is scheduled to be 18 months long, the current estimated duration of 22.5 months is too long. Using our rule-of-thumb that reducing the schedule by a quarter requires doubling the staff means that the schedule can be shorted to 75 percent of 22.5 months, or about 17 months, by adding the extra labor at the appropriate time.

The disadvantage of using the productivity approach is not knowing how to adjust the productivity when unexpected things happen on the project, such as the key designer leaving for personal reasons. Another disadvantage is that this method produces a duration and staffing level for the complete increment only, with no insight into what the duration and staffing is for each phase of the increment. This deficiency is critical because the staffing and duration for an incrementally built system need to increase for the integration and testing phase to account for the extra time required to test the new and legacy software.

COST ESTIMATION MODELS

A more powerful and flexible alternative for estimating cost and duration is to use software-cost estimation models. Cost models provide estimates of effort for the software development phases of requirements, architecture, detailed design, code and unit test, and integration and test. Effort is distributed for the activities of requirements analysis, architecture, programming, testing, verification and validation, project office, configuration management, quality assurance and documentation. The models provide estimates of duration by phases and staffing by phases and activities, as shown in Figure 17-4.

The size parameter for most cost models is source lines of code. The amounts of new code, reused code with modification, and reused code without

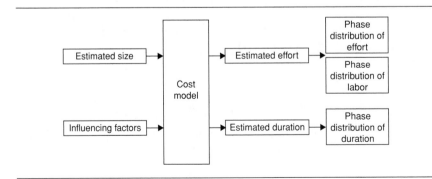

Figure 17-4 Cost model distribution of effort and duration

modification are used to adjust the estimated effort and duration by accounting for the extra work needed to incorporate and test these various sources of code.

One widely used cost estimation model is the Constructive Cost Model II (COCOMO II). COCOMO II addresses nonsequential process models, reengineering work, and reuse-driven approaches [Boehm 00a]. This model consists of two submodels, each offering increased fidelity the farther along one is in the project planning and design process [COCOMOII 02]. The COCOMO II model provides estimates of effort, schedule by phases, and staffing by phases and activities. Size inputs for COCOMO II are adjusted by an input called requirements evolution, or breakage, to account for new or evolving requirements.

Models can also be adjusted to account for *software product*, *software project*, *host platform*, and *personnel* factors that affect the software development. Software product factors include architecture and risk resolution, required reliability, product complexity, and database size. Software project factors include process maturity, development flexibility, team cohesion, use of software tools, and multi-site development. Host platform factors include host platform volatility, time constraints, and storage constraints. Finally, personnel factors include architect/designer capability, programmer capability, personnel continuity, application experience, host platform experience, and language and tool experience.

Recall that RSS requires experience with the legacy system, messaging, wrappers, adapters, a new implementation language, and design tools. Effort is impacted by the capability of the design, code, test, and documentation tools. Cost models can account for these special needs initially and as they change throughout the life of the project.

The most important feature of a cost model is its ability to account for increases and decreases in staffing because of the schedule compression or expansion. Again, the relationship between effort and schedule is nonlinear. Productivity ratios are for projects that have similar staffing and duration characteristics. The rule-of-thumb adjustment mentioned earlier is not accurate in all situations. Models make it easy to explore what happens when the required number of staff is not available or the required duration is longer than the schedule allocated to an increment.

A word of caution: Cost models need to be calibrated. The data required to calibrate a cost model is the actual developed software size, the staffing profile across the increment phases, and the duration of each phase. Calibration captures the differences in the type of work by changing the estimated effort and duration distribution.

Incremental Testing Cost.   The RSS incremental deployment plan requires that a fully functional system be deployed after each increment. A deployable system requires end-to-end testing for quality assurance. The cost of testing includes revalidating the legacy system that is still operational, the code modernized in the current increment, and the previously modernized code.

Testing cost can be estimated by a cost model based on an aggregated size input. The size input consists of the new increment, the sum of the previous increments, and the functioning portion of the legacy system converted into the implementation language, using a conversion ratio. This assumes that code is disabled as it is migrated to the modern system.

The cost of testing for each increment can be prohibitive. These costs can be reduced through the use of automated testing using testing tools or nondeliverable testing software. Automated testing can reduce the cost and duration to regression test previously modernized code and the remaining legacy system. The test suite can be continually expanded to detect the recurrence of previously corrected anomalies.

17.5   Costing the Preparation Work

Preparation work precedes the start of work on the first increment.[2] In Figure 17-2, the preparation work is similar to analyzing requirements and establishing the system architecture of the future system.

Lack of preparation work on the migration strategy and plan can increase the total cost of the system 32 percent.[3] The goal of the preparation phase is to reduce the uncertainty in key cost drivers: function and data migration, user interface, COTS software and hardware, and performance. The availability of tools for developing and verifying architectural specifications affects the efficiency of this phase, especially with a large legacy system.

Cost estimation for preparation work is performed using a cost model with the complete estimated modernized system size, estimated from the legacy code size and converted with the conversion ratio. With the system size and appropriate model inputs set to reflect the product, project, host platform, and people, an estimate can be produced for a big-bang—single-increment development and deployment—effort. The only part of this estimate we are interested in is the cost and schedule for the requirements and architecting phase, that is, only the portion of the estimate that applies to the preparation work.

There are additional factors that influence the effort required in performing the preparation work. They are the structure of the legacy code, the availability of complete documentation that describes the internals of the legacy system, availability of accurate user's manuals, availability of internal/external interface documentation, and the availability of architects/programmers who are familiar with the legacy system.

---

[2] This section appears out of order so that we could introduce the ideas of an incremental life cycle, sizing the work, and using cost models to estimate effort and duration.
[3] Based on varying the *architecture* and *risk resolution* input to the COCOMO II model from very low to high for a system of 713.6 KSLOC.

Assuming a complete estimated system size of 892 KSLOC—estimated 713.6 KSLOC + 25 percent growth—for RSS, relevant experience, availability of effective automated tools, and a compressed schedule, it could take from as many as 53 people for 17 months to as few as 27 people for 13 months to complete the preparation work. These numbers were calculated using the COCOMO II tool. Note that adjustments in the factors used by the formulas can result in widely varying estimates.

17.6   Costing the Final Database Migration

RSS data conversion involves three types of work: creating a new database schema, migrating the data, and converting the new system to use the newly structured data. When creating a new database schema, data fields in the old database are reallocated to new tables and rearranged. New fields may be created by either combining or splitting old fields. Data migration includes effort spent in mapping from one structure to the other, creating scripts to migrate the data, testing the scripts, and transferring the data from the old database to the new one. Finally, as explained in Section 15.4, the entity beans representing the data persistence layer have to be modified to use the new database structure and revalidated.

Costing for this type of work takes the lower path shown in Figure 17-1. The work is broken down into detailed tasks. Using engineering judgment, an estimate of the effort and time each task could take is used to build up a cost and duration.

Unfortunately, there usually is little data to support this kind of planning. The remedy is to collect data as soon as possible by closely monitoring the initial execution of data conversion tasks and then check the engineering-judgment figures. This bootstrap method means that the initial estimate will probably be low and that an updated estimate of cost and duration should be expected. Managing these risks is critical if the organization lacks a productivity factor for this type of work. One risk mitigation activity is to pilot an effort to collect the needed data to refine the initial estimate.

17.7   Data Collection

Measurements of development activity increase the credibility of future estimates. In an early stage of a project's life cycle, all estimates of cost must make assumptions because of a lack of knowledge. Reestimates need to be performed following the completion of each increment. Making measurements an integral part of the everyday operation of the project and using them to plan and make decisions is an indicator of a high-maturity organization.

The following data should be collected:

- **Amount of legacy code replaced by an increment.** Sizing data that represents the functionality replaced in the legacy system by the new system is used to improve the conversion ratio from legacy code to the new system.

- **Amount of new code developed during the increment.** This data is used in the conversion ratio and cost model calibration. This could get more difficult with each increment because of the difficulty of differentiating new from previously developed code. A good configuration management system could eliminate this problem.

- **New requirements.** New requirements may be introduced during an increment because of implementation differences in the new system or tweaking the functionality embedded in the legacy system. This information is used to track new growth, which is used in future planning.

- **Effort expended during the increment.** This data is used to calibrate the cost model. The effort data collected needs to specify which labor categories are included, which phases are covered, whether contract labor and overtime are included, and, if possible, the effort for each major development activity, such as architecting, designing, coding, testing, and repairing.

- **Duration for each project phase.** This data is used to calibrate the cost model. The duration data-collection procedures need to specify objective criteria for milestone completion. Ambiguous start- and end-phase dates produce useless duration data.

- **Quality data.** Collect quality data, such as the number of defects discovered, the type of defect, the source phase of the defect, and the discovery phase of the defect. This data is used to make succeeding increments more efficient and, within an increment, to give a realistic projection of readiness for deployment.

- **Data conversion.** Collect the effort and duration data for data conversion activities. This data needs to be collected and analyzed as soon as possible. The data is used to improve the engineering judgment used in the initial planning.

The initial estimates for the cost and duration may be only a rough order of magnitude in accuracy. Collecting data on pilot projects and on each increment will improve the quality of the estimates. This data should be used to check the assumptions in the estimates. The cost and duration should at least be reestimated based on past, demonstrated performance at the start of each increment.

17.8 Summary

In performing the cost estimate for the consensus profile, it was determined that the amount of time to complete the initial increments was prohibitively long, given the project requirements to deploy functionality every 18 to 24 months. The modernization plan, in this case, was determined to be infeasible but salvagable. The RSS stakeholders were sent back to rethink the consensus profile, given this new information about the cost estimate and schedule. At this point, we have learned what we need to learn from RSS and so end the case study.

In the next, and final, chapter, we generalize from our experiences in risk-managed modernization and provide some general recommendations to guide your modernization effort.

17.9 For Further Reading

- To learn about COCOMO II cost estimation model, see *Software Cost Estimation with COCOMO II* by Boehm et al. [Boehm 00b].

18

Recommendations

Those are my principles. If you don't like them I have others.
—Source unknown

In this, our final, chapter, we rise above the day-to-day struggles of modernizing legacy systems and consider the principles that can guide you along your path to fully evolvable, modernized systems.

18.1 Find a Better Way

Find a better way of doing things rather than simply trying to improve the way things have been done in the past. Many modernization efforts simply replace old legacy code with new legacy code. Although this extends the useful lifetime of the legacy systems, this approach often leaves possible moves unplayed.

When deciding how aggressively to approach a modernization effort, ask yourself, "When will the next opportunity to modernize come along?" On the other hand, being too aggressive in your modernization plans means increasing risk that could lead to project failure. Therefore, your plans must be well considered and plausible. In our experience, the best ideas reduce overall risk while providing needed capabilities.

Finding a better way may require you to ignore the existing system and processes and consider the underlying principles instead. This may provide a clearer vision of your goals and allow you to streamline your system and processes to this vision.

18.2   Use Commercial Components

The use of commercial off-the-shelf (COTS) products as elements of larger systems is becoming increasingly commonplace. Shrinking budgets, accelerating rates of COTS enhancement, and expanding system requirements are all driving this process. The shift from custom development to COTS-based systems is occurring in both new-development and maintenance activities. If done properly, this shift can help establish a sustainable modernization practice.

In general, incorporating off-the-shelf infrastructure products, although never painless, has great benefit in providing a standard infrastructure that can be more easily integrated with other systems and components, better quality of service, and more reliable and scalable communications. Off-the-shelf components that offer capabilities in domain-specific areas can also have a positive effect but are more difficult to integrate because they often require changes to existing business processes.

The SEI COTS-based systems (CBS) initiative is exploring the challenges of assembling systems from preexisting components, evaluating COTS products, and modifying legacy systems to take advantage of a CBS strategy.[1] The book *Building Systems from Commercial Components* [Wallnau 01] describes some lightweight, agile development processes for building COTS-based systems. Much of the philosophy underlying these processes is present in this book as well. In many ways, these two books could be considered companion volumes.

18.3   Manage Complexity

Complexity is always *a* and often *the* limiter in the modernization process. System architects and software engineers strive to control many variables, such as cost and schedule. At the same time, there is a tendency to let complexity expand unchecked. This may have something to do with our egos. After all, why make something simple when it can be complex and wonderful?

Unfortunately, complexity in a modernization effort is compounded by many factors: the size of the legacy system being modernized, the scale of the modernization effort, the number of people involved, the familiarity of the development team with both the legacy system and the modern technologies, and so forth. Therefore, complexity in a modernization effort should be constrained to the challenge of developing a migration plan that can be executed by a large team of individuals with disparate skills, on time, and on schedule.

---

[1] See http://www.sei.cmu.edu/cbs.

18.4 Develop and Deploy Incrementally

In theory, the most cost-effective way to develop and deploy a modernized system is all at once, in a big-bang deployment. A big-bang deployment eliminates adapters, bridges, and other connectors. It eliminates concurrently fielding both modern and legacy components, and it reduces the number of testing cycles to one. Again, this is in theory.

In practice, big-bang deployments are almost impossible in a large-scale modernization effort. In the time it takes to develop a modern system from the ground up, the target has typically moved. So although the modern system may achieve the original objectives, they may no longer be valid. Also, it is extremely difficult to reproduce the functionality of a legacy system that has been refined over many years by user involvement and feedback, without having the advantage of some user participation. In most cases, incremental deployment is necessary to obtain user feedback without completely disrupting the organization.

Incremental development can mean the difference between success and failure in a modernization effort. Once a modernization plan has been developed, it must be validated. The best way to do this is by selecting a small but difficult increment and demonstrating the validity of the plan.

Finally, it is unlikely that any plan will be implemented without modification. When developing and deploying in increments, it is possible to learn from past increments to improve both the process and the product. In a big-bang deployment, any lessons learned would be learned too late to affect the outcome of the modernization effort.

Once the plan has been proved, it can be scaled up to production levels. Any number of concurrent development efforts can be implemented simultaneously—limited only by the available resources.

18.5 Software Engineering Skills

There are two disparate views about software engineering. According to the first, improving the quality and reducing the cost of developing software-intensive systems requires improving the techniques, technologies, process, methods, and tools. According to the second perspective, the solution does not require that you improve the tools, only that you improve users' abilities to apply them. Both perspectives are equally valid in modernizing legacy systems.

Generally speaking, the old generation of developers must gain knowledge of new technologies. At the same time, the new generation must pick up best-of-breed development skills through teaching and experience. Both generations need to learn integration skills. The next generation integrator/developer will require many more skills and experiences and will have to adapt on the fly. This places a premium on developers who embrace new challenges and skill sets.

18.6 Component-Centric Approach

Component-based development is the current step in the evolutionary ladder of software development practices. As such, it represents our best understanding of how to build large, complex systems. The idea behind components is not a new one. It is really another means of managing complexity. For many years, we have practiced software decomposition—taking complex systems and decomposing them into simpler and simpler forms. Eventually, these designs were simple enough to translate to code. This code was then integrated with other code to form more complex constructs, until finally the entire system was assembled from these simple elements. The parallel with component-based development is obvious except that in this newer paradigm, components are formed into separately deployable units that are assembled during the integration process. This requires that more consideration be given to component interfaces. They must allow the component to be reused while conforming to a standard model that simplifies integration with other components.

A component-centric approach can be used to componentize legacy systems, develop small-grain components for a component framework—such as EJB—and to develop large-grained business object components. When modernizing legacy systems, each technique supports the others. For example, restructuring the legacy system into components makes it easier to replace them with modernized components. Developing reusable components at different levels of granularity enforces a reuse mentality at all levels of development.

Component-based development can be used with object-oriented programming techniques. A strict OO mind set, however, often results in highly complex and delicate class hierarchies. Component-based development can be thought of as "OO in moderation." Class hierarchies are maintained with limited levels of nesting, whereas components provide the primary means of functional decomposition.

18.7 Architecture-Centric Approach

Architecture drives the evolution of the system. Architecture both defines the desired end state and guides you to your goal. Of course, it is almost humorous to have a recommendation to use a component-centric approach directly followed by a recommendation to use an architecture-centric approach. After all, both the

Earth and the Sun cannot be at the center of our solar system. However, if we can adjust to the strange gravitational fields generated by a binary system, we can greatly benefit from the extra "light" created by a multicentric approach. Architecture can be used to encourage and enforce a component-centric approach, as demonstrated in Chapter 12. At the same time, the reuse mentality of an component-centric approach is orthogonal to architectural concerns.

18.8   High Levels of Concurrent Development

The relationship between the duration of a project and staffing is not linear. Achieving high levels of concurrent development through careful planning moves toward a linear relationship, allowing the schedule to be compressed in a fixed ratio to project staffing.

High levels of concurrent development are possible only in a highly structured, mature environment. The architecture must be well defined, and the development processes must be well understood and validated in practice. When successful, high levels of concurrent development allow projects to be completed in less time. This, in turn, allows functionality to be deployed quickly to the user community. It also allows systems that are not already obsolete to be fielded.

When executed poorly, high levels of concurrent development result in redundant efforts, incompatible system components, and software engineers standing around with nothing to do. These problems can quickly increase development costs and exhaust available resources. So although having high levels of concurrent development is a goal, it should not be attempted without adequate forethought and preparation.

18.9   Continuous Integration

Continuous integration has both advantages and disadvantages. The primary disadvantage is that it can disrupt the development process. A cost is always incurred when you are developing a component and are suddenly forced to deal with integration issues. The advantages, however, outweigh the disadvantages in this case because you can deal with integration issues while the consequences of integration decisions are still fresh in your mind. Continuous integration can also reduce schedule risk resulting from failures to identify integration issues that may cause significant rework to one or more components.

18.10 Risk-Managed Development

Risk-management is a cornerstone of our modernization approach. If you consider the inability to field sufficient functionality alongside other traditional risks, the entire modernization effort can be characterized as a risk-reduction effort. The process of continually evaluating risk factors and performing risk mitigation eventually results in the elimination of risks above the line separating success from failure.

18.11 Final Word

The risk-managed modernization approach can be applied to most modernization projects. The case study presented throughout this book is but one example, and the specifics of how this project was planned and managed may not be appropriate in your modernization effort. However you proceed, in the words of John Perry Barlow, "Let the words be yours, I'm done with mine."[2]

---

[2] "Cassidy," written in Cara, Wyoming, Feb. 1972. First performed on March 23, 1974, at the Cow Palace in Daly City, California.

References

[Agrawal 90] Agrawal, H., and J. R. Horgan. 1990. "Dynamic Program Slicing." *Proceedings of the ACM SIGPLAN '90 Conference on Programming Language Design and Implementation* (June) 246–256.

[Allamaraju 99] Allamaraju, Subrahmanyam. 1999. "Nuts and Bolts of Transaction Processing." http://www.sei.cmu.edu/activities/cbs/mls/links.html#allamaraju99.

[Altman 99] Altman, R., Y. Natis, J. Hill, J. Klein, B. Lheureux, M. Pezzini, R. Schulte, and S. Varma. 1999. "Middleware: The Glue for Modern Applications." *Gartner Group Strategic Analysis Report* (July 26).

[Barry 98] Barry, D. 1998. "ODMG 2.0: A Standard for Object Storage." *Component Strategies* (July): 48.

[Bass 98] Bass, Len, Paul Clements, and Rick Kazman. 1998. *Software Architecture in Practice.* Reading, MA: Addison-Wesley.

[Beck 93] Beck, J., and D. Eichmann. 1993. "Program and Interface Slicing for Reverse Engineering." *Proceedings of the 15th International Conference on Software Engineering.* Baltimore, MD (May 17–21): 54–63. IEEE Computer Society Press.

[Bernstein 97] Bernstein, Philip A. and Eric Newcomer. 1997. *Principles of Transaction Processing.* San Francisco: Morgan Kaufmann.

[Biggerstaff 93] Biggerstaff, T. J., B. G. Mitbander, and D. E. Webster. 1993. "The Concept Assignment Problem in Program Understanding." *Proceedings of the 15th International Conference on Software Engineering.* Baltimore, MD (May 17–21) 482–498. IEEE Computer Society Press.

[Biggerstaff 94] Biggerstaff, T. J., B. G. Mitbander, and D. E. Webster. 1994. "Program Understanding and the Concept Assignment Problem." *Communications of the ACM* 37, 5 (May): 72–82.

[Bisbal 97] Bisbal, Jesus, Deirdre Lawless, Bing Wu, Jane Grimson, Vincent Wade, Ray Richardson, and D. O'Sullivan. 1997. "An Overview of Legacy Information System Migration." *Proceedings of the 4th Asian-Pacific Software Engineering and International Computer Science Conference* (APSEC 97, ICSC 97). Hong Kong (Dec 1977). 529–530.

[Bisbal 99] Bisbal, J., D. Lawless, B. Wu, and J. Grimson. 1999. "Legacy System Migration: A Brief Review of Problems, Solutions and Research Issues" (07-TCD-CS-1999-38). Dublin, Ireland: Computer Science Department, Trinity College.

[Boehm 88] Boehm, B. 1988. "A Spiral Model of Software Development and Enhancement." *Computer* (May): 61–72.

[Boehm 91] Boehm, B. "Software Risk Management: Principles and Practices." 1991. *IEEE Software* 8, 1 (January): 32–41.

[Boehm 00a] Boehm, B., C. Abts, and C. Chulani. 2000. *Software Development Cost Estimation Approaches—A Survey.* Center for Software Engineering, Computer Science Department, University of Southern California, Los Angeles. USC-CSE 2000–505.

[Boehm 00b] Boehm, B., Ellis Horowitz, Ray Madachy, Donald Reifer, Bradford K. Clark, Bert Steece, A. Winsor Brown, Sunita Chulani, and Chris Abts. 2000. *Software Cost Estimation with COCOMOII.* Englewood Cliffs, NJ: Prentice-Hall.

[Bowman 99] Bowman, T., R. C. Holt, and N. V. Brewster. 1999. "Linux as a Case Study: Its Extracted Software Architecture." *Proceedings of the 21st International Conference on Software Engineering.* Los Angeles (May 16–22): 555–563. New York: ACM Press.

[Brodie 95] Brodie, M. L., and M. Stonebraker. 1995. *Migrating Legacy Systems: Gateways, Interfaces and the Incremental Approach.* San Francisco: Morgan Kaufmann.

[Buhr 96] Buhr, R. J. A., and R. S. Casselman. 1996. *Use Case Maps for Object-Oriented Systems.* Englewood Cliffs, NJ: Prentice-Hall.

[Buxton 70] Buxton, J. N., and B. Randell. 1970. "Software Engineering Techniques." *Proceedings of the NATO Software Engineering Conference.* Rome, Italy (April).

[Bye 01] Bye, Peter. 2001. *"Middleware Strategy and Products for ClearPath Systems Running OS 2200."* (Unisys white paper.) (April).

[Card 96] Card, D. N., S. A. Hissam, and R. T. Rosemeier. 1996. "National Software Data and Information Repository." *CrossTalk* 9, 2 (February). http://www.sei.cmu.edu/activities/cbs/mls/links.html#card96.

[Carr 98] Carr, D. 1998. "Web-Enabling Legacy Data When Resources Are Tight." *Internet World* (August 10): 24–25.

[Carriere 99] Carriere, S. J., S. G. Woods, and R. Kazman. 1999. "Software Architecture Transformation." *Proceedings of the Sixth Working Conference on Reverse Engineering (WCRE 99).* Atlanta, GA (Oct.): 13–23.

[Chappell 98] Chappell, David. 1998. "Microsoft Message Queue Is a Fast, Efficient Choice for Your Distributed Application." *Microsoft Journal* (July): 17–24.

[Chikofsky 90] Chikofsky, Elliot J., and J. H. Cross II. 1990. "Reverse Engineer and Design Recovery: A Taxonomy." *IEEE Software* 7 (January): 13–17.

[Cimitile 97] Cimitile, A., A. De Lucia, A. Di Lucca, and A. R. Fasolino. 1997. "Identifying Objects in Legacy Systems." *Proceedings of the 5th Workshop on Program Comprehension (WPC97).* Dearborn, MI (March, 1977): 138–147.

[Clements 02] Clements, Paul, Rick Kazman, and Mark Klein. 2002. *Evaluating Software Architecture: Methods and Case Studies.* Boston, MA: Addison-Wesley.

[Clements 03] Clements, P., F. Bachmann, L. Bass, D. Garlan, J. Ivers, R. Little, R. Nord, and J. Stafford. 2003. *Documenting Software Architectures: Views and Beyond.* Boston, MA: Addison-Wesley.

[COCOMOII 02] University of Southern California. 2000. "COCOMO." http://www.sei.cmu.edu/activities/cbs/mls/links.html#cocomoii02.

[Coleman 94] Coleman, D., D. Ash, B. Lowther, and P. Oman. 1994. "Using Metrics to Evaluate Software System Maintainability." *IEEE Computer* (August): 3–34.

[Comella-Dorda 00] Comella-Dorda, Santiago, John Robert, and Robert Seacord. 2000. "Theory and Practice of Enterprise JavaBean Portability." *International Journal of Computers and Their Applications* Volume 7, Number 3 (September): 139–145.

[Corsaro 02] Corsaro, A., and D. Schmidt. "Evaluating Real-Time Java Features and Performance for Real-Time Embedded Systems." *8th IEEE Real-Time and Embedded Technology and Applications Symposium (RTAS 2002)*. San Jose, CA (September 24–27): 90–100.

[De Lucia 97] De Lucia, A., G. A. Di Lucca, A. R. Fasolino, P. Guerra, and S. Petruzzelli. 1997. "Migrating Legacy Systems Towards Object-Oriented Platforms." *Proceedings of the International Conference of Software Maintenance (ICSM97)*, Bari, Italy (1–3 Oct, 1997): 122–129.

[ebXML 01] ebXML. 2001. "ebXML Technical Architecture Specification." February. http://www.sei.cmu.edu/activities/cbs/mls/links.html#ebxml01.

[Eichmann 95] Eichmann, David. 1995. "Application Architectures for Web-Based Data Access." http://www.sei.cmu.edu/activities/cbs/mls/links.html#eichmann95.

[Erlikh 00] Erlikh, L. 2000. "Leveraging Legacy System Dollars for E-Business." *IEEE. IT Pro* (May/June): 17–23.

[Fowler 99] Fowler, M., K. Beck, J. Brant, W. Opdyke, and D. Roberts. 1999. *Refactoring: Improving the Design of Existing Code.* Reading, MA: Addison-Wesley.

[Gamma 95] Gamma, E., R. Helm, R. Johnson, and J. Vlissides. 1995. *Design Patterns: Elements of Reusable Object-Oriented Software.* Reading, MA: Addison-Wesley.

[Garlan 02] Garlan, D., A. J. Kompanek, and S. Cheng. 2002. "Reconciling the Needs of Architectural Description with Object-Modeling Notations." *Science of Computer Programming.* Amsterdam: Elsevier Press. http://www.sei.cmu.edu/activities/cbs/mls/links.html#garlan00.

[Gosling 97] Gosling, J., and H. McGilton. 1997. "The Java Language Environment." http://www.sei.cmu.edu/activities/cbs/mls/links.html#gosling97.

[Grady 87] Grady, R. 1987. *Software Metrics: Establishing a Company-Wide Program.* Englewood Cliffs, NJ: Prentice-Hall.

[Haft 95] Haft, T. M., and I. Vessey. 1995. "The Relevance of Application Domain Knowledge: The Case of Computer Program Comprehension." *Information Systems Research* 6: 286–299.

[Hall 98] Hall, E. M. 1998. *Managing Risk.* Reading, MA: Addison-Wesley.

[Higuera 96] Higuera, Ronald P., and Yacov Y. Haimes. 1996. "Software Risk Management" (CMU/SEI-96-TR-012). Pittsburgh, PA: Software Engineering Institute, Carnegie Mellon University. http://www.sei.cmu.edu/activities/cbs/mls/links.html#higuera96.

[Houston 99] Houston, Peter. 1999. "Selecting Between Synchronous and Asynchronous Alternatives." Microsoft. http://www.sei.cmu.edu/activities/cbs/mls/links.html#houston99.

[IBM 01] International Business Machines. 2001. "Fundamental Information Aggregate Concepts." http://www.sei.cmu.edu/activities/cbs/mls/links.html#ibm01.

[IEEE 90] Institute of Electrical and Electronics Engineers. 1990. *IEEE Standard Computer Dictionary: A Compilation of IEEE Standard Computer Glossaries.* New York: Institute of Electrical and Electronics Engineers.

[IETF 01] IETF/W3C XMLDSIG Working Group. 2001. "XML-Signature Syntax and Processing—Internet Draft." October. http://www.sei.cmu.edu/activities/cbs/mls/links.html#ietf01.

[J2EE 01a] Sun Microsystems. 2001. "Session Façade Design Pattern." http://www.sei.cmu.edu/activities/cbs/mls/links.html#j2ee01a.

[J2EE 01b] Sun Microsystems. 2002. "Fast-Lane Reader Design Pattern." http://www.sei.cmu.edu/activities/cbs/mls/links.html#j2ee01b.

[J2EE 02] Sun Microsystems. 2002. "Java 2 Platform, Enterprise Edition." http://www.sei.cmu.edu/activities/cbs/mls/links.html#j2ee02.

[Jaworski 00] Jaworski, Jamie, and Paul J. Perrone. 2000. *Java Security Handbook* Indianapolis, IN: SAMS Publishing.

[Karolak 96] Karolak, D. W. 1996. *Software Engineering Risk Management.* Los Alamitos, CA: IEEE Computer Society Press.

[Kassem 00] Kassem, Nicholas. 2000. *Designing Enterprise Applications with the Java™ 2 Platform (Enterprise Edition).* Boston, MA: Addison-Wesley.

[Kazman 98] Kazman, R., S. G. Woods, and S. J. Carriere. 1998. "Requirements for Integrating Software Architecture and Reengineering Models: CORUM II." *Proceedings of the WCRE 98*, Honolulu (October): 154–163.

[Kazman 01] Kazman, Rick, Liam O'Brien, and Chris Verhoef. 2001. "Architecture Reconstruction Guidelines" (CMU/SEI-2001-TR-026). Pittsburgh, PA: Software Engineering Institute, Carnegie Mellon University. http://www.sei.cmu.edu/activities/cbs/mls/links.html#kazman01.

[Korel 88] Korel, B., and J. Laski. 1998. "Dynamic Program Slicing." *Information Processing Letters* 29, 3 (Oct): 155–163.

[Lakhotia 98] Lakhotia, Arun, and Jean-Christophe Deprez. 1998. "Restructuring Functions with Low Cohesion." *Proceedings of the 6th Working Conference of Electrical and Electronics Engineers.* Atlanta, GA (6–8 Oct. 1999): 36–46.

[Lanubile 97] Lanubile, Filippo, and Giuseppe Visaggio. 1997. "Extracting Reusable Functions by Flow Graph-Based Program Slicing." *IEEE Transactions on Software Engineering* 23, 4 (April): 246–259.

[Larman 00] Larman, Craig. 2000. "Enterprise JavaBeans 201: The Aggregate Entity Pattern." *Software Development Magazine* (April). http://www.sei.cmu.edu/activities/cbs/mls/links.html#larman00.

[Lehman 80] Lehman, M. M. 1980. "On Understanding Laws, Evolution and Conservation in the Large Program Life Cycle." *Journal of Systems and Software* 1, 3: 213–221.

[Lehman 85] Lehman, M. M. and L. Belady. 1985. *Program Evolution: Processes of Software Change.* London: Academic Press.

[Martin 83] Martin, J., and C. McClure. 1983. *Software Maintenance: The Problems and Its Solutions.* Englewood Cliffs, NJ: Prentice-Hall.

[Microsoft 00] Microsoft Corporation. 2000. "BizTalk Framework 2.0: Document and Message Specification." http://www.sei.cmu.edu/activities/cbs/mls/links.html#microsoft00.

[Moad 90] Moad, J. 1990. "Maintaining the Competitive Edge," *DATAMATION* 61–62, 64, 66.

[Müller 94] Müller, H. A., K. Wong, and S. R. Tilley. 1994. "Understanding Software Systems Using Reverse Engineering Technology." *The 62nd Congress of L'Association Canadienne Francaise pour l'Avancement des Sciences Proceedings* (ACFAS). Montreal, Que (16–17 May 1994): 41–48. Vol 26, No. 4.

[Nosek 90] Nosek, J. and P. Palvia. 1990. "Software Maintenance Management; Changes in the Last Decade." *Journal of Software Maintenance: Research and Practice* 23: 157–174.

[OAG 99] Open Applications Group. 1999. *Plug and Play Business Software Integration: The Compelling Value of the Open Applications Group.* Atlanta, GA: Open Applications Group. http://www.sei.cmu.edu/activities/cbs/mls/links.html#oag99.

[OASIS 01] Organization for the Advancement of Structured Information Standards (OASIS). 2001. "RELAX NG Specification—Committee Specification (December) http://www.sei.cmu.edu/activities/cbs/mls/links.html#oasis01.

[ODMG 98] ODMG. 1998. *ODMG OQL User Manual.* Release 5.0. February.

[OMG 01] Object Management Group. 2001. "Unified Modeling Language (UML) Specification," Version.1.4. December. http://www.sei.cmu.edu/activities/cbs/mls/links.html#omg01.

[OpenGroup 96] Open Group. 1996. *Distributed TP: Reference Model, Version 3, Open Group Guide G504.* Reading, England: X/Open Company.

[Ozsu 99] Ozsu, M. T., and P. Valduriez. 1999. *Principles of Distributed Database Systems.* Upper Saddle River, NJ: Prentice-Hall.

[Plakosh 99] Plakosh, Daniel, Scott Hissam, and Kurt Wallnau. 1999. "Into the Black Box: A Case Study in Obtaining Visibility into Commercial Software" (CMU/SEI-99-TN-010). Pittsburgh, PA: Software Engineering Institute, Carnegie Mellon University. http://www.sei.cmu.edu/activities/cbs/mls/links.html#plakosh99.

[Ransom 98] J. Ransom, I. Sommerville, and I. Warren. 1998. "A Method for Assessing Legacy Systems for Evolution." *Proceedings of the Second Euromicro Conference on Software Maintenance and Reengineering* (CSMR98). Florence, Italy (8–11 March 1998): 128–134.

[Reifer 02] Reifer, D. 2002. *Making the Software Business Case: Improvement by the Numbers.* Boston, MA: Addison-Wesley.

[RENAISSANCE 97] RENAISSANCE project. 1997. "ESPRIT" Lancaster University. http://www.sei.cmu.edu/activities/cbs/mls/links.html#renaissance97.

[RosettaNet 02] RosettaNet.org. 2002. RosettaNet Implementation Framework: Core Specification. March. http://www.sei.cmu.edu/activities/cbs/mls/links.html#rosettanet02.

[Seacord 02] Seacord, Robert. 2002. "Replaceable Components and the Service Provider Interface." *Proceedings of the First International Conference on COTS-Based Software Systems (ICCBSS).* Orlando, FL (Feb): 222–234. Berlin: Springer-Verlag.

[Seng 99] Seng, Jia-Lang, and Wayne Tsai. 1999. "A Structure Transformation Approach for Legacy Information Systems—A Cash Receipts/Reimbursement Example." *Proceedings of the 32nd Hawaii International Conference on System Sciences.* Maui, HI (5–8 Jan. 1999): CD Rom, 10 pages.

[Sharma 02] Sharma, Rahul, Beth Stearns, and Tony Ng. 2002. *J2EE Connector Architecture and Enterprise Application Integration.* Boston, MA: Addison-Wesley.

[Shaw 95] Shaw, Mary. 1995. "Architecture Issues in Software Reuse: It's Not Just the Functionality, It's the Packaging." *Proceedings of the IEEE Symposium on Software Reusability.* Seattle, WA (28–30 April 1995): 3–6.

[Shaw 96] Shaw, M., and D. Garlan. 1996. *Software Architecture: Perspectives on an Emerging Discipline.* Upper Saddle River, NJ: Prentice-Hall.

[Siddalingaiah 01] Siddalingahiah, M. 2001. "Overview of ebXML." August. http://www.sei.cmu.edu/activities/cbs/mls/links.html#siddalingaiah01.

[Singh-Rangar 00] Singh-Rangar, Bundeep. 2000. "One to Watch the Einstein of Legacy Data Migration." *Red Herring* (May). http://www.sei.cmu.edu/activities/cbs/mls/links.html#singhrangar00

[Sneed 84] Sneed, H. M. 1984. "Software Renewal: A Case Study." *IEEE Software* 1, 3 (July): 56–63.

[Sommerville 01] Sommerville, I. 2001. *Software Engineering, 6th Edition.* Boston: Addison-Wesley Higher Education.

[Standish 94] Standish Research Paper. 1994. "Chaos Study." http://www.sei.cmu.edu/activities/cbs/mls/links.html#standish94.

[Stets 99] Stets, Robert J., C. Galen Hunt, and Michael L. Scott. 1999. "Component-Based APIs for Versioning and Distributed Applications." *IEEE Computer* Vol. 32, no. 7 (July): 54–61.

[STSC 97] Software Technology Support Center (STSC). 1997. *Software Reengineering Assessment Handbook (SRAH) Version 3.0* (JLC-HDBK-SRAH). Hill Air Force Base, Utah.

[Sun 97a] Sun Microsystems. 1997. "Frequently Asked Questions—Applet Security." http://www.sei.cmu.edu/activities/cbs/mls/links.html#sun97a.

[Sun 97b] Sun Microsystems. 1997. "Overview of Java." http://www.sei.cmu.edu/activities/cbs/mls/links.html#sun97b.

[Sun 99a] Sun Microsystems. 1999. "Java Native Interface." http://www.sei.cmu.edu/activities/cbs/mls/links.html#sun99a.

[Sun 99b] Sun Microsystems. 1999. "JavaBeans Home Page." http://www.sei.cmu.edu/activities/cbs/mls/links.html#sun99b.

[Sun 02a] Sun Microsystems. 2002. "Java Remote Method Invocation." http://www.sei.cmu.edu/activities/cbs/mls/links.html#sun02a.

[Sun 02b] Sun Microsystems. 2002. "Java Technology Products and APIs." http://www.sei.cmu.edu/activities/cbs/mls/links.html#sun02b.

[Szyperski 98] Szyperski, C. 1998. *Component Software Beyond Object-Oriented Programming.* Reading, MA: Addison-Wesley and ACM Press.

[Tilley 91] Tilley, Scott R., and Hausi A. Müller. 1991. "INFO: A Simple Document Annotation Facility." *Proceedings of the Ninth Annual International Conference on Systems Documentation (SIGDOC '91).* Chicago (Oct. 10–12): 30–36.

[Tilley 92] Tilley, Scott R, Hausi A. Müller, and Mehmet A. Orgun. 1992. "Documenting Software Systems with Views." *Proceedings of the Tenth International Conference on Systems Documentation (SIGDOC '92).* Ottawa, Ontario (October 13–16): 211–219.

[Tilley 95] Tilley, S. R., and D. B. Smith. 1995. "Perspectives on Legacy System Reengineering." Pittsburgh, PA: Reengineering Center, Software Engineering Institute, Carnegie Mellon University. http://www.sei.cmu.edu/activities/cbs/mls/links.html#tilley95.

[Tilley 96] Tilley, Scott, and Dennis Smith. 1996. "Perspectives in Legacy System Reengineering." http://www.sei.cmu.edu/activities/cbs/mls/links.html#tilley96.

[Ulrich 90] Ulrich, W. M. 1990. "The Evolutionary Growth of Software Engineering and the Decade Ahead." *American Programmer* 3, 10: 12–20.

[Unisys 98] Unisys. 1998. *Unisys OS 2200 ASCII COBOL Programming Reference Manual.* Plymouth, MI: Unisys.

[Unisys 99] Unisys. 1999. *Unisys OS 2200 Universal Compiling System (UCS) COBOL Programming Reference Manual Volume 1: COBOL Statements.* Plymouth, MI: Unisys.

[Unisys 00] Unisys. 2000. "Java Virtual Machine on ClearPath." http://www.sei.cmu.edu/activities/cbs/mls/links.html#unisys00.

[van Hoff 96] van Hoff, A. 1996. *Hooked on Java.* Reading, MA: Addison-Wesley.

[van Vliet 00] van Vliet, H. 2000. *Software Engineering: Principles and Practice.* West Sussex, England: Wiley.

[Vigder 94] Vigder, M. R., and A. W. Kark. 1994. *Software Cost Estimation and Control.* Ottawa, Ont. National Research Council Canada—Institute for Information Technology.

[von Mayrhauser 94] von Mayrhauser, A., and A. M. Vans. 1994. "Comprehension Processes During Large Scale Maintenance." *Proceedings of the International Conference of Software Engineering (ICSE).* Sorrento, Italy (May 16): 39–48.

[W3C 01] W3C XML Encryption Working Group. 2001. "XML Encryption Requirements—W3C Working Draft." October. http://www.sei.cmu.edu/activities/cbs/mls/links.html#w3c01.

[Wallnau 97] Wallnau, Kurt, Edwin Morris, Peter Feiler, Anthony Earl, and Emile Litvak. 1997. "Engineering Component-Based Systems with Distributed Object Technology" (Lecture Notes in Computer Science). *Proceedings of the International Conference on Worldwide Computing and its Applications (WWCA'97).* Tsukuba, Japan. (March).

[Wallnau 01] Wallnau, Kurt, Scott Hissam, and Robert Seacord. 2001. *Building Systems from Commercial Components.* Boston, MA: Addison-Wesley.

[Warren 99] Warren, I. 1999. *The Renaissance of Legacy Systems: Method Support for Software Evolution.* London: Springer-Verlag.

[Weiderman 97] Weiderman, Nelson H., John K. Bergey, Dennis B. Smith, and Scott R. Tilley. 1997. "Approaches to Legacy System Evolution" (CMU/SEI-97-TR-014). Pittsburgh, PA: Software Engineering Institute, Carnegie Mellon University. http://www.sei.cmu.edu/activities/cbs/mls/links.html#weiderman97.

[Weiser 84] Weiser, M. 1984. "Program Slicing," *IEEE Transactions on Software Engineering* 10, 4 (July): 352–357.

[White 98] White, Seth, and Mark Hapner. 1998. *JDBC TM 2.0 API.* Palo Alto, CA. Sun Microsystems.

[Williams 99] Williams, R., G. Pandelios, and S. Behrens. 1999. "SRE Method Description, Version 2.0" (CMU/SEI-99-TR-029). Pittsburgh, PA: Software Engineering Institute, Carnegie Mellon University. http://www.sei.cmu.edu/activities/cbs/mls/links.html#williams99.

[Woods 99] Woods, S. G., S. J. Carriere, and R. Kazman. 1999. "A Semantic Foundation for Architectural Reengineering." *Proceedings of the ICSM 99.* Oxford, UK (Sept.): 391–398

Acronyms

A2A	application-to-application
ACID	atomicity, consistency, isolation, and durability
ADL	architecture description language
AIS	Applied Information Sciences
ANSI	American National Standards Institute
API	application program interface; application programming interface
APSEC	Asian-Pacific Software Engineering and International Computer Science Conference
ASC	Accredited Standards Committee
ASCII	American Standard Code for Information Interchange
AST	abstract syntax tree
ATAM	architecture trade-off analysis method
B2B	business-to-business
BDA	business data area
BFC	BizTalk Framework Compliant
BI	business intelligence
BMP	bean-managed persistence
BOD	business object document
BPR	business process reengineering
BSR	business service request
CBS	COTS-based systems
CEFACT	Center for Trade Facilitation and Electronic Business
CGI	Common Gateway Interface
CM	configuration management
CMP	container-managed persistence
CMU	Carnegie Mellon University
COBOL	common business-oriented language
COCOMO	constructive cost model
CODASYL	Conference on Data Systems Languages
COM	Component Object Model
COMAPI	communications application program interface
CORBA	common object request broker architecture

COTS	commercial-off-the-shelf
CPA	Collaboration Protocol Agreement
CPP	Collaboration Protocol Profile
CPU	central processing unit
CRM	communication resource manager
CRUD	create-read-update-delete
DB	Database
DBMS	database management system
DBRM	Database Resource Manager
DBTG	Database Task Group
DCE	Distributed Computing Environment
DDL	data description language
DLL	dynamic link library
DML	Data Manipulation Language
DMS	Data Management System
DOM	document object model
DOT	Distributed Object Technology
DPS	Display Processing System
DTD	document type definition
DTP	Distributed Transaction Processing
ECL	Execution Control Language
EDI	electronic data interchange
EDIFACT	Electronic Data Interchange for Administration, Commerce and Transport
EIS	enterprise information system
EJB	Enterprise JavaBeans
ERCOLE	encapsulation, reengineering, and coexistence of object with legacy
ERP	enterprise resource planning
ETL	extraction, transformation, and loading
FAA	Federal Aviation Administration
FIFO	first in first out
FORTRAN	formula translation
FRU	field-replaceable unit
FTP	File Transfer Protocol
GCOS	General Comprehensive Operating System
GIF	Graphics Interchange Format
GIG	Giga Information Group
GUI	graphical user interface

HTML	Hypertext Markup Language
HTTP	HyperText Transmission Protocol
HTTPS	HyperText Transmission Protocol, Secure
HVTIP	high-volume transaction processing
IDE	integrated development environment
IDL	Interface Definition Language
IETF	Internet Engineering Task Force
IIOP	Internet Inter-ORB Protocol
I/O	input/output
IP	Internet Protocol
ISO	International Organization for Standardization
IT	Information Technology
J2EE	Java 2 Enterprise Edition
J2SE	Java 2 Standard Edition
JAAS	Java Authentication and Authorization Service
JAF	JavaBeans Activation Framework
JAXP	Java API for XML Processing
JCA	J2EE Connector Architecture
JDBC	Java Database Connectivity
JDK	Java Development Kit
JIT	just in time
JMS	Java Message Service
JNDI	Java Naming Directory Interface
JNI	Java Native Interface
JPEG	Joint Photographic Experts Group
JRE	Java runtime environment
JSP	JavaServer Pages
JTA	Java Transaction API
JTS	Java Transaction Service
JVM	Java Virtual Machine
KLOC	thousands (kilo-) of lines of code
KSLOC	thousands of source lines of code
LAN	local area network
LOC	lines of code
MB	Megabyte
MCB	message control bank
MDB	message-driven bean
MIME	Multipurpose Internet Mail Extensions

MOM	message-oriented middleware
MQ	message queue
MQI	message queue interface
MSMQ	Microsoft Message Queue
NATO	North Atlantic Treaty Organization
NSDIR	National Software Data and Information Repository
OAG	Open Applications Group
OAGIS	Open Applications Group Integration Specification
OAMAS	Open Applications Group Middleware API Specification
OASIS	Organization for the Advancement of Structured Information Standards
OCL	Object Constraint Language
ODBC	Open Database Connectivity
ODBMS	object database management system
ODMG	Object Data Management Group
OLAP	on-line analytical processing
OLTP	on-line transaction processing
OMG	Object Management Group
OO	object orientation, object oriented
OODB	object-oriented database
OODBMS	object-oriented database management system
OQL	Object Query Language
ORB	object request broker
ORDBMS	object-relational database management system
OS	operating system
OSI	Open Systems Interconnect
OTS	Object Transaction Service
PBS	Portable Bookshelf
PC	personal computer
PIP	partner interface processes
PL	Programming Language
PM	Person Months
QA	quality assurance
QoS	quality of service
RAM	random access memory
RDBMS	relational database management system
RDMS	Relational Data Management System
REI	Rose Extensibility Interface

RM	resource manager
RMI	remote method invocation
RNIF	RosettaNet Implementation Framework
ROI	return on investment
RPC	remote procedure call
RPG	report program generator
RSF	Rigi Standard Format
RSS	Retail Supply System
SAM	System Analysis and Migration
SAP	Systems, Applications and Products
SAX	Simple API for XML
SEI	Software Engineering Institute
SGML	Standardized General Markup Language
SLOC	source lines of code
SMOP	Simple Matter of Programming
SMTP	Simple Mail Transfer Protocol
SNA	Systems Network Architecture
SOAP	Simple Object Access Protocol
SPX	Sequenced Packet Exchange
SQL	Structured Query Language
SQLJ	SQL with Java
SRE	Software Risk Evaluation
SRF	Standard Retail Framework
SSL	Secure Sockets Layer
TCP	Transmission Control Protocol
TIP	transaction processing
TM	transaction monitor
TP	transaction processing
TPA	trading partner agreement
TREX	Tree Regular Expressions for XML
TX	transaction
UC	UCS C
UCOB	UCS COBOL
UCS	universal compiling system
UDDI	Universal Description, Discovery, and Integration
UDS	Universal Data Management System
UFP	unadjusted function point
UI	user interface

UML	Unified Modeling Language
VOS	Virtual Operating System
W3C	World Wide Web Consortium
WAN	wide area network
WG	Working Group
WIP	work in process
WSDL	Web Services Description Language
XA	extended architecture
XATMI	extended architecture transaction management interface
XML	eXtensible Markup Language
XML4J	eXtensible Markup Language for Java
XSL	eXtensible Style Language
XSLT	eXtensible Style Language Transformation
Y2K	Year 2000

Index

Adapters. *See also* Data adaptation
use in Retail Supply System (RSS), 237–239
Aggregate Entity pattern, data components, 201, 202
Aggregation hierarchies, 64
Apache Xerces, 110
Applets, 98. *See also* Java
Application components, 126
elements of, 198
structure of, 198
Application Programming Interfaces (APIs), 97, 98–99. *See also* Java
Architectural compliance, 44
Architectural patterns
ad hoc query, 211
data access
with more than one business object, 207, 208
within one business object, 206, 207
data warehouses, 215–219
report, 209–211
roll-ups, 211–212
transactions, 215–216
Architectural views
component-and-connector (C&C), 76–83
decomposition, 74
deployment, 83–84
generalization, 74–75
hybrid, 85
layered, 76
module, 73–76
system context, 84–85
Architecture reconstruction, 32
definition of, 64–65
phases of, 65–66

Architecture representation, 64
as-built, 69
as-desired, 69, 70
levels of granularity, 72
purpose of, 71
requirements of, 71–72
Architecture transformation, 60, 221
adapters used in, 237–239
code migration. *See* Code migration
data migration. *See* Data migration
deployment options during, 235–236
operational risk in, 235
strategies for, 229–236
trail maps used in, 236–237
Artifact extraction, 61
Asynchronous communication, 114, 115
Automatic translation, 13, 14

Batch roll-ups, 212–213
B2B architecture, 173–174
availability in, 182
data integrity of, 183
evaluation of, 179
integrability of, 188
versus J2EE architecture, 176, 190
modifiability of, 184
performance in, 177
portability of, 187
reusability of, 187
security of, 180
Bean-managed persistence (BMP), 137, 138
BEA Tuxedo, 131–132
BEA WebLogic (EJB Server), 118
Behavioral pattern matching, 63
BizTalk
framework, 150
and XML messaging, 149–150

The SEI Series in Software Engineering

ISBN 0-201-73500-8

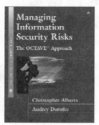

ISBN 0-321-11886-3

ISBN 0-201-73723-X

ISBN 0-201-54664-7

ISBN 0-321-15496-7

ISBN 0-201-70372-6

ISBN 0-201-70482-X

ISBN 0-201-70332-7

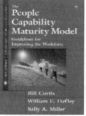

ISBN 0-201-60445-0

ISBN 0-201-60444-2

ISBN 0-201-25592-8

ISBN 0-201-54597-7

ISBN 0-201-54809-7

ISBN 0-201-18095-2

ISBN 0-201-54610-8

ISBN 0-201-47719-X

ISBN 0-201-77639-1

ISBN 0-201-61626-2

ISBN 0-201-70454-4

ISBN 0-201-73409-5

ISBN 0-201-85480-5

ISBN 0-321-11884-7

ISBN 0-201-70064-6

ISBN 0-201-17782-X

ISBN 0-201-52577-1

Please see our Web site at http://www.awprofessional.com for more information on these titles.